SANDISON'S
SCOTLAND

SANDISON'S SCOTLAND

A Scottish Journey

with

Bruce Sandison

BLACK & WHITE PUBLISHING

First published in this edition 2011
by Black & White Publishing Ltd
29 Ocean Drive, Edinburgh EH6 6JL

1 3 5 7 9 10 8 6 4 2   11 12 13 14

ISBN: 978 1 84502 369 0

Typeset by Ellipsis Digital Ltd, Glasgow
Printed and bound by ScandBook AB, Sweden

For Ann

"In her eyes I see the kindness of all ages"

Contents

Preface

This is a book about the land I love, about its people, mountains and moorlands and wild places. Most of the stories that appear here first saw the light of day in America by courtesy of my friends Neill and Lynn Kennedy Ray in their publications *Scottish Life* and *The Highlander*. Over the years, many Scots, often through circumstances beyond their control, left their native land to seek a new life overseas. They took with them little other than the strong beliefs and traditions that have made Scotland a byword for decency throughout the world.

The majority of the places visited in my travels are in the far north of Scotland because that is where my wife, Ann, and I have lived for the last thirty years, formerly in Caithness and presently in the small village of Tongue on the north coast of Sutherland. However, I was born and brought up in Scotland's capital city, Edinburgh, Auld Reekie, and I have warm memories of my days there and of expeditions from Edinburgh to the surrounding areas; the splendid Trossachs, the stormy Debatable Lands of the south west and amongst gently rolling Border hills.

Along the way, I have met many people who made my journeys memorable – courteous, considerate, kind and unfailingly welcoming. I have visited places that are the essential adjuncts in the shaping of Scotland's story, from croft to castle, ragged cliff to calm harbour. Together, they make us what we are, a nation at peace with its own identity, proud of its past and confident about its future. And today, for the first time in more than 300 years, we are governed by a Scottish parliament led by the political party that has devoted its lifetime to achieving full independence for Scotland. Could that time be now?

Whatever, I am just happy that I was born a Scot and have had the great privilege of growing up in this wonderful land, and of exploring and discovering the ethos which makes my country so special. My own ethos is pretty well summed up in words from John Barbour's (1320–1395) magnificent poem, "The Bruce": "A noble heart may haif nane ease, na ellis nocht that may him please, gif freedom failye." For everything that Scotland has given me, I am enduringly grateful.

Bruce Sandison

Foreword

Lady Fiona Armstrong-MacGregor

He's a Sandison, and a MacGregor, and I who am married to the chief of Clan Gregor cannot fail to like that. As you start to read, the infamous Rob Roy and the land he rampaged through leap from the pages.

My first meeting with Bruce was not in MacGregor country, in the Trossachs, but on a very wild Highland hill loch. It was more than twenty years ago and we were in search of brown trout. They were moving fast and furious but he carefully guided our rods to tantalising rises and made tiny feathery flies skit enticingly across the water. I was a fledgling angler and for me, he brought the world of fishing to life.

But Bruce is more than an expert angler: a first-class travel writer, a perceptive people-watcher, a hearty hill walker and a scintillating story-teller. He's one of the great exponents of Scottish life and now some of his best work has come together in this un-put-downable collection of tales.

From the heated passion of the Kirkwall Ba' Game, to the solitary and wind-whipped Seal Island, from mighty Edinburgh Castle to the elusive Berwick trolls, Bruce takes us from remote communities to the heart of big cities. Scotland is in his blood and with a pipe-tune named after him, he goes in search of bag-piping experts in Ross-shire.

Later, on a wild whisky tour, he brings to life the story of Macbeth and the three witches on the moor. At Ballindalloch, he finds out about the "doddies", the hardy Aberdeen Angus breed so loved by the late Queen Mother, and learns how the ghost of General James Grant stalks the castle corridors. The old warrior didn't just fight. He never stopped eating and became the fattest man in Britain.

Another man who liked his food and drink was Winston Churchill and as Bruce examines the Scottish Regiments, he reminds us that this famous bon viveur was one of their best-known soldiers. "Although an Englishman, it was in Scotland that I found the best things in my life – my wife, my constituency and my regiment," the war-time Prime Minister said.

We find out how hard life was, and still is, for the crofters of Assynt and, after a lifetime of cooking, I finally realise that a "skink" means soup, that old Scots' favourite of smoked haddock and potato, and it comes from Cullen. And did you know that according to Gaelic verse, the humble hazelnut was the source of all knowledge? From lairds to locals, we hear their stories. There is regret. There are the Clearances and there's the fishing port where you'll now find more yachts than fishing boats in the harbour.

"September is a good-to-be-alive month in the far north of Scotland," he tells us and we sense the dramatic wildness of Wester Ross, "as mountain and moorland resound to the roar of rutting stags and the hills are purple clad with heather." Or, "I stumbled into the shelter of the summit cairn, amazed by the wild landscape that lay before me, wave after wave of mountain crests guarding a blessing where all things were possible and all things equal." I love it! As Rob Roy MacGregor said, "My foot is on my native heath." Bruce MacGregor Sandison's is certainly on his.

Lady Fiona Armstrong-MacGregor

1.
The Trossachs, Clan Gregor Country

Ben Venue (729m) towers above Loch Katrine in the bristling heart of the Trossachs. As I climbed toward its twin peaks, I felt a complete sense of belonging. I was the hill and the rocks about me were my soul. I encompassed time and space. Wind screamed across the ridge. For a moment, I held eternity in my arms. Shivering, I stumbled into the shelter of the summit cairn, amazed at the wild landscape that lay before me; wave after wave of mountain crests guarding a blessing where all things were possible and all things equal.

The Trossachs command a special place in my mind. Not only for their supreme beauty, but also because of the central role they have played in Scotland's story. This is the domain of Clan Gregor, "the children of the mist", robbed of their rightful heritage by their rapacious Campbell neighbours. This is the land of Rob Roy MacGregor (1671–1734), the most famous and redoubtable of his clan. On the plinth of his statue in the town of Stirling are written the words, "My foot is on my native heath, and my name is Rob Roy MacGregor."

My grandmother, Jean MacGregor, was born in Callander by the banks of the tumbling River Teith and I carry her surname with pride. My own mother used to recount, proudly, that she was chosen to sing Clan Gregor's historic song, "MacGregor's Gathering" at a concert in the Usher Hall, Edinburgh, in the early 1920s. As a boy at the Royal High School of Edinburgh, I was thoroughly embroiled in the battles of Otterburn and Bannockburn and immersed in the romantic history of my native land. Sir Walter Scott (1771–1832), "the wizard of the north", was a former pupil and through his writing, Scott, more than anyone else, brought international fame to the Trossachs and to those who called it home. Sir Walter also wrote the words of the song my mother sang:

MacGregor's Gathering

The moon's on the lake, and the mist's on the brae,
And the Clan has a name that is nameless by day;
Then gather, gather, gather Grigalach!
Gather, gather, gather Grigalach!

Our signal for fight, that from monarchs we drew,
Must be heard but by night in our vengeful haloo!
Then haloo, Grigalach! Haloo, Grigalach!
Haloo, haloo, haloo, Grigalach!

Glen Orchy's proud mountains, Coalchuirn and her towers,
Glenstrae and Glenlyon no longer are ours;
We're landless, landless, landless, Grigalach!
Landless, landless, landless, Grigalach!

But doom'd and devoted by vassal and lord,
MacGregor has still both his heart and his sword!
Then courage, courage, courage, Grigalach!
Courage, courage, courage, Grigalach!

If they rob us of name, and pursue us with beagles,
Give their roofs to the flame, and their flesh to the eagles!
Then vengeance, vengeance, vengeance, Grigalach!
Vengeance, vengeance, vengeance, Grigalach!

While there's leaves in the forest, and foam on the river,
MacGregor despite them, shall flourish for ever!

Come then Grigalach, come then Grigalach,
Come then, come then, come then Grigalach!

Through the depths of Loch Katrine the steed shall career,
O'er the peak of Ben Lomond the galley shall steer,
The rocks of Craig-Royston like icicles melt,
Ere our wrongs be forgot, or our vengeance unfelt!
Then gather, gather, gather Grigalach!
Gather, gather, gather Grigalach!

By 1603, the lawlessness of Clan Gregor had become so notorious that James VI proscribed the clan, the consequences of which turned out to be very unpleasant indeed. His edict described them as: "that wicked race of lawless luminaries, callit the MacGregor." Henceforth they were to be pursued and hunted like animals. A reward was offered for the head of every MacGregor delivered to the laird; families were encouraged to betray their own people with promises of pardon; women were branded on the forehead; children were sold as little better than slaves to Lowland and Irish cattle dealers. Even the use of the name "MacGregor" was proscribed.

My wife, Ann, and I have experienced the sense of terror that these people must have felt because it still lingers to this day in the corries and glens in the Trossachs hills and mountains. Some years ago, we were walking to the south of Loch Tummel, heading to fish for trout in little Loch a'Chait, a hard tramp uphill from Lick. It was a hot morning with the sun beating down relentlessly and we found the going hard. Eventually, we arrived at a small, damp glen, peat and heather-filled, where insects hummed in the still air.

I was halfway across the floor of this glen when Ann came running past; when I say running, I mean as fast as she could stumble over the uneven ground, pack on her back, carrying her fishing rod. Her face was white with fear and she kept saying, almost whispering: "Quick, quick, get out of here, get out of here. Something terrible has happened." Without pausing, she hurried on and although I called after her, she didn't stop until she had reached the other side and scrambled up the rocky gully to the top.

When I caught up, Ann was still very distressed and I asked what on earth was wrong. She calmed down and told me that she had a sudden impression, walking across the glen, of women and children in great danger; nothing else, but a terrible feeling that women and children were about to be harmed. It was then that I decided to learn more about what had happened to the "Children of the Mist" during their years of persecution and found an amazing possibility.

Often, before the arrival of the hunters, the clansmen were warned that they were on the way. The first thing the men did, upon receiving this news and before fending for themselves, was to move their women and children to safety, generally into a secret corrie in the hills. But sometimes these hiding places were found and I think that Ann and I had stumbled into one of these hiding places where the women and children had lain, trembling with fear, listening to the sound of their approaching persecutors.

Some years later, talking to the owner of the estate upon which Loch a'Chait lies, he told me that neither he nor the members of his family ever visted the glen that Ann and I had passed through. He could give me no reason why, but said that they felt intensely uncomfortable there and always avoided it.

Rob Roy MacGregor lies asleep in the old churchyard on the Braes of Balquhidder at the east end of glorious Loch Voil. At his side lie his wife Mary, his second son Coll and his youngest son Robin Oig. Whilst Rob Roy died, surprisingly, peacefully in his bed, his son Robin met an altogether harsher fate. Convicted of kidnapping the twenty-year-old Jean Kay from Edinbilly near Balfron in Stirlingshire and forcing her to marry him, Robin paid the price of his crime on the gallows in Edinburgh on 14 February 1754.

Loch Lomond marks the western boundary of the Trossachs and visitors, to gain entry, sailed from Luss across the loch to Inversnaid on the east shore. Dr Johnson and the inevitable James Boswell (also a former pupil of the High School in Edinburgh) passed this way during their famous Highland tour. After enjoying the hospitality of Sir James Colquhoun of Luss and of the novelist Dr Tobias Smollet, Boswell noted: "The civility and respect which we found at every place, it is ungrateful to omit, and tedious to repeat."

William Wordsworth and Samuel Taylor Coleridge, accompanied by Wordsworth's sister Dorothy, also trekked this way in 1803. At Inversnaid, Wordsworth noticed the woman that inspired his poem "To a Highland Girl": "Sweet Highland Girl, a very shower of beauty is thy earthly dower." She was the daughter of the ferryman. Further along his journey, Wordsworth encountered another Highland beauty that prompted him to write one of my favourite poems, "The Solitary Reaper": "Behold her single in the field, yon solitary Highland lass, reaping and singing by herself, stop here or gently pass."

Inversnaid was a less peaceful place prior to the arrival of the literati, entirely due to the activities of Clan Gregor. Their exploits involved the removal of everything and anything not securely nailed down, including cattle, cash goods and chattels. In an effort to subdue the clan, the government built a fort there. But as soon as the fort was completed, the Macgregors attacked and burned it to the ground. As soon as the fort was rebuilt, the Macgregors, led by Rob Roy's nephew, attacked again and destroyed the fort.

Inversnaid was rebuilt for the third time and on this occasion command was given to a nineteen-year-old Lieutenant, James Wolfe, who later met his fate in 1759 at the Battle of the Plains of Abraham outside Quebec in Canada. Wolfe set about his Inversnaid duties with his customary efficiency, sending regular reports to his superior, General Bland, at Stirling Castle. Wolfe never liked either Scotland or its inhabitants, claiming that they were "better governed by fear than favour".

But when the Duke of Cumberland ordered him to shoot a wounded Highland soldier after the Battle of Culloden (1746) because he had looked at him, Wolfe refused to do so, offering to resign his commission instead.

When Walter Scott visited Inversnaid, the fort was still standing, but the soldiers were gone and the door was locked. A retired pensioner was in charge and he was busy working at a small crop of barley. Scott asked him if he could look around the fort and was told that he would find the key under a stone by the door.

The road from Inversnaid climbs past Loch Arklet to reach Stronachlachar on the shores of Loch Katrine. Thereafter, this road, which winds around the loch, is closed to motor vehicles but offers the possibility of a memorable ten-mile walk back to the Pier at the east end of Katrine. Along the way, you will find Rob Roy's birthplace at Glengyle at the foot of Meall Mor (747m). The initials "GM" and the date 1704 are carved on the lintel above the door. Rob Roy's mother is buried in the little graveyard here.

A mile or so west from the Pier is Brenachoile in the Gartney Forest. I never pass this way without paying my respects to Dr Archibald Cameron, brother of Cameron of Lochiel, "out" with Bonnie Prince Charlie during the 1745 Rebellion. The doctor's only crime was tending the wounded after the slaughter of Culloden. He was eventually captured, hiding at Brenachoile, branded a traitor and hanged at Tyburn in 1752.

The eastern boundary of the Trossachs enfolds the lovely Lake of Menteith, graced by the Island of Inchmahome with its thirteenth-century Augustinian priory. During the summer months, a ferry plies between Port of Menteith and the island. As a child, the future Mary, Queen of Scots, found sanctuary on Inchmahome before being hurried off to safety in France – beyond the avaricious grasp of King Henry VIII of England, who was determined that she should be betrothed to his sickly son, Edward.

As I walk the paths that she walked, I sometimes believe that I can hear her infant laughter, but remember with sadness the tragedy of her later life. Poor luckless Mary never stood a chance. Even today, we Scots tend to be wary of clever women but in those days, to be young, female, tall, beautiful, witty, talented and intelligent, and a Queen, was like writing one's own death warrant. The enduring shame of Scotland's lairds is that they connived in her downfall and judicial murder.

But it is hard to be somber for long in the Trossachs. Everywhere you look, around every corner and over every hill, heart and mind are ensnared. A lifetime's joy lives here. I remember one warm evening drifting over the calm surface of Loch Lubnaig, trout fishing in "Bonnie Strathyre", watching a bewhiskered otter splashing in the shallows and seeing the peak of Ben Vorlich (985m) covered in the fire of the setting sun.

And further back, as a boy sheltering from a storm on the shores of Loch Ard, I remember watching huge raindrops making the surface of the loch boil, whilst my father wrestled with the intricacies of an old paraffin stove to boil water to make tea. I remember white-foam-filled rivers urgent with leaping salmon hurrying to their ancient spawning grounds; the autumn scent of heather and the roar of stags on the hill; deciduous woodlands burnished brown and gold, waiting for winter, their branches sparkling with diamond crystals of frost; the first sprinkling of snow on the high tops.

Most of all, I treasure the memory of that singular moment on the windy summit of Ben Venue where I found such peace and content: "Now turn I to that God of old, who mocked not any of my ills, but gave my hungry hands to hold, the large religion of the hills." Get there if you can to the land of Clan Gregor and you will find there all that is finest in this land I love.

2.
The Kirkwall Ba' Game

On New Year's Day in Kirkwall a crowd of young and not so young men waited impatiently on Broad Street in front of St Magnus Cathedral for the start of the 2005 Ba' Game. At the Market Cross, west of the entrance to the old red-sandstone building, veteran Ba' player Ian Smith proudly held aloft a hand-made, brown and black patterned leather, cork-packed ball, which was the object of everyone's rapt attention. As the hands on the face of the clock reached one and the hour struck, Ian flung the ball into the midst of the waiting hoard.

Bedlam ensued as a forest of finger-wide human hands rose to catch the ball. When it was caught, it immediately disappeared into the centre of the throng. Several hundred determined and seemingly deranged men formed themselves into two opposing groups, shoving, heaving and shouting encouragement to those in the middle of the massive scrum. The traditional New Year's Day Men's Ba' game, played between the Uppies and the Doonies, was under way.

This is a fierce, hard-fought, no-holds-barred battle. It is played through the streets of the town, as it has been for over two centuries. To win, the Doonies must immerse the ball in the cold waters of the harbour, whilst the Uppies must touch the ball against the wall at Mackinson's Corner where New Scapa Road, Main Street and Junction Road meet. The game may last for less than an hour, or all day and well into the night. It only ends when one or other of the opposing sides reaches their goal and the single rule is that there are no rules.

The game is as demanding for spectators as it is for the players. Nothing stands in the way of those trying to move the Ba' through the narrow streets of the town. Often, because of the number of men in the scrum, the exact location of the Ba' is unknown. Is it in the pack or has somebody spirited it away? It is also difficult for visitors to identify who is an Uppie and who is a Doonie because the players don't wear distinguishing colours. In truth, the whole affair appears to be a near riot and as such, the authorities, to whom all riot is an anathema, have often tried to "civilise" the event but to no avail.

An imaginary line, drawn through Kirkwall and at right-angles to the Market Cross, divides the town. If you were born to the south of the line you are an Uppie and from "Up-the-Gates". Those born north of the line are Doonies, from "Down-the-Gates"; the word "gates" coming from the Old Norse "gata" meaning road. Team members are also known as being either Earl's Men (Doonies, from the old part of Kirkwall) or Bishop's Men (Uppies, from the newer part). These titles remind us of ancient quarrels between the church and Orkney's ruling earls, when, in times of strife, each side depended for support upon their servants.

Today, place of birth is less relevant, given that most children are born in the Balfour Hospital. The hospital is in Uppie territory and as such, Uppies would always outnumber Doonies and always win. Boys now usually adopt the side that their fathers played for. An exception to this rule is Uppie Jim Cromarty, another Ba' stalwart and Ba' Committee member; Jim's brother John was born at home, in Doonie territory, whilst Jim himself was born in the Balfour, making him an Uppie. Remarkably, both have won a Men's Ba', unique in the annals of the game: Jim wining an Uppie Ba' in 1983, John a Doonie Ba' in 1988.

Newcomers to Orkney, affectionately known as "ferryloupers" because they arrive in the islands by the ferry, carefully consider which way they first enter Kirkwall, as this will mark them forever as being either an Uppie or a Doonie. This also applies to those who arrive by air. Devious diversions are taken by all concerned to ensure that they enter town through the territory of their team of choice.

Street football has been played in Scotland for hundreds of years. Scone, where the Kings of ancient Scotland were crowned, had its game played on

Shrove Tuesday until 1785. Banffshire had a game, noted as being played in 1629. Church records from Elgin recount the banning of football being played through the town. When Ann and I were guests of the Lothian Family at Ferniehurst Castle near Jedburgh a few years ago, we heard the story of the origin of the Jedburgh "Fasternse'en" Ba' game: commemorating a defence of the castle from English attack when prisoners were decapitated and their heads used as footballs.

A lot of Orcadian heads were knocked about a bit during the 2005 New Year Men's Game. After two hours, the Ba' and the pack were still struggling furiously for supremacy in Broad Street, a few yards away from the Market Cross where the game had begun. The scrum was enveloped in a pall of steam from the heat of the mass of fighting bodies. Just before 2pm, it appeared that the Ba' had been "lost". One observer guessed that it had been smuggled out of the pack to the town library and everybody set off in pursuit, scattering the crowds of spectators in the process. The Ba' was found and the scrum wedged together again, striving for control.

After a further hour, with the Uppie goal in sight, deadlock was broken when the Ba' was thrown to a spectator standing on a nearby roof who hurled it back the way it had come. In spite of this, the Uppies grouped again for a final push. In darkness, four and a half hours after the Ba' had been thrown up at the Cross, the Uppies achieved their fourteenth victory in a row; the longest consecutive period of Uppie New Year Ba' and Christmas Day Game wins since the end of the last war. The Ba' was awarded to Gary Coltherd, who was then raised shoulder-high in triumph by his team-mates as he kissed his hard-won prize.

The 2005 Boys' Christmas Day Game, played on a snow-filled, freezing day, was a classic of its kind. Nearly two and a half hours after the "throw-up of the Ba'", and a few minutes before the start of the Men's Game, the youngsters were still struggling in Broad Street. At one stage, the pack was deluged in a huge fall of snow, sliding off an adjacent roof. With the Ba' and the players jammed into a tight corner, taking a breather whilst still trying to control the Ba', a snowball fight began in the middle of the pack. The Uppies, at one stage within sight of their goal, were gradually forced back and shortly after 4pm, the Doonies had the Ba' in the Harbour when young Jon Tait was awarded the Ba'.

I asked Gary Gibson, a former player and member of the Ba' Committee, how the Ba' winner is chosen. "The victors award the Ba' to one of their team, chosen not just for his performance on the day, but also for his performance over the years that he has been playing the game. There is always some who never get a Ba' and are disappointed, but we all play for the side until the game is over. It's a tremendous feeling, getting a Ba'."

Gary explained that four games were held each year, two on Christmas Day and two on New Year's Day. There is a Boys' Game in the morning, starting at 10.30am, followed by a Men's Game in the afternoon. Gary has won both a Boys' and a Men's Ba' – in 1949, when he was fourteen years old and in later life, in 1967. A further unique distinction is that on the day Gary won his Boys' Ba', his father, Edgar, won the Men's Ba'.

There used to be a Youth's Game as well, between 1897 and 1910, but spectators caused insurmountable problems. The Youth's Game was played after the Boys' Game and before the Men's Game and the temptation to lend a hand, or rather a shoulder, in support of your team was irresistible. Games ended in heated disputes between the players and spectators who had been drawn into the struggle; not only men intervened, but women also were just as likely to become involved. And with three games on the same day, Kirkwall was in chaos.

So how do you tell the difference between an Uppie and a Doonie? Gary was asked this question by a reporter from a women's magazine. "Well," he replied, "all the Uppies are tall, good-looking, Nordic types and all the Doonies are sort of Neanderthal, squat, ugly guys with low foreheads." Gary is an Uppie and his comments appeared in print, much to everyone's amusement. Gary continued, "The truth is that you tell them apart by knowing them, by playing against them since you were a boy. You grow up knowing who is on what side. You also recognise them as descendants of older people that you know."

Gary told me: "Immediately after the end of the game, everyone visits the home of the winner to celebrate. During the course of the evening, they disperse and go and get washed and cleaned up and then come back again. They often carry in a drink or so to help out the host family and the celebration goes on for, well, two or three days, certainly." The Kirkwall Ba' Game is entrenched in the history and culture of the community. The Game is a great leveller, when everybody – policeman, lawyer, doctor, farmer, fisherman, joiner, plumber or builder – meets and competes together in furious and friendly rivalry. As Jim Cromarty told me, "The Game will never die."

I am indebted to John D.M. Robertson, CBE, for information concerning the history and culture of the Kirkwall Ba' Game. His recently published study of the tradition, The Kirkwall Ba', Between the Water and the Wall, *has been revised and expanded from his earlier work,* Uppies and Doonies, *and is required reading for all with an interest in riotous behaviour.*

3.
Moray Drive

"When shall we three meet again? In thunder, lightning or in rain?" On a warm September morning the opening lines of Shakespeare's play *Macbeth* came to mind as I sped along the A96 road between Forres and Elgin. The moor here is where the Bard of Avon's three witches foresaw the fate of Macbeth, whilst Bothgowan, near Elgin, is where Macbeth foully murdered and usurped King Duncan of Scotland in 1039.

Elgin was to be the start of my journey, exploring the towns of Moray and the Banffshire villages that cling to the rocky coastline between Elgin and Portsoy. I would then follow the "Malt Whisky Trail" through the "Friendly Town" of Keith to Dufftown, "The Malt Whisky Capital of the World", and return to Elgin by the banks of the River Spey.

Elgin is a well-ordered, attractive town, dominated by the ruins of its cathedral on the banks of the River Lossie. Founded in 1224, the cathedral was so renowned that it became known throughout Europe as "The Lantern of the North", a lantern extinguished 200 years later by rapacious Alisdair Mor mac an Righ, the Wolf of Badenoch; Alisdair burned the cathedral and the town after he was excommunicated by the Bishop of Moray.

As I wandered the well-manicured lawns, I found the last resting place of another, more recent "wolf": Patrick Sellar, the infamous agent of the Countess Duchess of Sutherland, who played a major role in the brutal nineteenth-century evictions of thousands of Highlanders, driven from their homes in Strathnaver to make way for sheep. Sellar was born in Elgin and he and his wife are buried near the boundary wall at the north-east corner of the cathedral.

On the opposite bank are the premises of Johnstons of Elgin, one of the world's most excellent specialists in the manufacture of cashmere. The company was founded more than 200 years ago and their cashmere comes from China and Mongolia, as witnessed by a statue of three goats presented to Johnstons in 1993 by the South Trading Company of China to celebrate more than 140 years of experience of Chinese cashmere. The Mill Shop is a cacophony of colour and wonderful clothes.

I drove north through gentle fields to visit the Palace of Spynie, one of Scotland's most magnificent monuments and founded in 1107. Bishop David Stewart built the great tower of Spynie which is the principal feature of the palace. Spynie is hidden by wonderful woodlands and only the top of the tower can be seen from the road, but a palpable sense of peace and serenity surrounds you the moment you step within its walls.

A few miles from Spynie, near to the Royal Air Force base at Lossiemouth, I stopped to look at the remains of Duffus Castle. A tractor, trailed by a flock of seagulls, was ploughing a field nearby. Duffus Castle was the seat of the Moravia family who were of Flemish origin and came to England with William the Conqueror in 1066. They gave their name, "Moravia", to this part of Scotland.

The Moray Golf Club at Lossiemouth is a fine links course and as I putted out on the 18th green, I recalled its association with Britain's first Labour Prime Minister, Ramsay MacDonald (1866–1937). He was born in Lossiemouth and played there, but club members were so angered by his outspoken hatred of the slaughter taking place during the First World War that they expelled him. When he became Prime Minister in 1924, a vote to reinstate him failed. When he became Prime Minister again in 1929, the club invited him to rejoin their ranks. MacDonald didn't bother to reply.

The character of the coastline changed as I travelled east through Fochabers to Buckie. Broken cliffs tower over tiny, colourful villages: Gordonsburgh, Portessie, Findochty, Portknockie, Cullen and Portsoy. During the great days of the herring fishings in the nineteenth century, these communities thrived. Today, they are just as busy with holidaymakers who come to enjoy the sea air and the superb beaches that line the coast.

Findochty is perhaps one of the most attractive of these villages. The little harbour is crowded with boats of all descriptions, guarded by a white-painted statue of a seated man looking out to sea. Below the figure is a plaque with an inscription from Psalm 107, "These see the works of the LORD and his wonders in the deep." Starlochy Street, by the harbour, is narrow and winding and bordered by cottages, all of which seem to be painted in different colours – a splendid example of Scottish seaside domestic architecture.

Half an hour later, I drove down the steep hill into Cullen. Fading sunlight shadowed the dramatic pinnacles of the "Three Kings" sea stacks near the harbour. I was looking forward to dinner in Portsoy, the next village on my route and where I was to spend the night. There was no doubt what my first course would be: Cullen Skink, a traditional dish originating from Cullen and one of my favourites. "Skink" is the old Scottish name for soup and the main ingredient is haddock, complemented with finely chopped onion, chopped celery, potatoes, vegetable stock, milk and parsley, and perhaps a tablespoonful or three of double cream.

The Station Hotel in Portsoy is a friendly establishment and the proprietors, Euan and Susan Cameron, made my visit memorable; not only because of their welcome, but also because of the quality of the food they provided and believe me, the Cullen Skink was everything that I had hoped it would be. The following morning I explored the harbour, known for its annual Traditional Small Boat Festival (8–9 July), an event that attracts 20,000 visitors to the town and celebrates the maritime and cultural heritage of the north east of Scotland.

The next morning, I headed south west down the A95 towards Keith and the heartland of Scotland's famous single-malt whiskies. The landscape changed again, from the rugged grandeur of the coast to the fertile farmlands that grow the high-quality, golden barley used in the production of whisky. The Strathisla Distillery in Keith is the oldest in Scotland and has been in business since 1786. I pondered these matters as I stood on the Auld Brig that crosses the River Isla in the centre of Keith, built in 1609 and the oldest such structure in Scotland. Thomas and Janet Murray built the bridge after their son drowned there fording the river.

I arrived in Dufftown and fortuitously parked outside the Whisky Shop. Everything you ever wanted to know about *uisge beatha*, the Water of Life, will be found there and in the local Whisky Museum. The town sits at the confluence of the Dullan Burn and the River Fiddich, a major tributary of the River Spey. The Glenfiddich Distillery, opened on Christmas Day 1887 by its founder, William Grant, invites you to tour the distillery and sample their product.

Nearby is Balvanie Castle, a graceful thirteenth-century ruin that gives its name to another of Scotland's most outstanding malts, The Balvenie. Visitors are welcome at seven more distilleries in the immediate vicinity of Dufftown, at Pittyvaich, Dufftown, Benrinnes, Glenallachie, Mortlach, Glendullan and Convalmore.

Most of the barrels used by the industry come from the Speyside Cooperage, a few miles north from Dufftown. I stopped to have a word with Adeline Murphy, the Visitor Centre Manager. The cooperage makes and repairs 100,000 casks each year and they dominate the view. Some, positioned throughout the splendid gardens, are used as picnic shelters.

The principal river of Morayshire is the mighty Spey, the UK's fastest flowing stream. As well as being central to the production of malt whisky, the Spey is one of Europe's most famous salmon rivers and as an angler, I fell in love with it more years ago than I care to remember. Whisky and fishing are inextricably linked, so it was appropriate to visit Craigellachie and the home of my favourite whisky, The Macallan, often described as being the "Rolls Royce" of single malts.

After paying my respects to the traditional small, hand-beaten copper stills in the distillery, I drove down to the Spey where the company has a salmon beat. Afternoon sunlight sparkled on the crystal-clear stream. A best-bibbed black and white dipper hunted for insects amongst the stones along the margins whilst visiting anglers cast for salmon in the river. In the fishing hut, the talk was all about fishing, assisted by a comfortable dram of The Macallan.

My last call on this journey was in the small town of Rothes to visit the Glen Grant Distillery, one of the first to bottle its whisky as a single malt, rather than using it in blended whisky. The Glen Grant Distillery Gardens are just as impressive as their whisky; old apple trees and rhododendrons planted in the 1880s, ornamental areas filled with plants from America, China and the Himalayas, and a rustic bridge over the Black Burn which flows through the garden on its way to the distillery and the River Spey.

I climbed to the bridge where my guide opened a safe in the cliff face. It was constructed by James Grant, "The Major", in the 1870s so that he could serve his guests with a dram during an after-dinner stroll. The safe contained two bottles of the finest Glen Grant single malt and a cup on a chain so that water from the burn could be added to the straw-coloured liquid.

At the end of my fantastic journey, I drove home, back along the A96, my mind full of the sights and sounds that I had experienced on my travels through Moray and Banffshire; the serenity of the glorious ruins of the Lantern of the North; tumbled towers and quiet courtyards; of endless waves beating on strong harbour walls; colourful cottages clustered by the shore; the cry of wheeling gulls; the pleasure of Cullen Skink; the splash of a silver Spey salmon, and the warmth and pleasure of a golden glass of the Water of Life.

4.
Ballindalloch Castle

Ballindalloch Castle, "The Pearl of the North", is a wondrous surprise. The castle can't be seen from the road. Even as you approach along the tree-lined route through immaculately manicured grounds, it hides itself from view until almost the last moment.

I parked my car amidst the russet of an autumn afternoon and walked round a neatly trimmed beech hedge. This was when the beauty of Ballindalloch was exposed: calm, serene, turreted and towered, with crenellated gables that seemed to float above its pearl-grey walls.

Before me lay a lawn that dreams are made of, busy with black and white pied-wagtails. The sound of collared doves echoed from the woods. Trees that were old when I was a boy stood guard over the ancient home of the Macpherson-Grant families. Beyond the lawn, well-tended fields swept down to the banks of the swiftly flowing River Spey.

Scotland is resplendent with castles, most of which are grim reminders of the country's turbulent past. Hardly a square yard of my native land is untouched by signs of its violent birth and vigorous adolescence.

The ordered discipline of Ballindalloch belies this truth, although it has had its share of turmoil; during the religious wars of the 1640s, James Graham, Marquis of Montrose (1612–1650), knocked the castle about a bit. But Clan Grant, through their astuteness, weathered most of the storms that buffeted the Highlands.

This astuteness is as much in evidence today as it was in times past. The present Laird, Lady Clare Macpherson-Grant, and her husband, Oliver Russell, have lived at Ballindalloch for the past twenty-five years and their care for and love of this precious inheritance is self-evident.

Lady Clare was a Deputy Lieutenant for Banffshire from 1991 until 1998, when she was appointed Vice Lord-Lieutenant. In 2002, the Queen appointed her as Lord-Lieutenant for Banffshire. Oliver Russell is a former Page of Honour to Her Majesty and a member of the Queen's Bodyguard for Scotland, the Royal Company of Archers.

Lady Clare is a handsome woman with a wonderful smile. She said: "We have been continuing the renovations that my parents started in 1967. They took down the most recent wing which had been added in 1878. The family called it the carbuncle because it spoiled the entire castle.

"I was brought up here and educated by a Wee Free governess. I had seen my mother run the estate and when I took over, it had much the same staff. It's been a great challenge and it has been wonderful to have done the things that we have done together and survived.

"We try to refurbish a room every year. When I was five, there was one bathroom in the house and if it rained, we ran around with buckets. My parents did a lot to restore the property, including the installation of eight bathrooms. When we came back we did a lot, too, including more bathrooms. If one generation doesn't do any renovation, it nearly brings it all down."

The Grant ancestors came to Britain from Normandy with William the Conqueror (1066) and in the fifteenth century, King James IV (1488–1513) gave the lands of Ballindalloch to Patrick Grant. Different branches of Clan Grant have held the estate ever since. The original structure – the corner tower of the present building – built in 1546, took the form a Z-plan castle.

"We had to completely commercialise the whole estate when we returned because there was no income coming in," Lady Clare said. "We started opening the house to the public about eleven years ago and now have fifty people staying in our estate houses from March to October, fishing, shooting and playing golf on our new golf course."

Lady Clare's husband, Oliver, said: "We want to preserve the castle but not to preserve it in aspic. Some old castles are like museums and one tries to avoid that here. This is a family home and things have to work. When it comes to renovation, you must look 100 years ahead. I can be fairly sure that the things I have done here will still be around in 100 years time.

"They may not reflect me, or my personality, but they will still be here. It's a balance between the commercial aspects of the estate and its role as a home. The income comes from farming, forestry, shooting, fishing and tourism. Clare's great-grandfather started the Aberdeen-Angus breed [of cattle] and we still farm them today."

The Ballindalloch herd of Aberdeen-Angus is the oldest herd in the world, the result of the vision of three men: Hugh Watson of Keillor in Angus (1780–1865), William McCombie of Tillyfour in Aberdeenshire (1805–1880), and Sir George Macpherson-Grant, 2nd Bart of Ballindalloch, who inherited the estate in 1850 at the age of twenty-one years.

The herd is descended from Aberdeenshire's traditional black cattle, known locally as "doddies" and "hummlies", and the breed is now famous throughout the world. Sir George was determined to establish the Ballindalloch herd as the finest of the breed and this tradition continues under the guidance of the Macpherson-Grants and their stockman, Ian Spence.

The best-known breeder of Aberdeen-Angus cattle was the late Queen Mother. Her association with the breed began during her early years at Glamis Castle and she was Patron of the Aberdeen-Angus Cattle Society for sixty-five years until her death in 2002.

The Queen Mum, as she was affectionately known, established her own herd at the Castle of Mey in Caithness in 1964. Castle of Mey and Ballindalloch have always worked together to continue to improve the breed and the Queen Mother was a frequent visitor at Ballindalloch.

The Queen Mother was also Patron of Queen Mary's Clothing Guild, one of her favourite charities founded in 1882, and Clare Macpherson-Grant Russell has been Scottish chairman of the Guild since 1986.

The Guild is a nationwide network of women who knit with wool donated to them by supporters of the charity. Each year, Ballindalloch Castle is the gathering centre for the items completed in Scotland and for those who did the knitting. The Queen Mother invariably attended this happy occasion and, no doubt, also took the opportunity to have a shrewd look at the Aberdeen-Angus herd when she was there.

I turned from the splendid lawn and entered the castle. Almost immediately, I was aware of being in a family home, rather than a castle. Nothing seemed to be on display, but everywhere you looked there was something of interest, some beautiful object, piece of furniture or portrait to catch the eye: eighteenth-century pistols over the fireplace, a Sheraton corner cupboard and Chinese Chippendale-style chairs.

This "lived in" look pervades the whole house; the library, with its amazing collection of more than 25,000 books, collected mainly by Colonel William Grant in the early eighteenth century and by Sir John Macpherson-Grant; Lady Macpherson-Grant's room, with its wonderful four-poster bed made in cherry wood in 1860.

Family portraits adorn the walls, including one of General James Grant (1720–1806), who in 1770 built the part of the house that contains the present-day drawing room. Grant was born at Ballindalloch but spent most of his life fighting Britain's wars around the world.

Grant took part in the Battle of Fontenoy in Flanders in May 1745 and was back in Scotland in April 1746 to join in the rout of Bonnie Prince Charlie's rebel force at Culloden. He fought against the French and the Cherokee Indians and was briefly Governor of Florida (1763).

Most famously, when illness forced him to return to England in 1771, on the brink of the American War of Independence, he declared in parliament that he could "march from one end of the continent to the other with five thousand men". He learned different at Bunkers Hill, Trenton, Boston, New York and other engagements.

The General was famous for his love of fine food and drink. As I stood in the dining room, the largest room in the castle and formerly the Great Hall, I swear I heard him calling for a toast to His Majesty. A portrait of King George III, painted by Allan Ramsay, was presented to Grant in recognition of his military service in America and it hangs in the dining room.

Lady Clare said of her illustrious ancestor, "He died the fattest man in Great Britain and still wanders along the passage handing out drams."

Ballindalloch is well-endowed with ghosts. A bedroom in the Pink Tower, the oldest part of the castle, holds the spirit of an unknown woman, seen sitting in a chair, wearing a pink crinoline gown and a large straw hat. The ghost of the General, mounted on a white horse, is said to ride the estate boundaries every night. The ghost of a daughter of the castle, jilted in love, has been seen crossing the bridge over the River Avon to post a letter to her errant lover.

Another love is to be found at Ballindalloch, in Lady Clare's latest book, *I Love Food*. The book is, like the house, as much a celebration of family as it is about her love of cooking. "We wanted it to be a bit different. There are favourite recipes, family photographs, prayers, poems and paintings, as well as information about the castle. And it's the only recipe book around with a section on food for dogs!" she said.

I left the house and stepped out into the warm evening. The pied-wagtails still played on the lawn and doves still called from the woods. Lengthening shadows touched the old castle, sending shafts of sunlight dancing amidst its towers and turrets. It was hard to leave. My enduring memory of Ballindalloch is of a wonderful, happy, family home.

Ballindalloch Castle lies twelve miles to the north of Grantown-on-Spey on the A95 Grantown to Craigellachie road at Bridge of Avon. For further information, contact: The Estate Office, Ballindalloch Castle, Banffshire, Scotland AB37 9AX; Tel: 01807 500 205; Fax: 01807 500 210; Website: http://www.ballindalloch castle.co.uk; Email: enquiries@ballindallochcastle.co.uk

5.
Helmsdale

I stood at the end of the pier at Helmsdale Harbour. A silver-grey sea merged into the cloud-darkened sky. The breakwater of the old harbour wall was clustered with the black, statuesque shapes of cormorants, crowded together like semi-quavers on a page of music. Arctic tern wheeled overhead. A group of white-cloaked eider ducks probed for food in the shallows. The deep throb of the engine of a returning fishing boat filled the air.

The opposite wall, at the entrance to the harbour, sparkled with light reflected from a huge, sculptured fish-like shape, part whale and part salmon; a work commissioned by Timespan, the Helmsdale heritage organisation, from the artist Julian Meredith. It is constructed out of a series of stainless steel, triangular-shaped pieces, each piece being of a different size. It celebrates the whales that are often seen from the harbour and the salmon that return through the harbour to their natal home in the Helmsdale River.

Behind me lay the little village, clinging to the sides of the yellow-bright, gorse-covered hills that guard the village and the mouth of the Helmsdale River; one of Scotland's most famous salmon streams, much loved by HRH Prince Charles and countless numbers of other anglers who come to the far north from all over the world to fish in its peat-stained waters for *Salmo salar*, the King of Fish.

The story of Helmsdale is inextricably linked to the sea and to fishing. People have lived and worked here for thousands of years. The village has weathered the less-than-friendly visitations of Viking invaders, endless clan squabbles and the depredations of the dreadful days of the Highland Clearances during the nineteenth century when Kildonan Strath was cleared of people to make way for more profitable sheep.

Some of the dispossessed were allotted small plots of land at Gartymore, to the south of Helmsdale, where they were expected to set up home and support their families. These harsh beginnings gave birth to the Land League, through which the crofters fought a long and acrimonious battle with their landlords and with the government for security of tenure of their properties. Eventually, in 1886, this was won by the passing of the first Crofting Act.

I got lost once in Helmsdale, which is difficult to do because the village has few streets. But it was a happy accident. Until then, I had passed through, either travelling south from our home in Caithness or hurrying north again with never enough time to stand and stare. Since then, I often visit Helmsdale to explore its history and walk its well-ordered streets. The village was laid out by the Duke of Sutherland to accommodate those cleared from his lands, a fact commemorated in the street names he chose for his new town.

The streets parallel to the river were named after the Duke's Sutherland holdings: Sutherland Street (the family owned most of the county in those days) and Dunrobin Street (in honour of his fairytale castle to the north of Golspie). The streets running in the opposite direction were named after his lands in England: Stafford Street and Stittenham Road. Before the clearances, Helmsdale and its hinterland areas had 2,000 people. Today, it is home to about 600.

I had come that morning to speak to some of the people who call Helmsdale home, and to ask them about the life and history of their village, and my first call was on Adam Macpherson at his general store in Dunrobin Street. Adam was born in Helmsdale. His grandfather started the business and his father followed in his father's footsteps. Adam himself has been there for the past twenty-five years. He told me, "I love staying here. I think that it is a very beautiful little village. I won't be moving. No, I'll be here forever. I was born just next door to the shop."

In the nineteenth century, Helmsdale was one of the most important herring fishing stations on the north-east coast. During the short summer season, more than 200 boats crowded the harbour, setting out to sea each day in search of the "silver darlings". The village bustled with the activity of cleaning and curing the herring, which were salted and packed into barrels and exported to the Baltic and Europe. Such was the efficiency of the operation that fish caught in July could be on the table in Europe by early September.

The advent of the Great War and the Russian Revolution brought these glory days to an end and by the 1960s, the fleet had turned to fishing for white fish, cod and haddock. When stocks of these fish began to decline, Helmsdale's importance as a fishing port declined with them. Today, the few boats left primarily fish for prawns, lobsters and crab, which provide a good living because they are under less pressure than white fish stocks. Alex Jappy is the Harbour Master and I met him in the nineteenth-century Red Herring House, a herring curing yard built by the Duke of Sutherland, which now serves as the Harbour Master's office.

I asked Alex what he saw as the future for Helmsdale Harbour and his answer was unequivocal: yachts. Until not so long ago, fewer than eight or nine yachts visited the harbour each year. Now, the number has risen to over ninety. Most are visitors from England, sailing up the west coast of Scotland and through the Caledonian Canal to Inverness. From there, it is a day's sail to Helmsdale. This makes Helmsdale the ideal place to rest before an onward journey to Wick, thence across the broken waters of the Pentland Firth to the Orkney Islands.

Alex told me that additional pontoons were being installed to meet the growing demand and that this increase in visitors was bringing new life to the community. "To start with, most of the boats just stopped overnight. Now, some are staying for a week, hiring a car to explore the area, enjoying its culture and history, and enjoying the fresh sea food and local produce available in our restaurants and pubs. For centuries, Scotland's most notable export was its people, now, it seems to me, the position is reversed as more and more people from the south recognise the quality of the life that we have and want to share it," he said.

The confidence Alex Jappy has in the future of Helmsdale is nowhere better reflected than in Timespan. This award-winning heritage centre has become a focal point for the community. Indeed, it owes its existence to the determination of the community to record its history and commemorate those who helped to shape it. At the wheel of this enthusiastic juggernaut is Timespan Director, Rachel Skeen, who steers the ever-expanding interests of Timespan with consummate skill, supported by an equally enthusiastic staff and a hard-working board of directors and volunteers.

Timespan has just completed work on a "geology garden", overlooking the river. The garden is peopled with huge rocks from virtually every period of geological time, each stone accompanied by a brief description of its place in the making and formation of the north of Scotland. The Timespan gallery, the only public art gallery in Sutherland, hosts exhibitions and workshops from visiting artists from around the world – this year, artists from Finland and Canada, as well as from Scotland. Alex Jappy is helping with the restoration of a Fifie, a design of fishing boat that was in use in Helmsdale from the 1850s until well into the twentieth century.

However, the key function of Timespan is to record and display records and artefacts that illuminate the life and times of Helmsdale, and it does this with unparalleled success, attracting thousands of visitors each year. Timespan has also introduced the UK's first ever GPS (Global Positioning System) visitor experience, which leads visitors round the site of Scotland's only Gold Rush. The Gold Rush began in 1869 when Robert Gilchrist returned to his native village from prospecting in Australia. Gilchrist found gold in Kildonan Burn at Baile an Or and shortly thereafter, 300 men had arrived at the site to seek their fortune. Gold may still be found in the Kildonan Burn today and visitors can try their luck panning for it.

One of Helmsdale's most famous recent residents was the novelist Barbara Cartland, author of 723 books. Barbara Cartland married into the McCorquodale family who lived at Kilphedir and fished the river. She was famous also for her love of pink chiffon clothing and jewellery. One of her great friends, the late Nancy Sinclair, shared this love. Nancy, a happy, welcoming woman, was a Helmsdale institution and lived surrounded by an astonishing array of mementos and artefacts, not the least of which is a life-sized figure of Marilyn Monroe, skirt blowing, in a bathroom, and a similar-sized one of Elvis Presley in the sitting room.

Rather than setting off to a fashion career in Paris, Nancy came north to help her mother run the Navidale House Hotel to the north of Helmsdale. I asked what she thought of her decision now: "All I could think was that there was nothing here but sheep!" In time, Nancy opened La Mirage restaurant in Dunrobin Street, which became one of the north's most notable places to dine. Decorated entirely in her favourite pink style, La Mirage was featured in press and on television and attracted a clientele that included household names from stage and screen. Last year, Nancy was appointed Chieftain of the Helmsdale Highland Games.

Back at the harbour, I called at an Aladdin's Cave of a shop in one of Helmsdale's oldest buildings in Helmsdale to meet the owner, Lorna Sangster, an ebullient woman with a sparkling smile and a deep love of her adopted home. Lorna was born in Edinburgh but has lived in Helmsdale for many years. The shop hosts an amazing display of local and worldwide craft items, including the famous Helmsdale Pottery made by David and Penny Woodley.

The building dates from 1745, when it housed government troops billeted there after Bonnie Prince Charlie's sad uprising. The lower part was used as stables for the soldiers' horses; the narrow slits that ventilated the stables have been uncovered. The upper floor was living quarters, whilst the officer in charge lived in the house next door. Later, the building was used as a granary; tenants paid their rent to the laird in money and in produce.

In the aftermath of the Clearances, when people where starving throughout the Highlands, the grain that they grew for their laird was shipped south. A statue of a family – father, mother and child – has been erected on the hill overlooking the harbour to commemorate these times and the suffering of the people who were evicted. The family is looking out to sea, which so many were destined to sail, to Canada, Australia, New Zealand and South Africa. Today, their descendants return to search the straths of Sutherland for lost stories of their loved ones, and to pay their respects to the land and people that gave them birth.

As I turned from the harbour, the day had ended. The sea glistened steely blue and I drove home thinking of Alex Jappy's parting words when I asked him what was special about Helmsdale: "The people, really, they are always kind and friendly. That is what makes Helmsdale such a special place, the people." Amen to that, I thought.

6.
Assynt Revisited

~~~~~~~~~~~~~~~~~~~~~

Alastair MacAskill is a big man with a big personality. His soft voice resonates with love for his Assynt homeland and he is Chairman of the Assynt Foundation, a community group that now owns 44,000 acres of land in the area. I met Alastair at Glencanisp Lodge near Lochinver and asked him how the 450 families in this remote corner of North West Sutherland managed to acquire Glencanisp and Drumrunie, two of Scotland's most magnificent estates.

Alastair told me, "I had heard on the grape vine that the estates were coming up for sale and a short time later my friend Bill Ritchie put to me the idea that the community should bid for them. I was not sure. However, he suggested that it was possible that they would fall into the hands of owners who might be less than conscious of their responsibility to the community and that the only way to avoid this happening was for the community itself to buy the land."

Bill Ritchie had been one of the leaders of the historic crofter-led £300,000 buy out of the 21,300-acre North Assynt Estate in 1993. The estate had been placed on the market when the company that owned it went into liquidation. It was proposed that it should be broken up into seven lots – showing little regard for the impact that this would have had on the crofting families who lived and worked there, as their forefathers had done for generations before them.

Within a short space of time, the crofters had prepared a bid to buy the estate and reports began to appear in the press about this 'audacious attempt by a few crofters in the North West Highlands' to win back the land taken from their ancestors during the terrible years of the nineteenth-century

Highland Clearances. The crofters' campaign caught the public's imagination and six months after the decision to launch the bid, the newly-formed Assynt Crofters Trust took back their land.

Thus, when Glencanisp and Drumrunie came on the market, there was an in-built support mechanism for a local buy out. At a meeting in Lochinver in February 2005 the community voted by a margin of two to one in favour of bidding for Glencanisp and Drumrunie; the estates had been run in the past as sporting "playgrounds", with an abundance of game and very few people. Now, however, the local community would have to raise nearly £3 million to complete the purchase. They did but it was a close-run thing.

Under land reform law introduced by the Scottish Parliament, a community wishing to buy their land has six months in which to do so, starting from the date that it first announces its intention to submit an offer. The Scottish Executive Land Fund, set up to help land purchase, and the Community Land Fund, a similar fund operated by Highlands and Islands Enterprise, pledged £2 million towards the cost of the purchase, but for the people that Alistair led, time would run out on 3 June.

With six weeks left to go, the community was still short of £900,000 pounds and it was beginning to look very much as though their famous bid was heading for failure. At that time, Alastair MacAskill commented, "No one is giving up hope but we don't have long, and unless we have a clear idea of where the money is coming from, we couldn't even ask the owners for an extension on the time we have to buy their estates."

But help was at hand. In May, at the instigation of the John Muir Trust, named after Scotland's most famous conservationist, the England-based Tubney Trust came forward with a surprise donation of £550,000. When the news was announced, Alistair said, "We are going to do it. We are highly optimistic that we will get the necessary funds by the deadline. Three weeks ago we were short of £900,000. Since then we have raised £700,000. Not bad for such a small community. We are hopeful that some of the other funding bodies will now help to close the gap." They did.

I asked Alastair how he had felt when it was signed, sealed and delivered.

He smiled and touched his head, "Do you not see all these grey hairs? But I will tell you how I felt. Yes, we were elated, but it was tempered with the realisation of the enormity of the task that we were undertaking. I think that it was the writer John Galsworthy who said, 'Idealism can be directly measured in proportion to a person's distance from the problem.' We are at no distance at all from the problem. This is our home and we went into this with our eyes wide open."

My first visit to Assynt and Drumrunie, many years ago, opened my eyes. Our children were at school at the time and the school had arranged an adventure weekend at Elphin, near Drumrunie. A woman was required to "chaperon" the girls in the group and since our daughter was in the party, my wife, Ann, agreed to go along. I accompanied them in my capacity as an angler, to introduce some of the children to the joys of fishing for wild brown trout. We arrived after dark and the next morning I went outside to see what I could see.

When I was confronted with the vastness of the landscape, my heart missed a beat. It was as though I had stepped into a paradise of mountains and moorland. Dramatic, uncompromising peaks crowded the view: Cul Mor (849m); Cul Beg (789m); the long, grey shoulder of Canisp (846m); and Suilven (731m), the "Pillar Mountain" of the Vikings. They were etched into a clear, cloudless sky, almost as if I could reach out my hand and touch them. Mirror-calm lochs, stippled with rising trout, reflected their image; the long, silver-blue ribbon of Veyatie, crooked Cam Loch and, at the centre of the Inverpolly Nature Reserve, magnificent Sionascaig, winding around a jagged shoreline for a distance of more than seventeen miles.

Later that morning, I tramped a track on the north shore of the Cam Loch with a few of the boys, trout rods at the ready. After a mile or so, we climbed north west into the hills to find two lochs where I knew that catching trout was virtually guaranteed: little Loch a'Chroisg and finger-like Lochan Fada. With Canisp to our right and the enormous, intimidating bulk of Suilven ahead, we spent a happy few hours and caught enough trout to provide breakfast for the whole party the following morning.

I have been returning to Assynt and Drumrunie ever since and every time I do so, I still experience that sudden shock of pleasure as I descend from Glen Oykle and catch the first glimpse of this splendid wonderland. One of my heroes, who had a life-long love affair with Assynt, is the late Norman MacCaig, awarded the Queen's Gold Medal for Poetry in 1986. My great regret is that I never called to see him because we had a lot in common. Like me, he was born in Edinburgh, went to the same school that I attended, The Royal High, and, again like me, he loved hill loch fishing for wild brown trout.

You will find copies of his books at Scotland's most remote bookshop, Achins, at Inverkirkaig, where the River Kirkaig tumbles into Enard Bay. MacCaig's works are constant best sellers at Achins. Here is one of my favourite's poems:

On the North Side of Suilven

The three-inch-wide streamlet
trickles over its own fingers
down the sandstone slabs
of my favourite mountain.

Like the Amazon it'll reach the sea
Like the Volga
it'll forget its own language.

Its water goes down my throat
With glassy coldness,
Like something suddenly remembered.

I drink
Its freezing vocabulary
And half understand the purity
Of all beginnings.

The broken bounds of Assynt and Drumrunie instil in all who know them a deep love for this amazing landscape. Few express this love more eloquently and passionately than Allan MacRae, the present chairman of the Assynt Crofters Trust. His determination to enhance and preserve the crofting way of life is self-evident, from the moment he begins to recall how the Trust has survived and expanded since that momentous day in 1993 when they bought back their land. Allan encapsulated this for me when I met him recently. He told me, "Without our land, we are nothing."

Allan's Crofters Trust supports the aspirations of "new boys" in town, the Assynt Foundation, of which more than 25% of the community are now members. Derek Louden is the Foundation development manager and he, too, is passionately committed to the aims of the Foundation: to create opportunities for local people to live and work on the land; encourage and support the entrepreneurial ambitions of local people; get people back on the land by creating crofts and smallholdings; create employment; safeguard and enhance the natural heritage and landscape on behalf of the nation.

You, too, can help the Foundation achieve these objectives by joining "Friends of Assynt Foundation". As such, you will receive regular newsletters and progress reports. The Foundation is based at Glencanisp Lodge, a traditional Highland sporting lodge set amidst ancient woodlands overlooking little island-dotted Loch Druim Suardalain. Eventually, the Foundation hopes to let out Glencanisp Lodge to visitors, as they intended to do with other properties that they now own. I can think of no finer place in all of Scotland in which to spend precious time.

The face of land tenure in Scotland was radically altered by the primary actions of the Assynt Crofters Trust and this, in my opinion, encouraged other Scottish communities to follow suit – including the bold, spectacular decision of the Assynt Foundation to bid for and win the ownership of Glencanisp and Drumrunie for the local community. Before I left the lodge, Alastair MacAskill told me, "We do not view ourselves as landowners – we see ourselves as custodians of the land." As I drove home through the mountains, I knew that I had left Assynt in safe hands.

7.

Durness

Not so many years ago, a few days before Easter, a crofter was herding half a dozen donkeys along the narrow road from Rhiconich to Durness in North West Sutherland. In the process, he collected behind him a convoy of motorists who were angry about being unable to get past.

Eventually, the crofter left his donkeys and walked back to the leading vehicle. The agitated driver wound down his window but before he could utter a single word, the recalcitrant crofter politely asked, "Excuse me, Sir, can you tell me, is this the way to Jerusalem?"

It is this wry, laconic sense of humour that marks out the Highlander from the Lowland Scot and it is a characteristic I have always admired. The story is true and I first heard it during one of my early visits to this most glorious and dramatic part of the land that I love and call home.

I am an angler and hill walker, and was first drawn to Durness by the lure of its famous wild brown trout lochs and salmon and sea-trout fishing on the River Dionard and in the Kyle of Durness – and by the urge to explore the ragged ridge of Foinaven (914m), grey-shouldered Arkle (787m), green Cranstackie (801m) and the wilderness hills of Cape Wrath.

The township of Durness clings to the edge of the sea-bird-clad cliffs that protect this remote community from Atlantic storms. People have lived here for thousands of years, from the Mesolithic hunter-gatherers who arrived at the end of the last Ice Age some 8,000 years ago, to the Neolithic men who followed them and, subsequently, their Pictish descendants.

Warrior Vikings invaded in the later years of the ninth century and ruled the Highlands and Islands for more than 500 years. During this time, this part of Sutherland became home to Clan Mackay: "The first Lord of

Reay was a Mackay and he and his relations owned all of the land that extended from the western seaboard, between Assynt and Cape Wrath, to the Caithness frontier in the east. He was described as the leader of four thousand fighting men."

On a spring morning last April, I set out for Durness from my home in Tongue to speak to a less-warlike member of the clan, Iris Mackay. My intention was to try to discover what it was that had made, and still makes, Durness (population 350) one of the most vibrant communities in Scotland. Iris is an immediately striking personality, with a wonderful smile and a wonderfully soft, Highland voice. A black Labrador dog, tail-wagging, also greeted me and we relaxed in Iris's sitting room chatting over home-baked scones and shortbread.

Iris Mackay owns a treasure trove of a shop, Mather's Mini Market, close to her house on the main A838 Tongue to Durness road. The shop overlooks the golden sands and blue seas of Sango Bay and has been a family business for 100 years. Iris is still known as Iris Mather although she has been married to her husband, Donnie, for more than thirty-eight years.

I asked Iris what made Durness special for her and she paused whilst considering her reply: "It is the community spirit and the life style that we have here. People are important. Everybody is equal. I grew up here and could never survive in a town or city. Of course, over the years, things change, attitudes change, but there is still the same sense of communal responsibility for where we live, and for the way in which we live."

One of the best-attended events in North Sutherland is the Durness Highland Gathering, held on the last Friday in July. Iris has been a member of the Gathering committee for more than three decades and has been chairperson for fourteen years. The competitions – from tossing the caber to highland dancing – are free of charge and open to everyone, no matter from which country they come, and in the evening there is a Highland Gathering dance in the village hall, which always attracts an enthusiastic full house.

Iris Mackay also plays an active role in the Durness Community Council, which has an affiliated charitable organisation, the Durness

Development Group. The Group has promoted a wide range of activities to sustain the community and to provide employment and tourist opportunities for locals and visitors alike.

Their work has had an enormous impact, particularly through the establishment of the "Cape Wrath Challenges". The week includes what is generally regarded to be the toughest marathon in the UK – forty-two kilometres with a climb of over 736 metres, beginning at the east side of the Kyle of Durness, out to Cape Wrath Lighthouse and then back again. The event takes place in May and attracts more than 200 runners.

There are other, less taxing runs during the festival: a half marathon, the Sangmore and Loch Meadaidh hill run, and a ten kilometre run. But the Cape Wrath Challenges are not only about testing your stamina along some golden strand or heather-bordered track, they are also about people: a wide range of social events are organised, designed to involve every member of the community, their guests and visitors.

On the first evening of the week there is a Meet & Greet wine and cheese event with a welcome talk about the area. This is held in the Village Hall and is free of charge. During the week, there is a general knowledge Quiz Night with teams of local people and visitors in the Sango Sands Oasis pub, as well as abseiling down Smoo Cave – sixty-one metres long, forty metres wide and fifteen metres high, once the haunt of smugglers and brigands. Local wine producers, Balnakeil Wines, arrange wine tasting and there are sheepdog trial demonstrations where top-class dogs work with their shepherds.

There is also time to brush up on your Scottish Country Dancing skills, accompanied by local musicians and expert dancers. "Square Wheels" offer mountain biking and instruction for exploring the peat tracks around Durness, and there is angling on the world-famous Durness limestone lochs, Caladail, Borralie, Croispol and little Lanlish. Visitors can also enjoy a round of golf, where players must drive across the Atlantic, a wide bay dividing the 9th tee from the flagpole that marks the position of the cup on the distant green.

As well as the activities noted above, the local Countryside Ranger organises guided walks to bird-watching sites – puffins galore – and areas renowned for the diversity of their flora and fauna, including wonderful plants such as the unique Scottish primrose, *Primula scotica*. Members of the Durness Archaeology Field Group are also on hand to guide visitors to sites of historical and archaeological interest nearby.

If you need to test your sea legs, then the Cape Wrath Charters Company's vessel, *The Nimrod*, carries up to twelve passengers and offers the chance to see, close-up, some of the most dramatic sea-cliffs to be found anywhere around the British Isles. Finally, the Cape Wrath Challenges week ends on the Saturday evening with a splendid ceilidh, complete with a traditional ceilidh band and a buffet featuring the best of locally produced and prepared food.

In September, Durness bustles again with the annual Sheepdog Trials at Keoldale Farm, overlooking the Kyle of Durness and backed by the mountains of Strath Dionard. The event attracts some of Scotland's finest dog-handlers, thanks to the hard work of the small band of enthusiasts who organise the event and to Keoldale Farm manager, Jock Sutherland, a well-kent face at trials around the country. It is always an early start, from 7am, with business being completed at about 6pm, but entirely enthralling, as much for visitors as it is for those taking part.

As well as the September Sheepdog Trials, a Music & Food Festival is generally arranged and last year this was incorporated into the John Lennon Northern Lights Festival. As a youth, John Lennon, the famous member of the "Fab Four", The Beatles, used to visit Durness on holiday when he stayed with his aunt, Elizabeth Sutherland. This connection is commemorated by a splendid John Lennon garden next to the Village Hall.

The Festival featured some of Scotland and the UK's most prestigious musicians and composers, including Sir Peter Maxwell Davies, Master of the Queen's Music. There were classical, jazz, traditional Scottish music and popular music performances. Theatre and film were also represented, as well as poets and writers. The event was an enormous success and captured the title "Best New Festival" in the UK Festival Awards competition.

However, the heart of any community is its school and, after leaving Iris Mackay at her shop unloading the weekly delivery of supplies, I went in search of Graham Bruce, head teacher at Durness Primary School, where he and his colleague look after nineteen pupils. I found Graham at the School House and asked him what it was that had attracted him to Durness.

"When I was ten years old, we came north on a family holiday and I never forgot the experience, particularly the seemingly unending drive along the north coast from Caithness to get here. It took all day. The road was very narrow, with passing places, and there was no causeway over the Kyle of Tongue then. But I never forgot it and when I saw an advert for a teacher in Durness, I immediately applied. That was twenty-four years ago."

Like Iris Mackay, Graham identified the strong sense of community spirit as being the well-spring of life in this remote corner of Scotland: "It is a good community to live in," he told me. "People pull together and work together in an almost old-fashioned way. If something has to be done, they simply do it and make things happen. They are really nice people."

Graham is chairman of the Durness Development Group and is immensely proud of what the Group has achieved, not the least of which was the communal effort involved in funding the building of the new village hall; in use seven days a week by the local youth club and for badminton, indoor football and bowls, table tennis, country dancing, social events and meetings. The hall has become the key venue for groups throughout North West Sutherland.

I left the school house and drove to the Loch Croispol Bookshop and Restaurant for lunch. No visit to Durness is complete without a visit to the bookshop, run by Kevin Crowe and his partner Simon Long. They serve simple, excellent food in a comforting atmosphere, surrounded by books, where you may browse for as long as you please.

After lunch I visited Balnakeil to watch golfers attempting the "shot across the Atlantic", and wind-surfers and canoeists splashing amongst the green, white-topped waves. Also, to pay my respects to Rob Don (1714–1778), the Gaelic poet, revered in the north and known as the Robert Burns of the Highlands: "I was born in the winter, among the lowering mountains, and my first sight of the world, snow and wind about my ears." He lies at rest here in the old graveyard overlooking the bay.

With the afternoon sun setting, I turned for home. One more stop along the way, near Portnacon, by deep Loch Eriboll, and the remains of an earth-house built and inhabited some 2,000 years ago, now barely visible amongst the bracken and heather that has grown over the roof. I climbed down the broken stairs to the dark inner chamber and listened to the silence. I know that it was just my imagination but I thought that I could faintly hear the voices and laughter of the people who had once lived there – along their road to Jerusalem.

8.
Bagpipe Music

When I served with the East Lowland Divisional District Territorial Army Column, I used to give the commentary for our Pipes & Drums as they Beat Retreat on Edinburgh Castle esplanade. The ceremony of Beating Retreat grew out of the days when troops retreat into a defensive positions at nightfall. It was an honour for our band to be asked to Beat Retreat and it was the principal social event in our year, followed by a drinks party in Edinburgh Castle's Officer's Mess and a magisterial piobaireachd from our Pipe Major.

One year, I invited my wife's parents to be our special guests. At the start of the ceremony, from my eagle's nest commentary position on the Half Moon Battery, I announced: "The Pipes and Drums will march across the drawbridge playing . . ." and as I did so, I saw my father-in-law slip from the back of the VIP enclosure and set off down Castlehill. At the junction of Bank Street and George IV Bridge, he turned left and disappeared into the all-enveloping embrace of Deacon Brodie's Tavern.

Well, I thought, pipes and drums are not for everyone and, after all, my father-in-law, Charles Rhodes, was Yorkshire born and bred. However, with faultless timing, ten minutes before the end, I saw him scuttling back to resume his seat. Later, in the Mess, over a dram, I asked him, "Well, Charles, what did you think of it – did it stir your soul and rouse your spirits?"

He looked at me and smiled: "You know, don't you?"

"Yes," I replied, "and I am never going to let you forget it."

Bagpipe music is as natural to me as is breathing. Perhaps Scots are born with the sound of the bagpipes in their blood. I can't remember ever being far from their magical melancholy. From my earliest years in Edinburgh, we always seemed to be surrounded by pipers; at weddings, sports days, school prize-giving, commemorative events, visits to Auld Reekie by members of the Royal Family, and visits to our school by seriously ermine-robed, sombre City dignitaries.

I attended the Royal High School of Edinburgh and was a member of our Army Combined Cadet Force. We had our own pipe band and I remember once marching proudly behind the band from our school building on the side of Calton Hill, down Regent Road to Holyrood, where we had an open day for parents. My mum and dad were there. They were Scottish Country Dancers and I was soon captivated by that music as well; which is, I suppose, how I came to know Pipe Major Sandy Forbes.

In my mother's later years, she stayed near us at Caladh Sona, a residential home in Melness, across the Kyle from where we live in the township of Tongue. Sandy is a skilled musician and regularly entertained the residents, playing piano, piano accordion and, of course, the pipes. Sandy recognised my mother's love of music and always played her favourite tunes, including the Scottish Country Dance melodies that she loved so much. Sandy brought a lot of joy into her life and when he asked me if I could arrange a day's trout fishing for himself and one of his friends, I was happy to do so.

It was a wonderful outing but when Sandy and his friend tried to pay me for acting as their gillie, I refused even to consider it. But as much as I insisted that it wasn't necessary, so they insisted that it was. In desperation, I struggled to find a solution. It came to me in an inspirational flash. "Sandy," I said, "why don't you just write me a pipe tune instead?" In due course, the tune arrived, a rousing jig which Sandy called "The Bruce", and it is included in his latest book, *The Ben Loyal Collection, Ceòl Beag and Ceòl Mor – Tunes for the Highland Bagpipe*.

Sandy learned to play the pipes as a boy and he served during the war with Royal Armoured Corps. He became a piper in the Seaforth Highlanders and studied under the legendary Pipe Major Willie Ross at the Army School of Piping in Edinburgh Castle. The School was founded in 1910 on the initiative of the Piobaireachd Society. At the age of nineteen, Sandy had the distinction of being the youngest holder of the Pipe Major's Certificate in the British Army. Sandy is a well-known figure in the piping world, at home and abroad, and he has spent a lifetime playing, teaching and judging.

It was through Sandy that I met one of his friends, also a famous figure on the Scottish piping scene, Pipe Major Andrew Venters. Andrew lives at Culloden near Inverness and he is a bright-eyed, sprightly man with an enormous sense of fun and a ready smile. He was born in Edinburgh in 1935, and started his piping career with the Boys Brigade and playing with the Thurso Pipe Band in Caithness in 1948 during a summer camp at Castletown.

Andrew joined the Queen's Own Cameron Highlanders in 1953 with the sole aim of becoming a piper. He told me, "I had played for the Pipe Major and thought that I hadn't done too badly, but I didn't hear any more. Until one day, as we were training on the barrack square, the Pipe Major saw me. "What are you doing there?" he asked. I tried to explain but he said, "Right, you, come wi me, now!" Andrew served in Austria, Germany and Korea before being demobbed from the army in 1956.

Andrew rejoined the army in 1960 and graduated from the Army School of Piping's Pipe Majors course in 1963. After the Cameron and the Seaforth Highlanders were amalgamated, in 1969 Andrew became the regimental Pipe Major. He served and played with the band in Singapore, Borneo and Germany, and toured with them throughout much of Europe and the USA. After leaving the army in 1982, he became the piping instructor to the schools on the Black Isles. He recruited and trained the Black Isles Schools Pipe Band, famous throughout Scotland for its high standard of piping and drumming, and for its immaculate turnout and drill.

Andrew became Pipe Major to the Queen's Own Regimental Association Pipe Band in 1984 and still holds that position in 2011. Like Sandy Forbes, Andrew has also built up a reputation as a composer whose melodies have instant appeal. I was privileged to hear Andrew and five of his companions playing at the Queen's Own Highlanders Pipe and Drums annual dinner in Inverness on St Andrews Night 2010. The programme promised, after dinner, a "Selection of pipe tunes from Pipe Major Andy Venters and others," and it was one of the most memorable and amazing performances of pipe music that I have heard.

The following morning I travelled west, to the Summer Isles and Achiltibuie, to meet one of the world's most renowned and respected pipers, Major Bruce Hitchings, MBE, BEM. Bruce lives with his wife, Alison, and their two boys, Seamus and Finlay, in an isolated house by the sea in Coigach, the "fifth part" part of Ross-shire. Their home is backed by the vast bulk of Ben More Coigach (743m) and looks westwards over the broken waters of the Minch to Skye and the Outer Hebrides. It seemed to me to be an entirely appropriate setting for someone who plays our music with such extraordinary skill and dramatic passion.

Bruce was born in Huntersville on the North Island of New Zealand. His grandfather, a Gunn from Dunnet in Caithness, emigrated to New Zealand during the later years of the nineteenth century, taking with him one of his most prized possessions, a fine set of 1886 MacDougall bagpipes. Bruce revered his grandfather's pipes. He told me, "When I was a boy, I knew that I would be a piper. That is all that I ever really wanted to be." By the age of nine, he was playing with the local band, and by fifteen, with the prestigious City of Wellington Pipe Band.

When the band went to the UK to play in the World Championships in 1975, Bruce went with them, and also on their subsequent tours around the UK and Canada. But when the band returned to New Zealand, Bruce stayed on in Edinburgh to follow the competition circuit and finally, in 1977, to be offered a place in the Black Watch Territorial Army Pipe band. A year later, he enlisted in the Queen's Own Highlanders and in 1979, he won the Silver Medal at the Argyllshire Gathering.

His career in the army encompassed twenty-two years, during which time he served in Northern Ireland and Hong Kong, but in 1980, he was offered a place on the Pipe Major's course at Edinburgh Castle and, by 1986, Bruce was Pipe Major of the Queen's Own Highlanders. As Warrant Officer Class 1, Bruce was the senior pipe major in the British Army and he ended his military career in Edinburgh Castle as the Chief Instructor at the Army School of Piping.

We sat round the kitchen table for lunch, Scotch broth and freshly baked bread served by Bruce's wife Alison. From somewhere around the house, I heard the sound of a chanter. "The boys?" I asked. Alison smiled. "Yes," she replied, "I think that you will understand that they didn't really have any other option. And they love it." Alison herself plays the bagpipes and was Pipe Major of the Ullapool Pipe Band. As a girl, she studied with Andrew Venters at Dingwall High School and has many happy memories of her playing days.

After lunch, Bruce took me to his workshop, where he developed his revolutionary "Balance Tone" drone reeds, now used in bagpipes around the world. The reeds are easily set up, "strike in" every time, take a minimum amount of air, are rock steady and have a telescopic adjustment to alter their pitch. You can find out more about these remarkable reeds by logging on to Bruce's website at: www.highlandreeds.com, where you will also find everything you ever need to know about Highland bagpipes and everything associated with playing them.

Finally, as the sun was setting over the Summer Isles, Bruce showed me the miraculous MacDougall pipes, the ones that his grandfather had taken to New Zealand with him and that had so inspired a young boy that he had devoted the rest of his life to making music with them. I thanked Bruce and Alison for their courtesy and as I got into my car to drive home, I heard again, in the background, above the sound of the wind on the moor, the lyrical cry of a chanter.

9.
Seal Island

On a wild night in December 1938, the last inhabitants of Eilean nan Ron boarded a small boat and set off into the gathering storm. Their destination was Skerray Harbour, one mile distant across the broken seas that constantly torment the north coast of Scotland. Shattered waves drenched them with ice-cold spray as the boat pitched and tossed on the angry waters. The homes that they had left behind them quickly merged into the all-enveloping wall of darkness. Ahead, on the mainland, lights from cottages around Skerray flickered and beckoned. But that night, on the island that they had called home, the lights went out forever.

Eilean nan Ron, more commonly known today as Island Roan, lies in the parish of Tongue in North Sutherland, east of the entrance to the shallow waters and golden sands of the Kyle of Tongue. The Gaelic meaning of the name is "The Island of Seals", because Island Roan is a favoured breeding ground for these mystical creatures. The island is one and a half kilometres long by up to a kilometre wide and it covers an area of 700 acres. The highest point on the island is seventy-five metres above sea level and to the north west, separated by a narrow channel, lies a satellite isle, little Eilean Iosal. The only safe place to land on Island Roan is at Port na h-Uaille, where there is a landing stage from which steps have been cut into the cliff face leading up to the village.

In the early years of the nineteenth century, during the harsh times of the Sutherland Clearances, families trekked north from the fertile straths in which they had lived to the exposed coastal lands overlooking the North Sea. After the Strathnaver evictions in 1819, many of the destitute settled at Skerray, "between the rocks and the sea", and in 1820, four families crossed over to Island Roan to start a new life there. Eventually, the community expanded to more than seventy people and they lived and sustained themselves by fishing and farming, raising sheep and cattle and whatever crops they could grow – oats, hay, potatoes, turnips – on the small, cultivable area of land around which they built their homes.

But by the 1930s, it had become clear that the few people remaining on the island could no longer sustain themselves. The impact of two world wars and the departure of families to the mainland and overseas to Australia, Canada and America, overshadowed the lives of those who remained. This movement of young people away from their homes was mirrored throughout the Highlands of Scotland, when many once-inhabited islands suffered the same fate as Island Roan; also, stocks of fish in the seas around the island, upon which those who lived there relied for food and a source of income, had been badly damaged by the influx of large, modern vessels over-exploiting this finite resource. The lack of able-bodied men to carry out the essential everyday tasks required to exist in such a remote environment meant that, ultimately, evacuation was inevitable.

On a warm morning in October 2009, I set out from Skerray Harbour in search of memories of the people who had lived and loved and thrived on Island Roan and, as the boat headed across the crests of gently rolling waves, sunlight sparkled the sea silver. Graceful gannets, white stars against a blue sky, wheeled and dived for fish. Black shags and busy guillemots bobbed on the surface and as we approached the island, the ruins of the deserted houses were starkly etched above a foreground of ragged, scarred cliffs. I used to work as the archivist for the Skerray Historical Association and was familiar with the history of Island Roan and fascinated by its story. As I looked at the houses, I thought that I caught the scent of peat smoke drifting to greet us.

The people of the island were renowned for the gracious and friendly welcome they always afforded visitors, and this is well documented in a Visitors Book that records these events. The book was maintained from 1883 until 1999 and was gifted to the islanders by Lady Millicent, the Duchess of Sutherland, whose family owned the island then and still do so to this day. The book names the more than 2,500 people who came to Island Roan during these years, to meet friends and relatives or simply to enjoy the peace and serenity that imbued the island. In July 1884, Charles Cooper, from Edinburgh, left this message: "Where's health and happiness? / In places alone? / Or in the humble cottage / On this bare Island Roan."

After 1938, when the island was evacuated, the Visitors Book records the many, many, times that former inhabitants came back to their island: "Donald Mackay of Island Roan" and "Donald P Mackay, Late of Island Roan" in 1961. "George Mackay, Late of Island Roan" in 1962 and in 1963, Helen C Mackay wrote, "Last visit to the island." In July 1968, the Shanks family from near Glasgow left this message: "Island of cliffs, of seagulls and sheep / Happy the day we spent on your braes / Haven of peace where empty crofts keep / Sweet memory of the folk of the old days – Thanks for a golden day. An island whose spell has captured us."

Perhaps, however, the most poignant entry is an account of the "Island Roan Re-Union of Survivors" held at Coldbackie, between Skerray and Tongue, on 15 December 1973. "Tonight we drank a toast to Island Roan and to all its people, wherever they may be." The last entry in the Visitors Book, on 28 September 1999, was written by Williamina Mackay Megally from Canberra, Australia: "A wonderful experience to see the island where I was born – leaving for Australia in 1928."

When I was with the Skerray Historical Association, I was entranced by a series of wonderful black and white photographs of the island. What puzzled me was when they had been taken and by whom, although I suspected that they were for a feature article in a magazine or newspaper. I found the answer in the Visitors Book in an entry dated 12 June 1937: "Ian M Templeton, Scottish Daily Express, Edinburgh Office." I had brought copies of these photographs, the objective being to identify and photograph the houses and places in which these pictures had been taken.

I found the school house, where the last two pupils had been taught by their elder sister, and as I stood where the blackboard had been, I thought of the classroom in the early years of the twentieth century, when eighteen children crowded into the small space, attentive to the careful direction of their teacher. Happily, an account of these days has been written by one of the islanders, the late John George Mackay, who published a booklet in 1962 describing his experiences growing up on the island. It is a marvellous story and in his preface to the work, John George explained:

> My reason for putting in book form the story of Eilean-nan-Ron is to help to preserve the memory of this once prosperous and happy little island.
>
> I was born on the island and spent my childhood and adolescent years there, and now, with old age creeping over me, and having to spend most of my days alone, I often think of those happy times on the island.
>
> Now that the island is desolate and its surviving natives getting fewer and fewer, I feared that soon there would be no one left to recall the old days. The thought grieved me. Why, I said to myself, why allow the memory of my island to die? But then, how was it going to be kept alive? There was no one left capable of writing a history of its habitation.
>
> I knew full well, with my limited education, that I could not do this either. Nevertheless, I decided to try, and I thought, however simply written the book might be, it might serve as a dedication to the memory of the industrious and God-fearing people who spent their lives on the island.

John George Mackay's book admirably achieves the aims that he set himself and it is a delightful account of the life and times of Island Roan. Although the book is out of print at present, you can find the text at: http://www.scottishweb.net/articles/40/1/The-Story-Of-Island-Roan/Page1.html with a forward written by John George's grandson, Stewart Mackay.

I explored the remains of the nine houses, built so laboriously by the islanders, and then walked over the land that they had cultivated to find the huge cave on the north side where the fish they caught were hung up to cure naturally in the salt spray. As I sat on the cliffs above the cave, lulled by the sound of endless waves breaking on the rocky shore, I was overwhelmed by a feeling of profound content. I walked on to the narrow gap separating Island Roan from Eilean Iosal and to the bay at Ann Innis, spiked with sentinel rock stacks springing from the sea like the fingers of an outstretched hand. On the highest point of the island, we were rewarded with a God-like vista of mainland mountains Ben Loyal, Ben Hee, Ben Hope, Arkle, Foinaven and Cranstackie, coloured blue and silver and grey in white shafts of sunlight.

Later, back at the harbour, we threw out anchors and we sat in the stern of the boat with cups of coffee, enjoying the cry of seabirds and the haunting call of curlew. From time to time, a seal's bewhiskered head would surface and survey us with sad-eyed caution. It was hard to leave but the wind was rising. Reluctantly, we recovered the anchors, cleared them of silky purple and brown seaweed and stowed them safely. The noise of the engine reverberated round the high cliffs as we pulled away from the island and headed back towards Skerray Harbour. I watched the old houses fade into the distance and tasted salt spray on my lips; I said a silent prayer for the souls of those who had lived on Island Roan.

Further information: Any visitor to Island Roan is entirely dependent upon the weather. The best time to plan a visit is during the month of June, July and August. But even then, do not be surprised should adverse weather conditions make the journey impossible.

Landing on the island can be awkward, as is ascending the steps up from the harbour up to the cliff top. The steps have not been maintained and should be approached with caution. All of this requires a reasonable degree of fitness and, if in doubt, you should confine your visit to a sail around the island.

Either way, your visit will be eminently memorable. For information about arranging a visit to Island Roan, telephone Jimson's Shop in Skerray, tel: 01641 521445.

10.
Gairloch

September is a good-to-be-alive month in the far north of Scotland. Mountains and moorland resound to the roar of rutting stags, hills are purple-clad with heather, whilst majestic salmon, fish that have survived in Scottish waters since the end of the last Ice Age, surge upstream to their ancestral spawning grounds. Ann and I invariably spend a week away at this time of year, exploring the land we love, and this autumn we decided to revisit Wester Ross, one of the most dramatic and welcoming places in all of Scotland.

One of our objectives was to find Ross-shire's oldest Scots Pine (*Pinus sylvestris*), a tree that was young in the days before the Union of Parliaments in 1707, when Scotland lost its separate identity and joined "the auld enemy", England, to give birth to the United Kingdom. It seemed to be an appropriate thing to do, given that Scotland now has a new government led, for the first time ever, by the Scottish National Party.

We also wanted to explore Loch Maree and historic, tree-clad Isle Maree, one of the many islands that grace this lovely, nineteen-kilometre-long loch; named after St Maelrubha (The Red Priest), the Irish saint who introduced Christianity to the area in 671–673AD. We intended to spend time at Osgood Mackenzie's famous gardens at Inverewe, which contain more than 2,500 species of plants gathered from around the world, and to explore the wild peninsula that lies between Loch Ewe and Loch Gairloch.

Trees have always played an important part in the culture and heritage of Scotland. For instance, a Gaelic verse hails the humble hazelnut as being the source of all knowledge: "Thou nut of my heart / Thou face of my sun / Thou harp of my music / Thou crown of my sense." The same tradition suggested that knowledge could be acquired by eating a salmon caught in a pool surrounded by nine hazel trees.

Our Celtic ancestors revered their natural habitat and, in particular, the oak woods where they worshipped their gods and burned oak in sacred fires. Oak wood was also used to build the boats from which they fished for salmon. Salmon were considered to be a sign of wisdom and were often portrayed on intricately-carved symbol stones.

Remnants of these ancient forests, the Great Wood of Caledon, which covered 90% of Scotland, still survive today but less than 1% remains; by Loch Rannoch in Perthshire, Loch Affric in Inverness-shire, Strathspey, Mar Lodge on Royal Deeside, and around the shores and islands of Loch Maree.

The forests were destroyed to make a way through the woods secure from wolves and robbers, for building dwellings and, significantly, to build warships during the Napoleonic Wars. From 1610 onwards, the trees were burned in the process of producing iron and this is remembered in the names of locations where iron smelting flourished – Bonawe on Loch Etive and at Furnace on the shores of Loch Maree.

Ann and I found our Scots Pine when we followed the Beinn Eighe Mountain Nature Trail up to the skirts of Meall a'Ghiubhais (878m), one of the outriders of the mighty Beinn Eighe range that embraces six Munros – Scottish mountains over 914.4 metres in height – including Sail Mhor (981m) and, the highest point, Ruadh-stac Mor (1010m).

Beinn Eighe is Britain's oldest National Nature Reserve, established in 1951 to protect and preserve the ancient pinewoods near Kinlochewe. The reserve extends to some forty-eight square kilometres and is now owned and managed by Scottish Natural Heritage, the government agency charged with caring for Scotland's precious inheritance of wildlife habitats and landscapes. The aim of the organisation is to help people to enjoy Scotland's natural heritage responsibly, understand it more fully and to use it wisely so that it can be sustained for future generations.

The Beinn Eighe Mountain Nature Trail is not a walk for the faint-hearted and should not be undertaken lightly. You must be properly prepared and dressed for whatever the weather decides to throw at you, and although the trail is less than five kilometres in length, it climbs steeply in places to almost 550 metres. Allow three to four hours for the round trip.

As we descended from the high point of the trail, past Lunar Loch – so named to commemorate man's first landing on the moon on 21 July 1969 and strangely similar to a lunar landscape – we followed the crystal waters of the An t-Allt burn down into the dramatic gorge where the Lone Pine holds court. It is an awesome tree, gnarled and majestic. We sat for a while beneath its branches and told it about the advent of the new parliament, headed at last by those who value Scotland's independence. As we left, I swear that I heard the tree mutter, "And about time, too!"

The main population centre here is the village of Gairloch (the Short Loch) extending to include the neighbouring community of Charlestown. It is a bustling holiday centre where children play on golden sands or splash in clear waters warmed by the Gulf Stream. There are excellent hotels, restaurants, craft centres, an outstanding heritage museum, golf course, pony trekking, hill walking and climbing, sail boarding, organised wildlife safaris, game fishing for salmon, trout and sea-trout, sea fishing and whale-watching trips, stalking and shooting – indeed, something to keep every member of your party well-exercised, amused and happy.

But the shores of the Short Loch were not always so peaceful. Famine and evictions during the nineteenth century brought ruin to the north. When Lowland granaries were full, Highlanders starved. People went barefoot, clothed in discarded meal bags, whilst Free Church ministers appealed to Edinburgh and London in vain for help. Lord Napier, leading a Royal Commission into the unrest in the Highlands in 1882, reported: "A state of misery, of wrong-doing, and patient long suffering, without parallel in the history of our country."

The open-air pulpit of the Free Presbyterian church at Gairloch is a reminder of these sad times, when sheep were preferred to people and old and young alike laboured building roads for Destitution Boards, or accepted the blandishments of Emigration Societies and took ship for the Colonies.

Much of the history of these events can be found in the Gairloch Museum and will give you an overview of how the community coped with these depredations and yet survived to fight another day.

For our visit, we found a comfortable self-catering cottage in the straggling crofting township of Melvaig – about seven miles to the north of Gairloch along the narrow, tortuous road that leads out to Rua Reidh Lighthouse. Our cottage overlooked the sea and was within a couple of hundred yards of the nearest beach. The views were magnificent and sunsets an unforgettable joy – westwards, beyond the Shiant Isles, to the long islands of Lewis, Harris, North Uist, Benbecula and South Uist in the Outer Hebrides; south west to the Island of Skye, dominated by the stark outline of the Trotternish Ridge – an enduring fusion of light and time and space.

We drove out to the white tower of Rua Reidh Lighthouse, perched precariously above the broken waters of the Minch, guarded by myriads of endlessly wheeling gulls. Rua Reidh offers simple, inexpensive accommodation and when we arrived, a young couple were waiting to book in. They were from Spain, engaged to be married and as much in love with the Scottish landscape as they were clearly in love with each other.

The following morning, Ann and I set sail for Isle Maree. Our guide was Nick Thompson and we met Nick at the Loch Maree Hotel. The hotel used to be one of the most famous fishing hotels in Europe because of the quality of the sea-trout fishing on the loch. Each season, from March to September, anglers could catch upwards of 1,500 sea-trout in Loch Maree, as well as good numbers of salmon. Tragically, because of disease and pollution from fish farms, sea-trout and salmon numbers have collapsed in recent years and the hotel has closed its doors to anglers.

However, because of the scenic beauty of the loch and the historical importance of Isle Maree, Nick spends much of his time during the year taking parties out to the island. The story of the island is as much myth as it is factual but it is probable that in Celtic times Isle Maree was revered as being a sacred isle, dedicated to Rhiannon, the Celtic goddess of the moon. It was definitely the site of pagan rituals, as there are records of bulls being sacrificed there well into the seventeenth century.

What is beyond dispute, however, is the date of the "druid circle", which is one of the most remarkable features of the island. According to archaeological research, it has been dated at around 100 BC. The Vikings also knew the island: two graves, reputedly of a prince and princess thwarted in love, lie within the stone circle and show an inscription that may depict a Viking axe. Oak trees abound on Isle Maree, as well as holly, birch and beech, but, strangely, few birds sing. Tradition also notes that anybody who removes anything from the island will meet with a serious, if not fatal, accident.

There is also the "money tree", close to the ruins of Saint Maelrubha's cell and the site of the long-since-vanished "sacred well". Exactly when visitors to the island began the practice of hammering coins into the trunk of the tree is not clear but the oldest coin has been dated at 1828. The wish made whilst fixing the stone would be granted, provided that the coin remained in place and did not fall out. When Queen Victoria visited Isle Maree in 1877, she also left behind a coin in the tree.

We left Isle Maree and on our way back to the mooring bay, we passed amongst the other islands on the loch, Eilean Subhainn, Eilean Ruairidh Mor, Garbh Eilean and Eilean Dubh na Sroine. They were very lovely, also tree-clad and some with amazing, white sand beaches, but none had that special feeling which I had experienced on Isle Maree. It was not a feeling that evoked fear or anguish; the reverse was the case, it was a feeling of happiness. Later, as we talked about our day, Ann said that she also experienced a sense of calmness as she walked amongst the ancient stones on this enchanted isle.

Inverewe Gardens are much more organised than Isle Maree but none-the-less engaging and special for being so. We spent our last afternoon exploring the 100-acre gardens, adjudged by many to be one of the finest gardens in the world. As evening slowly silvered the sky, we watched the changing light play on the black Boor Rocks in Loch Ewe, whilst, in the distance, the gathering darkness shrouded the mighty Beinn Eighe peaks in mystery and settled them to rest.

For Melvaig self-catering properties see: http://www.cottageshighlands.com; for other accommodation see: http://www.celticfringe.org.uk/gairloch-breakfast.htm; to arrange boat trips to Isle Maree, call Nick Thompson at the Loch Maree Hotel on tel: 01445 760288; for further information about the Beinn Eighe National Nature Reserve, see: http://www.snh.org.uk or contact the Reserve Visitor Centre on tel: 01445 760254 during working hours.

11.
Scottish Regiments

Clan Mackay and Clan Sutherland fought their last battle in 1431 at Druim na Coup on the northern slopes of Ben Loyal. I see the site from my window as I write and, sometimes, when I walk that way, I think I hear the cry of angry voices. But it is the rush of the wind across the moor echoing amidst the corners and corries of the mountain.

We Scots are a warlike race. From the Borders to the Shetland Isles, hardly a square inch of my native soil is free from association with some deadly struggle. But the carnage of Culloden on 14 April 1746 destroyed the warrior clans. Their land was stolen and they became the tenants and slaves of their English-educated lairds. To enhance their own dignity and impress London society, the lairds raised companies of soldiers – led, of course, by the lairds themselves.

Out of these beginnings, many Scottish regiments were born. It is not unreasonable to suggest that without the fighting quality of the Scottish soldier, Britain could never have sustained its far-flung Empire. They played a major role in protecting the commercial interests of the nation, often at terrible cost to themselves. The story of their battles, triumphs and disasters is one of astonishing courage, vividly told in regimental museums throughout the land.

Edinburgh is a good starting point for a journey of military discovery. I was born and brought up in Auld Reekie and by the time I was ten years old, I was convinced that it was my solemn duty to die, not in bed, but on the battlefield. My maternal grandfather was a Drum Major in the Royal Scots and he survived the carnage of Flanders Fields during the First World War. Joining the school Army Cadet Force was the natural thing to do. I was proud to be associated with our parent regiment, the Royal Scots, whose badge we wore.

The regimental museum is in Edinburgh Castle, where, above the entrance, after crossing the drawbridge, are written the words, "Nemo me impune lacessit" – nobody harasses me with impunity or, to put it in broad Scots, wha dar meddle wi me. The Regimental cap badge, one of which I still have and treasure, has the figure of St Andrew, worn with a red felt backing.

The Royal Scots Museum in the Castle was opened in June 1991 by the Colonel in Chief of the Regiment, HRH The Princess Royal. As a youth, I used to haunt Edinburgh Castle and there is no more appropriate place to read the history of the city's famous regiment. This proud regiment is the oldest in the British Army and takes precedence by being on the right of the line on parade.

There has always been rivalry between Scotland's two major cities, Edinburgh and Glasgow, but there is no dispute about the courage of the Glasgow Regiment, the Royal Highland Fusiliers, Princess Margaret's Own Glasgow and Ayrshire Regiment; a core of which was originally employed in 1678 to keep "Watch on the Braes" to suppress Highland lawlessness.

One of the best known soldiers of the Royal Scots Fusiliers was Lt Col Winston Churchill. In 1915, the future Second World War leader commanded the 6th Battalion of the Regiment at Ploegsteert, called "Plug Street" by the soldiers, in the hellhole that was the Ypres Salient. Churchill earned respect by leading his men into battle and survived thirty-six forays across no man's land. He is reputed to have said later: "Although an Englishman, it was in Scotland that I found the best things in my life – my wife, my constituency and my Regiment."

Stirling Castle is one of Scotland's most dramatic fortifications, dominating the flat lands that enfold the River Forth and Flanders Moss. It has played a central role in Scotland's story and is the home of the Argyll and Sutherland Highlanders Regimental Museum. The regiment was formed in 1881 when the 91st Argyllshire Highlanders and the 93rd Sutherland

Highlanders were amalgamated as Princess Louise's Argyllshire and Sutherland Highlanders.

The 93rd were raised in Strathnaver in Sutherland by Elizabeth, Countess of Sutherland, in 1799, primarily by coercion; families unwilling to give up their men faced almost certain eviction from the land they rented from the Countess. In the event, it didn't really matter, because a few years later the Countess, who had promised the soldiers' families her protection "for all time coming" evicted them anyway to make way for sheep farming.

The history of both regiments is displayed in Stirling Castle's museum. The 91st first saw action at Cape of Good Hope and later played a major part in the Peninsular Wars when it protected Sir John Moore's retreat to Corunna. The regiment was demoralized, however, when, in 1809, it lost the right to wear the kilt, adjudged at the time to be "objectionable to the natives of South Britain".

The members of the 93rd were revered for their self-discipline and firmly held religious beliefs. They gained great honour during the Battle of New Orleans when, under appalling leadership, they stood firm amidst fire from General Andrew Jackson's defending force, suffering 557 casualties in the process out of a total for the defeated army of 2,000. The Americans had six men killed and seven wounded.

Perhaps the most famous moment for the 93rd came when they formed the "Thin Red Line" at the Battle of Balaclava in 1854 during the Crimean War. Standing in line, two deep, they faced a furious charge by Russian cavalry. Sir John Campbell, their commander, called: "There is no retreat from here, men, you must die where you stand."

"Aye, Sir John. And needs be we'll do that."

The line held, and their courage and fortitude broke the charge and saved the day.

Am Freiceadan Dubh, the Black Watch, have their regimental base in the fair city of Perth by the swiftly-flowing River Tay. Balhousie Castle, built in 1860 and incorporating an earlier, sixteenth-century L-plan tower house, was acquired by the Army after the Second World War and in 1962, the castle became the Black Watch regimental headquarters and museum.

The force was raised in 1729 in an attempt to subdue discontent amongst the mainly Catholic Highland clans, caused when a Protestant, William of Orange, usurped the Catholic King James in 1688. The young men who flocked to join the new independent units were called the "Black Watch" to distinguish them from regular troops, the Saighdearan Dearg, or "Red Soldiers", because of their red uniforms.

These independent companies soon proved their worth and were amalgamated into a single regiment on the outbreak of war with Spain in 1730. This coming-together was carried out on the Birks of Aberfeldy between Tay Bridge and Aberfeldy in Perthshire. The new force was designated as the 43rd (Highland) Regiment but they are still known to this day as the Black Watch.

The regiment fought bravely in 1815, facing and defeating the full might of Marshal Ney's 2nd French Army cavalry charges. They distinguished themselves at the Battle of Alma in 1854 in the Crimean War, and fought with honour and courage in the wars and skirmishes leading up to the Boer Wars and the Great World Wars of the twentieth century. Memorials of these times – medals, uniforms, equipment and mementoes – adorn the museum.

The last part of our military journey takes us north east from Perth to the Granite City of Aberdeen on the cold shores of the North Sea – the home of the museum of the Gordon Highlanders, raised in 1794 by the 4th Duke of Gordon. The regiment draws its strength from Aberdeenshire, Kincardine and Morayshire and to encourage men to join the regiment, it is said that each recruit was kissed by the Duchess of Gordon herself.

The regiment fought alongside the Black Watch at the Battle of Les Quatre Bras in 1815 and they were so eager to engage with the enemy at Waterloo that many soldiers clung to horse-riders' stirrups to speed their progress into battle. As Britain's Empire flourished during the nineteenth century, the Gordons saw action in India, Egypt and the Sudan, and in South

Africa during the Boer Wars. During the nightmare of the First World War, the Gordons, out of a total complement of 50,000 men, lost 27,000 killed or wounded in the conflict.

Their regimental museum in Aberdeen displays a unique collection of artifacts, including twelve Victoria Crosses won by members of the regiment. The museum also has an audio-visual theater showing an absorbing film of the history and activities of the regiment. And, for children, a "handling area" where boys and girls can dress in Gordon Highland uniforms and wear the equipment that soldiers had to carry.

There are other, equally famous Scottish regiments, each with their rightful place in Scotland's military history and each celebrated and remembered in individual regimental museums: the Scots Guards (Birdcage Walk, London), the King's Own Scottish Borders (Berwick upon Tweed), the Cameronians (Hamilton), the Queen's Own Highlanders (Fort George, near Inverness).

And there are more personal, poignant reminders of Scotland's soldiers in every Scottish community: the poppy-bedecked, inscribed memorials that commemorate the ultimate sacrifice tens of thousands of my fellow Scots made during two World Wars. Across the Kyle of Tongue from my home is a tiny graveyard with one such memorial. It stands on a green hill by the shore. Gulls cry and curlew call over the sleeping bodies gathered there, home at last.

The museums noted above can all be visited during the course of a single week. Edinburgh is an excellent centre from which to do so, by train or bus. Auld Reekie also offers a full range of other activities to keep every member of your party amused whilst you journey through Scottish military history.

Further details and opening times from:

The Royal Scots Regimental Museum, The Castle, Edinburgh EH1 2YT. Tel: 0131 310 5016; Fax: 0131 310 5019; email: rhqrs@btconnect.com

The Royal Highland Fusiliers, 518 Sauchiehall Street, Glasgow G2 3LW. Tel: 0141 332 5639; email: reg.sec@rhf.org.uk

Argyll and Sutherland Highlanders Regimental Museum, The Castle, Stirling FK8 1EH. Tel: 01786 475165; Fax: 01786 446038; email: museum@argylls. co.uk

The Black Watch Regimental Museum, Balhousie Castle, Hay Street, Perth PH1 5HS. Tel: 0131 310 8530; Fax: 0131 310 8525; email: rhq@theblackwatch. co.uk

The Gordon Highlanders Regimental Museum, St Luke's, Viewfield Road, Aberdeen AB15 7XH. Tel: 01224 311200; email: museum@gordonhighlanders. com

12.
An Island For All Seasons

Islay – pronounced "I-la" – is a speck on God's great map. People from this tiny island, a two-hour sail from the jagged west coast of Argyllshire, have flourished in the four quarters of His planet but they never lose their love for "The Queen of the Hebrides", the fertile island that they call home.

I thought of these truths as I waited with Ann at Kennacraig on the Mull of Kintyre for the arrival of the Caledonian MacBrayne ferry to Islay. Flying is not for me. The best way to arrive on a Scottish island is by sea, as our ancestors did. Caledonian MacBrayne's fleet of ships is the heartbeat of the Hebrides, as a well-known West Coast rhyme reminds us,

> The Earth belongs unto the Lord
> And all that it contains,
> Except the Clyde and Western Isles,
> They're Caledonian MacBrayne's.

It had taken us seven hours to drive from North Sutherland to the ferry, built on Eilean Ceann na Creige, an islet connected to the mainland by a causeway. I walked to the pier-head to stretch my legs. It was a grey afternoon with a grey mist on the sea's face and a grey evening breaking. A flight of geese arrowed by in perfect formation. An ink-black cormorant dived for supper in the waters of West Loch Tarbert.

As I watched, a brown-bewhiskered head appeared above the waves. Dark, shining eyes gazed up at me. It was a dog otter, going about its lawful business, curious and unafraid. He swam towards me until only a few yards away. Did he smile and bid me welcome? I think so and I knew then that we were going to experience all that is finest about Scotland's islands when we crossed the sea to Islay.

The island offers something for every member of your tribe, young and old alike. For Clan Sandison, it is a complete paradise encompassing all that we love: unspoiled, yellow-sand beaches washed by white-topped green waves; golden moors guarded by hen harrier, buzzard and golden eagle; wonderful trout lochs and streams where salmon lie; myriad dragonflies, wild flowers and butterflies, including the rare Marsh Fritillary (*Eurodryas aurinia*); cliff-top walks and kindly hills that beckon.

Islay is also famous for whisky distilleries, all of which welcome visitors. There are seven, giving the chance of sampling a different dram each day of the week. They are: Caol Ila, Bunnahabhain, Bruichladdich, Bowmore, Ardbeg, Lagavulin and Laphroaig. I particularly liked Caol Ila, light-coloured and comforting, which I had never tasted before. The distillery stands in a sheltered cove close to Port Askaig. David Graham of the Ballygrant Inn, over a pint, told me a tale about two regular Caol Ila visitors.

"Duncan MacGregor, whose father was gamekeeper on Dunlossit Estate, was friendly with crew members of the *Loch Ard*, a trading vessel that called at Port Askaig. The captain of the *Loch Ard* was known as 'Polaris' because he always steered a straight course and Duncan used to take Polaris and the ship's engineer, 'Paraffin Dan', to the Caol Ila distillery to stock up with whisky for the crew. [I hesitated to ask how Paraffin Dan came by his name.]

"In those days, distillery workers were given two drams of clear spirit a day. Polaris and Paraffin Dan just joined the end of the queue. When their turn came, the jug containing the whisky was often less than empty because the brewer invariably filled it too full. After the other men had gone back to work, the brewer disposed of the surplus into lemonade bottles brought by Polaris and Paraffin Dan for that purpose – much to their shipmates' delight on a cold night at sea."

The distilleries are as distinctive for their appearance as they are for the wonderful quality of the malt whisky that they produce. It is almost as though, before dawn each morning, a team of cleaners brush and polish the premises from top to bottom. They are pristine, shining white and none more so than Bowmore Distillery by the colourful, boat-bobbing little harbour in the town that gave it its name.

Bowmore is the oldest Islay distillery and it has graced the shores of shallow Loch Indaal since 1779. It is one of the few remaining distilleries in Scotland that still produces its own malt barley, hand-turned on the floor by the Maltman using traditional wooden malt shovels. The whisky is stored in damp vaults below sea level in Spanish and American oak casks that give the whisky its distinctive mellow flavor – maturing it into a dream-like, marvelous, memorable drinking experience.

Bowmore has a magnificent, wide, main street dominated by the Round Church (1769). The oldest houses are between the Harbour Inn and the Pier. They have external stairs to the upper floors. House and shop fronts are painted in various colours, with the dominant colour being white. Another dominant aspect of Main Street is one of Scotland's most inviting bakeries, "The Bakery", where bread and scones and other delights are baked on the premises. The smell alone is reason enough to linger and the bread is to die for.

Islay exudes self-confidence and this is evident from the way in which properties, like the distilleries, are maintained. It seems to be a matter of a community pride, rather than official dictate, that has achieved this standard. This "philosophy" perhaps reaches its highest expression in the Rinns, the most westerly part of Islay. You will find here two of the most attractive villages in all of Scotland, Port Charlotte and Portnahaven, both amazingly lovely and welcoming.

Also amazing is the wind. As we walked the Big Strand Beach one afternoon, along the shore of Laggan Bay south from Bowmore, the wind was so fierce that it lifted the sand and sent it flying like a white wave before us. The sea was in constant turmoil, meeting the sky in a fury of blue and green foam. But by the following morning, the storm had passed and we hurried north to visit the Loch Gruinart Nature Reserve in search of the geese that make Islay as famous as its whisky.

The Royal Society for the Protection of Birds (RSPB) bought the reserve in 1984 and 45% of the world's population of Greenland barnacle geese come to Loch Gruinart during the winter months. There is an excellent Visitor Centre at Aoradh Farm, which the RSPB runs as a model example of environmentally-friendly agriculture. A few hundred yards north, a track leads down to the shore of Loch Gruinart to a splendid bird-watching "hide", accessed by a sunken track so that approaching visitors can't be seen by the birds.

The hide has windows overlooking the fields that border the loch and a more than adequate supply of books to help you identify the different species. When Ann and I arrived, in mid-October, we were confronted by a spectacular display: 20,000 barnacle geese, more than 1,000 white-fronted geese, Canada geese, brent geese, wigeon, teal, mallard, shoveler, pintail, pochard, long-tailed duck, goldeneye, a pair of statuesque herons, and even a brace of brightly-plumed pheasant. It was one of the most unforgettable sights that I have ever seen and the music the birds made was a miraculous symphony of sheer delight.

Another rare Islay bird, the chough, a member of the crow family with a distinctive red beak, proved more difficult to find. Accompanied by an invigorating wind, we walked the RSPB reserve at the Oa on the south-west coast of Islay in search of it and were rewarded by a brief glimpse of a pair cart-wheeling in the storm. However, the dominant feature here is the American Monument, on the edge of the cliffs on the headland at Mull of Oa. It was built by the United States Government to commemorate the 266 Americans who drowned when the *HMS Tuscania* was torpedoed by a German submarine ten miles offshore on 5 February 1918. The bodies of some of those who died lie at rest in a small graveyard close to the ruins of Kilnaughton Chapel to the west of Port Ellen.

Being an angler, I visited Loch Finlaggan near Ballygrant. Only one salmon has ever been caught in Finlaggan and that was taken in 1930 by one of Scotland's best-loved song writers and comedians, Sir Harry Lauder. But the real treasures here are the tiny islands at the north end of Finlaggan,

Eilean na Comhairle (The Council Isle) and Eilean Mor (The Great Isle). From these inconspicuous sites, the Lords of the Isles, Clan MacDonald, ruled a vast, independent kingdom for nearly 400 years.

But evidence from excavations at Finlaggan has shown that people lived there long before the Lordship of the Isles; Eilean Mor is a natural island but Eilean na Comhairle and another island off the east shore are in fact crannogs, man-made islets that could date back to Neolithic times (4000–2000 BC). As we explored the islands, in my imagination I saw these people netting the loch for trout, smelled the smoke from their cooking fires and heard the laughter of their children at play.

In all of my travels round Scotland, I have rarely come across anywhere else that is as visitor-friendly as Islay. The Ileachs make you welcome and try hard to ensure that your stay amongst them is enjoyable and enriching. Our last day found us in the north of Islay, where we discovered a heavenly, deserted beach, Traigh Baile Aonghais. The sea was calm and autumn sunlight warmed our walk. It was hard to leave. Islay is an enduring joy, an island for all seasons.

For further information about Islay, contact the Islay Development Company, Distillery Road, Port Ellen, Islay PA43 7JX; Tel: 01496 300010; Email: info@ islay.org.uk

For ferry information and bookings, contact: Caledonian MacBrayne Limited, Ferry Terminal, Gourock PA19 1QP; Tel: 01475 650100; Email: enquiries@ calmac.co.uk; Website: www.calmac.co.uk

For information about the RSPB Loch Gruinart Reserve, contact RSPB Loch Gruinart Reserve, Bushmills Cottage, Gruinart, Bridgend, Isle of Islay, Argyll PA44 7PR; Tel: 01496 850505; Email: loch.gruinart@rspb.org.uk; Website: www.rspb.org.uk

13.
Lerwick Ablaze

The night sky was starless. A Presbyterian wind buffeted me and it was raining hard. I hunched into my waterproof jacket, captivated by the mounting excitement. Suddenly, a signal rocket was launched, splashing the darkness red as more than 800 torches were lit and held aloft by the members of forty-six squads of local people, nearly 1,000 participants, waiting for the arrival of the Guizer Jarl and his helpers. Viking axes, horned-helmets and studded shields sparkled in the glow. Everyone cheered. It was 7.30pm in Lerwick, Shetland, on Tuesday, 28 January 2003, and the highlight of "Up Helly Aa" had begun: the ceremonial burning of a nine-metre-long Viking Galley.

Earlier, Niall Cruickshank, a storyteller and singer, had explained the importance of Up Helly Aa. "Celebration in the winter time has always been part of Shetland life. The winters are lang and dark. In the past, this was when people repaired their fishing nets and agricultural implements and in the evenings, they gathered together in somebody's house, to tell stories, play music and sing. From Norse times, Christmas was a twenty-four-day celebration because there was precious little else to do. Up Helly Aa has always been associated with fire, and dressing up and disguising yourself and visiting friends."

Up Helly Aa was also important because it chased away Trolls – supernatural, heathen goblins, little people who lived in the hills. On that night of the year, Trolls were free to roam, to steal people's milk and food, and even to kidnap children. A cross made of straw pinned to the front door helped to ward them off. Young men would make and wear a straw skirt, cape and hat to frighten the Trolls. The use of fire and dressing up scared the

Trolls back to their caves and it was out of these beginnings that the present-day festival evolved.

In nineteenth-century Lerwick, it is recalled that, "Sometimes two tubs were fastened to a great raft-like frame knocked together at the Docks, whence combustibles were generally obtained. Two chains were fastened to the bogie supporting the tub or tar barrel . . . eked [joined] to those were strong ropes on which a motley mob, wearing masks for the most part, fastened. A party of about a dozen men stirred up the molten contents to keep them burning." Matters frequently got out of hand and Lerwick jail was often full the morning after. Eventually, it became difficult for the town to enlist sufficient Special Constables to deal with the riots.

The name "Guizer" comes from this tradition of dressing up, of disguising oneself, and it is a great honour to be the Guizer Jarl. Alex Johnson, a chemist, holds the position this year and he posted his personal three-metre-high "Proclamation" at the Market Cross to announce his ascendancy. This is full of personal humour and wit, specifically written to entertain the people of Lerwick. Up Helly Aa is a local tradition, not a spectacle mounted for visitors, although, of course, visitors are well entertained, as I found out over a few drams.

The Guizer Jarl is granted the freedom of the town for Up Helly Aa day and his Raven Banner is flown from the Town Hall. He takes a Viking name for the ceremony; Alex Johnson choosing Olaf Sitricson – Olaf of the Sandals – a tenth-century Viking who commanded a fleet of 600 longships in an effort to expand Norse influence south of Shetland and who eventually died on the island of Iona in 981. A Junior Up Helly Aa festival, with pupils from Anderson High School, is held in tandem with the adult event, when a smaller, six-metre galley is burned two hours before the start of the senior "Burning". This year's Junior Jarl is Shane Jamieson, who took the Viking name of Magnus of Marasetr, a Danish settler who lived on the Island of Whalsay. Before a battle, Magnus, for safety, threw a gold ropework ring amongst his horses. In 1903, a gold ropework ring was found at Marasetr by one of Junior Jarl's ancestors.

The night before, I had visited the Galley Shed where the longship had been built. The final colour of the boat is kept a closely guarded secret until it appears in public. Shields adorn the sides of the boat and round the walls of the Galley Shed are paintings of previous Jarls in scenes from Norse times – longships coming ashore, battles and raids. Bruce Leask, Guizer Jarl in 2002, explained the significance of the shields. "The first shield has a cartoon drawing of the Guizer Jarl, the second shows his seal. Tomorrow is going to be excellent. Regardless of the weather, we always have a great day. The ceremony will never die. Up Helly Aa will never die." I asked Billy Goudie, Guizer Jarl in 2001, if the Up Helly Aa tradition was flourishing: "Younger ones are coming up through the ranks all the time and starting to take over. Lots of people who used to live in Shetland come home for Up Helly Aa."

The following morning, I watched as the galley, named "Aaksytrik" this year and gleaming white, finally arrived at the British Legion Club premises. It looked far too precious for immolation. School children with their teachers began to line the street. The Lerwick Brass Band formed up, ready to begin. Police stopped traffic. The Guizer Jarl and his party emerged from the Legion building and took up position around the galley – sheep-skin cloaked, hugely bearded, brandishing axes, their helmets sparkling in the morning sun. Shops and offices emptied. With three cheers, they were off, striding along Commercial Street towing the galley, the brass band leading. As they passed, members of the squad called for more cheers: "Three cheers for the man on the roof," "Three cheers for the bus station!"

It was a happy day, full of laughter and good humour. The Junior Jarl Squad was royally entertained for lunch by Captain Wheeler of the NorthLink Ferry vessel *MV Hjaltland*, whilst the Guizer Jarl and his squad visited Lerwick schools, the hospital and residential homes. In the afternoon, I enjoyed a concert of music and song, Fiery Sessions, presented by local people at the Garrison Theatre. Now, at 7.30pm precisely, as I watched the signal rocket burst, it was time for the torchlight procession to begin. And it was still raining, if anything even harder. But nothing seemed to dampen the spirits of the torch bearers waiting to accompany the galley to its fate.

They were lined up on either side of the road below the Town Hall, singing in the rain. The Guizer Jarl and his team marched down the ranks through a stream of flame and the whole procession counter-marched, falling in behind them, the Lerwick Brass Band again leading. As the formation moved off, they sang the "The Up Helly Aa Song", learned by every Shetland child at school:

> Grand old Vikings ruled upon the ocean vast,
> Their brave battle-songs still thunder on the blast;
> Their wild war-cry comes a-ringing from the past;
> We answer it "A-oi!"
> Roll their glory down the ages,
> Sons of warriors and sages,
> When the fight for Freedom rages,
> Be bold and strong as they!

The final resting place of the galley was the centre of the King George V Playing Field and the procession followed a circuitous path to reach it. From my vantage point I could see most of the route. The squads filled the street from side to side, sparks flying from their torches, faces aglow with excitement. Fathers hoisted little ones aloft to give them a better view. The ribbon of flame reached the north entrance to the park and filed in to surround the galley. A circle of fire encompassed the vessel. The Guizer Jarl mounted his galley for the last time, axe aloft. Another signal rocket burst overhead and all the Guizers roared out "The Galley Song":

> Floats the raven banner o'er us,
> Round our Dragon Ship we stand,
> Voices joined in gladsome chorus,
> Raised aloft the flaming brand.
> Bonds of Brotherhood inherit,
> O'er strife the curtain draw;

Let our actions breathe the spirit
Of our grand Up-Helly-A'.

A bugle call echoed through the night and the Guizer Jarl rejoined his companions. As the last note sounded, they began to hurl their torches into the galley, spiraling upwards then falling into the doomed vessel in a sheet of startling brightness. One by one, the other squads moved forward to add their torches to the inferno. The sail of the galley was ablaze, the proud figurehead alight. Slowly, the mast tumbled and the Raven Flag was laid low. As the vessel burned, the thousands-strong crowd roared their approval and tension was tangible. The spell was broken as a glorious firework display set the very sky itself afire.

Up Helly Aa celebrations continue well into the next day. Immediately after the Burning, each of the forty-six squads visit eleven private parties in Lerwick community halls to perform a topical sketch, sing a song, dance, drink and celebrate. If visitors wish to join one of these parties, they simply ask the party hostess for permission to do so. Otherwise, they may prefer to enjoy the many lively gatherings in Lerwick hotels and pubs: nobody goes to bed on Up Helly Aa night. But my enduring Up Helly Aa memory is of watching the wonderful torchlight procession and witnessing the proud end of that magnificent, shining white galley – and Up Helly Aa must work, because, you know, I never once saw a single Troll.

14.
Practise Your Swing in Scotland

Like most Scots, I was born with a golf club in my hand. The game is one of Scotland's most popular participant sports. We Jocks have been bashing various designs of golf balls around since the twelfth century. In the time of King James II (1430–1460), the game so captivated the nation that it was banned because it interfered with archery practice and other more urgent military pursuits. The preferred golfing venue in the Middle Ages was Leith Links near Edinburgh, conveniently close to the Scottish Parliament Buildings in the High Street; Scotland's political luminaries, judiciary and the like, could comfortably draft their laws and edicts in the morning and still have plenty of time for a hack round the links before supper.

The world's oldest golf club is the Honourable Company of Edinburgh Golfers. They played their first competition on Leith Links in 1744, one year before Bonnie Prince Charlie arrived in town to temporarily disrupt their swing. Ten years later, twenty-two good-men-and-true in St Andrews formed what has become known as the Royal & Ancient (R&A). They subscribed to the purchase of a silver golf club, to be played for in competition, the winner becoming the club captain for the next year. In recognition of the winner's achievement, a silver ball inscribed with his name was attached to the club. To this day, as a mark of respect, newly elected R&A members at their inaugural dinner are required to kiss the captain's balls.

Two of my most unnerving golfing experiences occurred on two of Scotland's most famous courses. The first was on the Old Course at St Andrews on a cold morning when tee-off time was 9.28am, precisely. I was so over-awed by the occasion that I could barely balance the ball on the tee. The second happened at Old Prestwick, where the first Open Championship was played in 1860. By the time I reached the 9th hole, I had lost nine balls in the unforgiving rough bordering the narrow fairways. As I courageously prepared to address the ball on the 10th tee, my caddie muttered to me: "Och, Sir, this is nae a course for beginners." Still, I did manage a par at the 18th and thus ended the round shaken, with my honour shredded but relatively intact.

This is why I now play most of my golf north of the Great Glen. Golf in the Highlands is much less of a "goldfish bowl" experience than on southern courses such as St Andrews, Carnoustie, Gleneagles, Troon or Turnberry. It is also a lot less expensive, more readily available and, although I admit to being biased, a lot more fun. I have often played round Durness, in North West Sutherland, without meeting another soul. The most taxing hole is a 7 iron shot across the Atlantic. The tee is perched on basalt cliffs above the sea and golfers play over a scallop-shaped inlet, known in these airts as a "geo".

A local man playing this hole recently struck his tee-shot superbly. The ball soared over the geo, bounced on the edge of the green and rolled into the cup. A rare hole-in-one, whereupon he turned to his companion on the tee and announced somberly, "Well, Hamish, you have got this for the half," meaning that his opponent couldn't win, but could even the score if he also managed to get a hole-in-one. The story may be apocryphal, but it encapsulates the way in which the noble game is played in Scotland – with no holds barred; a gentleman's game, yes, but one which gentlemen and ladies play to win.

I should also confess that this delightful little course has another attraction for me apart from the "shot across the Atlantic". The 6th hole borders what is, in my view, one of the finest wild brown trout lochs in Europe. So I sometimes pack a fishing rod in my golf bag and have a few casts along the way.

Another of my favourite courses is at Reiss near Wick in Caithness, a traditional Scottish "links" course sheltered from cold east winds by high sand dunes. Wick Golf Club claims to be the oldest club in the north of Scotland and a new club house, built at a cost of £250,000, was opened in 1994. The 18th tee is one of the most dramatic from which I have ever duffed a drive. It is set high on the sand-dunes bordering the blue and gold sweep of Sinclair Bay and dominated by the tall, gaunt fortress of Ackergill Tower, where Oliver Cromwell's officers were billeted during the religious wars of the seventeenth century, when they brought their Protestant army north to subdue un-Christian-like mirth and jollity.

The newest Highland course, officially opened in April 1998, is at Ullapool in Wester Ross, although there is mention of a golf course at Ullapool as far back as 1903. The present course, designed by Souters of Stirling, took two years to construct and was built by Messrs ATF Urquhart. Ullapool is a busy fishing port and a hub of activity during the summer months. The course lies on a raised beach close to the sea by the banks of the Ullapool River. The surrounding scenery is magnificent with splendid views north west to Isle St Martin and the Summer Isles, and south over Loch Broom to Beinn Ghobhlach (635m) and the hamlet of Altnaharrie, once famous for the food and comfort of its Inn.

Just as famous, although for an entirely different reason, is Fortrose & Rosemarkie Golf Club on the Black Isle to the north of the City of Inverness. The course looks south over the Moray Firth to Fort George – built in the years after the 1745 Rebellion to help "quell" any future Scottish-based insurrection. Before the Second World War, officers stationed at Fort George were given honorary membership of the club. Bandmaster Rickets of Fort George used to play Fortrose & Rosemarkie regularly with his colonel. On one occasion, another player tried to attract the colonel's attention by "whistling" to him. Rickets later used the sounds made in a tune he composed that became internationally renowned as "Colonel Bogey".

North of Inverness, up the busy A9 road, brings you to further golfing delights, not the least of which is Royal Dornoch, where golf was being played as long ago as 1616. This Sutherland links course ranks in the top ten of British courses. Some of the most noted names in golf are associated with Royal Dornoch: Ben Cranshaw, Tom Watson, Greg Norman, Nick Faldo and HRH the Duke of York, who is an honorary member. Another new course is at Skibo Castle, once the home of multi-millionaire Andrew

Carnegie, now a prestigious watering-hole for the world's rich and famous. But I am more concerned here with the less well-known courses and one of the finest in Sutherland is Brora Links.

The Brora golf course, established in 1891, was re-designed in 1923 by James Baird (1870–1950), five-time winner of the Open Championship. Baird won his first title at Muirfield in 1901. He is credited with being involved with the design of more than 180 courses, including the King's Course at Gleneagles and the medal course at Carnoustie. Baird's fee for re-designing the Brora course was £25 and Brora is now the home of "The James Baird Golfing Society", formed in 1997 by Peter Thomson, another five-time winner of the Open Championship. A room at the Royal Marine Hotel in Brora is given over to memorabilia of the great man and the test of Baird's course lies in some wonderful holes: the 13th, "The Snake", with its little burn flowing below the tee; the 15th, "Sahara"; and the spectacular 17th, "Tarbatness", where the lighthouse gives the line to follow.

The beauty of the far north of Scotland, with its grand mountains, heather moorlands, foaming rivers and peat-stained lochs, is extolled throughout the world. Less well known is the fact that it is also a golfer's paradise. Apart from the courses I have mentioned, there are dozens more: Gairloch, where the first hole is known as "Leabaidh". After the Disruption in the Church of Scotland in 1843, the lairds locked dissident Free Church ministers out of their premises. At Gairloch, they preached their sermons out of doors, at Leabaidh, Gaelic for "a bed". Other splendid courses include Golspie Golf Course, another links affair designed by James Baird; Reay Golf Club in north Caithness undoubtedly contains unexcavated Neolithic settlements buried in its sand dunes; Helmsdale, Bonar Bridge and Tain all have excellent courses.

North over the turbulent waves of the Pentland Firth, beyond the red-scarred cliffs of the Island of Hoy, there are splendid courses in Stromness and Kirkwall in Orkney and the most northerly golf course in the UK, at Burrafirth on the Island of Unst in Shetland. But my most enduring memory of playing golf in Scotland is of the course at Askernish, near the birthplace of Flora MacDonald on the Island of South Uist in the Outer Hebrides. It was in June. The fertile machair lands were at their finest, a fifty-kilometre-long riot of glorious multicoloured wildflowers. The clubhouse, a broken-down hut, was closed but visitors were invited to leave their green fee in "the box provided". It was hard to do so, the box in question being otherwise engaged rearing a family of starlings. The course is being "modernised" but is still wild and beautiful. Come along and find the magic of the outstanding golf courses in the glorious Northlands of Scotland.

Further Information: Highland Golf, *published by The Northern Times Ltd, Sutherland Press House, Golspie, Sutherland, Scotland KW10 6RA; Tel: 01408 633993.*

15.
The Silver Tay

We slept in the heather beneath an ink-black, star-bright sky. A velvet cloud of pipistrelle bats whisked out into the darkness from ruined croft buildings. A fox barked sharply in the distance. A solemn owl ghosted by on silent wings. Late curlew called hauntingly. Loch water lapped the shores of my dreams and sleep came easy in that warm night.

This resting-place was on the margins of Loch Ordie in Perthshire, high above the River Tay near the cathedral City of Dunkeld. Our Boy Scout camp was based on the banks of the river at Inver Park and we had set out earlier that morning on an adventure hike into the wilderness crags of Deuchary Hill (240m). In these few hours, I fell hopelessly in love with the River Tay.

From its source in the west amongst the thread-fingered busy streams of Ben Lui (1,130m) by Tyndrum, to the vast expanse of the Firth of Tay, the river runs 193 kilometres. It draws strength from an area of more than 7,300 square kilometres. Waters from the mountains of Breadalbane and Glen Lednock feed mighty Loch Tay. They flow from the ribbon of lochs of Laidon, Rannoch and Tummel, and from autumn-purple Forest of Atholl tributaries and mingle in the sea-salt tide by the fair City of Perth.

The constant Tay encapsulates Scotland's story. Neolithic man has left his mark in stone circles near Killin, and at Dowally four miles north from Dunkeld. There is evidence of 4,000-year-old homesteads in the lands of Strathtummel, Strathardle and Glenshee. Crannogs, defensive homes built on natural or artificially created islands, edged Loch Tay. A crannog reconstruction may be seen at the east end of the loch near Kenmore.

In AD 85, the Romans built fortifications at Inchtuthil, north from

Perth. Apart from unsuccessful attempts to subdue the natives, they indulged in pearl fishing. Scottish pearls were highly prized by the glitterati back in Rome.

Dunkeld Cathedral's links with Christianity go back as far as the sixth century when Celtic monks from Iona established a settlement on the banks of the Tay. St Columba is thought to have visited Dunkeld during his missionary work amongst the Picts. In AD 884, King Kenneth MacAlpine chose Dunkeld as one of the capital cities of his newfound kingdom, the other being Scone near Perth.

During the Scottish Wars of Independence, Clan MacDougall won a victory over Robert Bruce at Dalrigh in the hills above Killin at the west end of Loch Tay. The Clan possesses a magnificent brooch, torn from the plaid of the fleeing King of Scots.

James V hunted in Glen Tilt, where the River Tilt hurries to join the River Garry, a once important tributary of the Tay, now sadly robbed of most of its water to service hydro-electric power generation. In 1529, the Earl of Atholl built a hunting lodge there for King James V when 1,000 men were employed to herd deer down from the corries of Beinn a'Ghlo for His Majesty's pleasure. His daughter, Mary, Queen of Scots, was similarly entertained in Glen Tilt in 1564, before she became the hunted one.

The most famous "hunted" ones of the Tay are, however, its Atlantic salmon. The Tay is the pre-eminent European salmon fishery. For hundreds of years, *Salmo salar* has provided sustenance and sport for local fishermen and visitors alike. John Richardson described the Tay salmon fishings thus in 1788: "The fishings employ between two and three hundred fishers. Six vessels are employed during the season running to and from London which is the principal market. A considerable part are sent fresh in the spring season, and for the past two years, the greatest proportion of the fresh salmon has been packed in ice."

In 1969, 104,492 salmon were caught in the Tay District alone. Sadly, today, because of the sheer greed and stupidity of regulators and river owners, the total number of salmon caught in the whole of Scotland has sunk to less than 50,000. Indeed, many distinct populations of fish may now face extinction. Great efforts are being made to reverse the decline, but whether or not it will be in time to save Scotland's salmon remains to be seen.

Salmon were abundant in 1922 when Miss Georgina Ballantine – fishing with her father, who had rented the fishing from the Laird of Glendelvine, Sir Alexander Lyle – landed Scotland's heaviest rod-and-line caught salmon, a fish weighing 64lbs. It was displayed in the window of PD Malloch's shop in Perth. Georgina listened to two elderly men as they marvelled at the great fish. She said later, "One said to the other, 'A woman? Nae woman ever took a fish like that oot of the water, mon. I would need a horse, a block and tackle, tae tak a fish like that oot. A woman – that's a lee [lie] anyway.' I had a quiet chuckle up my sleeve and ran to catch the bus."

The Tay has always been famous for the quality and size of its salmon, and more than twenty fish of over 50lbs in weight have been taken from the river. A salmon of 71lbs was recorded as being hooked and played, but not landed, in 1868 by Dr Browne, Bishop of Bristol. He was fishing near the mouth of the River Earn, a tributary of the Tay that flows into the Firth of Tay from the south. After a battle lasting ten hours, the fish broke free.

The closest I have come to Tay salmon happened near the end of our Boy Scout camping trip. We had built a raft, and a friend and I thought that we would give it a "Viking" send off: floating down stream on it, and then diving off and leaving it to its fate before reaching the point where Thomas Telford's graceful bridge spans the Tay. The river, seventy-five yards wide at that point, was high after rain and we soon realised our folly as the strong current gripped us. It was impossible to paddle to the bank. We dived in and struck out for the shore.

I immediately felt a stomach-churning pang of panic as the flood hit me. I swam hard, vividly aware of the approaching rapids below the bridge. I made the bank just above the bridge, 300 yards down the river from where I had dived in. My companion joined me a moment later. Glad to be alive, we climbed the steps up onto the bridge and hiked shamefaced and embarrassed back to camp in our swimming trunks.

In earlier times, the bridge caused embarrassment of a different kind to its owner, the Duke of Atholl. The Duke built the bridge in 1809 and for seventy years charged a toll for crossing. Dunkeld people had to pay to meet trains in Birnam, across the river, and Birnam people paid to go to church in Dunkeld. Either way, the laird won. Locals meekly coughed up for half a century before complaining. When riots broke out in 1856, the military were called in to quell them but, even so, it was not until 1879 that the Duke was persuaded by the County Council to give up his rights.

Dunkeld is a perfect centre for exploring the Tay and its tributaries and the scent of evening woodsmoke drifting above the clustered houses is one of my enduring memories. The surrounding woodlands are quite magnificent: beech, oak, sycamore, birch, ash, pine and fir. A Douglas fir of more than thirty metres in height, by the banks of the River Braan on a walk to view a glorious waterfall, is said to be the tallest tree in Britain.

One night, whilst walking in the woods above Birnam, I surprised a capercaillie, the Gaelic "great cock of the wood". This magnificent bird was hunted to extinction in Scotland by the mid-seventeenth century. The Campbell Earls of Breadalbane reintroduced it in 1837 at Drummond Hill, which overlooks the north shore of Loch Tay at Kenmore.

Another object of great size may be viewed from Drummond Hill: the dark, blue-grey bulk of Taymouth Castle on the banks of the river. The castle was enlarged extensively by Breadalbane lairds over the years and visited by Queen Victoria in 1842. It is reported that she was pleased by her reception, commenting that it was "princely and romantic". Hundreds of Breadalbane's tenants were employed to build and light fires on the surrounding hills for the entertainment of the diminutive Queen.

When the grey finger of dawn inched its way into my sleeping bag, I awoke to find mist shimmering over the calm waters of Loch Ordie. Around me in the heather lay my companions, one by one stirring to greet the coming day. We cluttered about, washing in the loch, making breakfast. It was sad to leave, to tramp back down the hill to civilisation. But as we cleared the lower forest, like a silver thread, the River Tay lay before me and I felt as though I had returned home.

Further information about the River Tay and Perthshire may be obtained from the Perthshire Tourist Board, Lower City Mills, West Mill Street, Perth PH1 5QP, Scotland; Tel: 01738 450600; Email: perth@visitscotland.com

16.
George Heriot, the Royal Banker, Goldsmith and Jeweller

As the sun rose over Edinburgh on Wednesday, 19 June 1566, the town's goldsmiths brushed sleep from their eyes, breakfasted on porridge, haddock and oatcakes and set off for their kraams – wooden workshops built against the walls of St Giles Kirk.

In the kraams, apprentice goldsmiths tended their Master's furnace fires whilst nearby the wool and linen merchants of the Lawnmarket prepared for their weekly sale. Across the street from St Giles, the stench of rotting fish and poultry innards emanating from Fishmarket Close filled the air.

Picking his way carefully through the littered wynds, master goldsmith George Heriot greeted two colleagues, James Mossman and James Cok. All three wore the uniform of their profession, scarlet coat and black cocked hat. Each carried a gold-tipped stick. One topic dominated their conversation: the birth that morning of a son to Mary, Queen of Scots.

As the day lengthened, servants cleaned dusty rooms, laid fires and emptied their masters' chamber pots onto the streets where barefoot children begged for food and played amidst the middens. Bonfires were lit and the great and good gathered in St Giles to pray for the royal child.

Heriot lived in the High Street amidst the tall buildings that crowded either side of the "Royal Mile" from Holyrood Palace to the castle. Paved with stone, the street was narrow in its beginnings. However, from the Netherbow, the gateway to the city, the buildings were tightly packed; a maze of dark passageways constricted by the city's defensive Flodden Wall; a warren of humanity embracing 7,500 souls.

When Mary's son, James, became King of Scotland on the enforced abdication of his mother, the country divided into two factions: those who supported the Queen and those who supported the King. But in May 1573, Mary's hopes of restoration ended when Edinburgh Castle fell to the King's Party.

The town hangman, the "Doomster", was busy. He lived in Fishmarket Close near to the Tolbooth where executions were carried out. Nick-named "The Magpie" for his black silver-laced coat, he "attended" to Kirkcaldy of Grange, who had held the castle for the Queen's Party. Grange was hung and dismembered and his head spiked on the Castle wall. Next followed Heriot's friends and fellow goldsmiths, James Mossman and James Cok. Their "crime" was minting coins for the Queen's Party.

By European standards, sixteenth-century Scotland was impoverished. Gold and silver was most noticeable by its scarcity. But during Mary's reign, and both before and after her sad tenure of the Scottish Crown, Scotland was remarkable for the beauty of its coinage.

The goldsmiths guild that produced these pieces had authority to search out and destroy the work of anyone who was not a Master Goldsmith. After an apprenticeship of seven years, those who wished to become masters had to make "ane sufficient assay, pruiform try of all his cunnyng and experience in baith workmanship and knowledge of the fyenes of the metils".

Some test pieces may still be seen today. In 1586, John Mossman made the Roseneath Communion Cup, a slender bowl above a simple spreading foot, now in Huntley House Museum in the Canongate. But the most famous is "The Heriot Loving Cup" – "a Nautilus shell with silver mounts, set on a slender stem spreading into a stepped, chased foot".

The cup is erroneously named because Robert Denniestoun in fact made it. George Heriot (Snr) only supervised its production. The "Loving Cup" is owned by the famous Edinburgh school named in honour of Heriot's son, also George, who left the bulk of his fortune to establish a hospital and school "for the maintenance relief and bringing up and education of poor fatherless bairns, freemen sons of Edinburgh".

William Wallace, Master Mason, and his successor, William Aytoun, supervised the building of the school and work was completed in June 1659. That caustic commentator on all things Scottish, the Welshman Thomas Pennant, visiting Scotland in 1771, said: "Heriot's hospital is a fine old building, much too magnificent for the end proposed, that of educating poor children."

As James VI asserted his authority, the rising financial star in the crowded town was Heriot's son. He followed his father into the Goldsmiths Guild, married and set up in business on his own account and father Heriot lived to see his son rise to the peak of his profession.

Heriot was appointed goldsmith to Queen Anne in 1597. Four years later, he was appointed jeweller to the King. Such was the volume of business he conducted with the royal family that private rooms were made available to him in Holyrood Palace. Heriot was in effect the Royal Banker and became known as "jingling Geordie" because of the sound of gold coins rattling in his pockets.

The permanence of the established order that sustained Heriot ended on the evening of 26 March 1603. Sir Robert Carey cantered through the gates of Holyrood Palace bringing momentous news from London. He was ushered into the King's presence: "The Queen is dead, Your Majestie is King of England."

James had instructed Heriot to follow him to London but in the midst of this triumph, Heriot's wife Christian died. Shortly afterwards, his two sons, sailing from Leith to join their father, were drowned when their vessel foundered in a storm.

Nevertheless, Heriot prospered mightily in London, buying and selling jewellery on the Queen's behalf, making new pieces for her and for her friends, lending money whenever Anne needed it. The King also made frequent recourse to Heriot's services, as did his immediate circle and Heriot decided it was time to set aside grief and remarry.

He travelled to Edinburgh to seek a wife, the lady in question being a daughter of James Primrose, Clerk to the Privy Council. Heriot was forty-five, his bride, Alison, sixteen. The couple married in the autumn of 1608.

When Heriot returned to London, he realised he needed more staff.

Because of his special relationship with the King and Queen, Heriot made sure he employed only the best. In March 1609, a proclamation was issued requiring every magistrate in the Kingdom to recommend suitable tradesmen for the Royal Jeweller.

Whilst Queen Anne remained Heriot's most important customer, her debts, amounting to some £20,000, had become scandalous. It required a delicate touch to raise the matter with the King. James was incensed but had little option other than to pay up and hope to curb her future excesses.

Heriot paid his raw material suppliers in Portugal and Spain and set to work with a will, proud of his young wife and hopeful of starting a new family with her. But fate struck again: on 16 April 1612, Alison died. Heriot had a monument erected to her in St Gregory's Parish Church, now part of St Paul's Churchyard, and wrote, "She cannot be too much lamented who could not be too much loved."

His misfortune was compounded by the fact that Queen Anne was again up to her ears in debt and Heriot was the principal creditor. But James and Anne had also suffered personal loss. Young Prince Henry, heir to the crown of England and Scotland, had died. Heriot was loath to bring up the subject of the Queen's debts but his creditors were pressing.

Heriot petitioned the King: "Having served Your Majesty for the long period of twenty-four years without ever having sought or obtained any recompense for the same . . ." The King's response to his banker's cry for help was less than complete. Only part of the debt was paid. But it was enough to stabilise Heriot's affairs. As for the King, he was finally rid of his profligate Queen when she died in 1619 at the age of forty-five.

Heriot had been badly shaken and considered returning to Edinburgh. In the meantime, however, he found consolation in the arms of mistresses by whom he had two daughters, both of whom he acknowledged. He lived in a fine house in St Martin's-in-the-Field and even in his declining years, retained tight control over every aspect of his business. As the end came, he began to make decisions about how the fortune he had amassed was to be used after his death.

He had no immediate heir, being childless apart from his two "love-begotten" daughters. As matters stood, his estate would pass to Franchischetta Heriot, the only child of his brother Patrick who had died in Genoa in Italy, but Heriot wanted to do more with his fortune. He decided to leave the bulk of his money to Edinburgh City Council to establish his school and hospital.

Heriot died in London on 12 February 1624 and was buried at St Martin's-in-the-Field. Sir Walter Balanquall, his nephew and Dean of Rochester, preached the sermon. Digging the grave and other funeral duties cost £7.6s 0d, the wake, £14.13s 4d. Heriot would not have begrudged these expenses: the motto of the school that bears his name is "We distribute chearfullie".

As the sun rises over Edinburgh today, boys and girls, dressed in their distinctive cobalt blue jackets, cross the High Street by St Giles Cathedral and make their way up George IV Bridge past Greyfriar's Church to George Heriot's School. Although now mainly a fee-paying school, it still cares "for the maintenance relief and bringing up and education of poor fatherless bairns, freemen sons of Edinburgh" and Heriot's legacy lives on.

17.
The City of Inverness, "Inversneckie", the Capital of the Highlands

Lady Mackintosh lived stylishly at No. 43 Church Street, Inverness, in 1745. Bonnie Prince Charlie was her guest before he and his kilted host headed south in hot pursuit of his father's lost crown. The following April, after the rout of the Jacobite army on Drumossie Moor, the victorious Duke of Cumberland also put his Hanovarian feet under Lady Mackintosh's dining room table. She said later, "I have had two king's bairns living with me in my time, and I wish I may never have another."

I first put my toes under an Inverness table as a young man when attending a Royal Highland Show there in 1955. Or it could have been 1956. I can't remember. Whatever, it was the last time the event was held in the Capital of the Highlands – "Inversneckie" to its friends – prior to finding a permanent home at Ingliston on the outskirts of Auld Reekie. This was my introduction to the north and I loved it, particularly the grace and charm of the old town on the banks of the fast-flowing River Ness.

Today, Inverness has been elevated to the status of City, the first Scottish town to be granted such honour in more than 100 years. The douce inhabitants greeted this achievement with their customary reserve but Provost Bill Smith said: "To be granted city status from the Queen is a magnificent honour for Inverness and will give businesses in the town and throughout the Highlands a tremendous marketing tool in attracting additional income to our fast-growing economy."

Clan Sandison has played a significant role in promoting that "economy". For a quarter of a century, Inverness has been our principal shopping centre.

A function it performs superbly. Given the choice of stumbling about Princes Street in Edinburgh or Sauchiehall Street in Glasgow, Inverness wins hands down, every time. It has all the facilities and range of choice to be found in a major city with none of the attendant hassle. We live 100 miles north from Inverness in the small township of Tongue and do not begrudge the journey. It is time and money well spent.

The population of Inverness has doubled over the past twenty years and is now more than 40,000. At the time of the Jacobite Rebellion, however, it was little more than 3,000. Four principal streets of a few hundred houses clustered around the Mercat Cross and the Town House. Then, as now, Inverness was the most important town in the north of Scotland. Most of the great Highland Clan Chiefs owned a house in Inverness and all business, trade and commerce was conducted at the Mercat Cross.

A northern "Stone of Destiny" is incorporated in the Mercat Cross: the "Clach-na-Cuddain Stone". Woman returning from the River Ness with washing or water used this stone as a resting-place. Local lore claims that so long as this famous stone remains undisturbed, so long will Inverness flourish. The original Town House, built in 1708, was the residence of Lord Lovat, who earned himself the dubious distinction of being the last man to be publicly beheaded in Britain – his reward for the part he played in Bonnie Prince Charlie's disastrous rebellion.

In the aftermath of the Battle of Culloden, the people of Inverness hastily rearranged their political sympathies and warmly greeted the government army and its fat commander, Cumberland, known to this day as "Stinking Billy". The town's jails and kirkyards were soon packed with prisoners – fit men, the wounded and the dying huddled together with little food, water or medical attention to alleviate their suffering.

The Provost of Inverness, John Fraser, and his predecessor in that office, John Hossack, petitioned General Hawley on the prisoners' behalf. The General, who had set up headquarters in the Town House, had Hossack kicked down the stairs and into the street. Fraser was ordered to clean the General's stables but allowed to pay others to do the loathsome work on his behalf. They became known as "Provost Kick" and "Provost Muck".

The oldest surviving building in Inverness is Abertarff House on Church Street, built in 1594 and now the Highland office of the National Trust for Scotland. Also in Church Street, on the walls of numbers 77–79, is a carved stone with the initials AS and HP, separated by a heart and commemorating a marriage in the Schives family. The practice of erecting "marriage lintels" was commonplace in seventeenth century Scotland. Near-by Bow Court, dating from 1720, was attractively restored in 1972 and is now home to a splendid group of flats and shops.

Inverness, ancient and modern, is ideal for a Highland adventure. Within a thirty-mile drive from the centre of town, hill walkers and climbers will find more than enough to keep them fully energised. Local golf courses are of world-class standard. There is excellent game fishing for salmon, trout and sea-trout. Indeed, Inverness is one of the few cities I know where you are likely to meet a fully kitted-out angler, complete with waders, landing net and fishing rod, strolling unconcernedly and unremarked down the High Street to do business in the River Ness.

One summer afternoon, I was walking by the river near Inverness Cathedral when an excited visitor grabbed me by the arm. "Look, Look!" he exclaimed, pointing to the middle of the stream. "It's the Loch Ness Monster!" He was almost correct. The fish was a monster but going to Loch Ness, not from it. A huge salmon was surging upstream, its vast back out of the water. I estimated the weight of the fish to have been at least 40lbs, if not more. As we anglers say, it would have been "worth the hauding", which means worth hooking, playing and landing.

Inverness Castle dominates the city and river. It is perched on a grassy hillock in the centre of town. The present red sandstone structure was built between 1834 and 1846 but it stands on the remains of much older fortifications, variously bashed about a bit by successive waves of less than friendly visitors – the last being Bonnie Prince Charlie's army, who blew up the castle to prevent it being used by their enemies. A graceful monument to one of my most-loved Scottish heroines, Flora MacDonald, guards the front door.

After helping Prince Charles to escape, Flora was incarcerated in the Tower of London. The Duke of Cumberland visited her there to ask why she had assisted his father's enemy. Flora is said to have responded that she would have done the same for any man in such a position, regardless of politics or religion. The statue is inscribed with the comment Samuel Johnson made when he met Flora during his tour of the Highlands: "The preserver of Prince Charles Edward Stuart will be mentioned in history and if courage and fidelity be virtues, mentioned with honour."

One man who knows the nooks and crannies of Inversneckie better than most has the same Macdonald surname and similar lineage: the late John Macdonald, editor of the *Inverness Courier*, whose crofting ancestors lived for generations on the Island of Skye. The *Inverness Courier* celebrated its 175th year of publication in November 1992 and is required reading throughout the north. I asked John what he thought about his town's grand new status. "Well," he replied laconically, "if it doesn't do you any good it won't do you any harm."

John Macdonald believes passionately that Inverness is "as near perfect an urban community as any place can be". An exile for much of his journalistic life, working with the *British Reader's Digest*, *Daily Telegraph* and *The Times*, John is also an authority on the American Civil War. His book, *Great Battles of the Civil War*, published by Michael Joseph in 1989, was greeted with wide critical acclaim and is a definitive work on the subject. He told me when he last visited Gettysburg, walking up the Confederate lines and down the Union lines, a visitor driving a car stopped him.

"What are you doing?" the man asked.

John told him he was walking the lines.

"Are you mad?" came the reply. "Nobody walks!"

Walking is the best way to discover the heart and soul of the "Capital of the Highlands" and there are seven bridges over the river to help you do so. There is enduring pleasure to be had in mingling with local people as they go about their business. Listen to their soft Scottish accent, adjudged to be the purest form of spoken English heard anywhere in the world. Listen to the sound of the old stream hurrying by to greet the cold waters of the Moray Firth. Look over the River Ness to the fourteenth-century Parish Church of St Mary. Say a silent prayer for the Jacobite prisoners who suffered and died there for Bonnie Prince Charlie so long ago.

Further information from: Inverness Tourist Centre, Castle Wynd, Inverness IV2 3BJ; Tel: 01463 234353; Fax: 01463 710609.

18.
Dornoch

On a mild autumn morning I wandered amongst the grey tombstones surrounding Dornoch Cathedral in east Sutherland. The dew-wet sparkling grass bore the imprint of my passing footsteps. Jet-black jackdaws croaked from the cockerel-capped weather vane above the tower. Collared doves cooed on the branches of ancient trees nodding round the quiet city square. The sense of peace was palpable.

There are grander cathedrals than Dornoch, more awe-inspiring buildings more magnificently designed and decorated, but I know of no other cathedral that so immediately captivates the spirit. A contract has been struck here between man and his maker, a happy union that neither intimidates nor demands obsessive obedience. The old sandstone structure exudes life and love.

The Royal Burgh of Dornoch has been the religious and administrative centre of Sutherland for more than 800 years. Today, the busy A9 Inverness/Thurso road bypasses it and this may be the reason why this small community on the shores of the sea-blue firth has retained its unique character. The next time you pass this way, visit Dornoch. Your only problem will be in leaving it.

You will be following famous names when you do so, particularly names of people afflicted with golf: Nick Faldo, Greg Norman, Tom Watson, Bob Charles, Andy North and Chip Black, all of whom have extolled the excellence of world-famous Royal Dornoch Golf Course. Earlier visitors included Tom Morris, Harry Vardon, Bobby Locke, Bobby Jones and Bing Crosby.

Old Tom Morris from St Andrews designed the course and he greatly influenced two Dornoch men, Donald Ross and his brother Alec. Donald went on to become one of the most famous course designers in the history of the game. He and his brother immigrated to America at the end of the nineteenth century where Donald designed more than 500 courses, including Pinehurst No. 2 course and the Seminole Course in Florida.

Multi-millionaire and philanthropist Andrew Carnegie had a "holiday cottage" nearby at Skibo Castle and he and his wife, Louise, were introduced to the Royal and Ancient game at Dornoch. The magnate presented the Carnegie Shield to the Royal Dornoch Golf Club and it is said to be "one of the most beautiful golf trophies in the world". The Shield is on display in the clubhouse.

Golf and Dornoch are inseparable. People have been playing Scotland's national game on the links here for more than 400 years. The course was laid out in 1616, although it is more likely than not that the clerics of Dornoch disported themselves thus well before that time. After all, monks from St Andrews, the home of golf, were "posted" to Dornoch and I'll bet they lugged their clubs along with them.

The religious importance of Dornoch reaches even further back in time. By AD 1140, a cell of Benedictine monks from Dunfermline had established themselves in Dornoch, when King David I, "for the love of him", asked the Earl of Orkney and Caithness to protect the monks from injury and shame.

That they needed such protection was beyond doubt. Two previous Bishops had come to a grisly end in Caithness: Bishop John was mutilated and murdered at Scrabster in 1202 and Bishop Adam met a similar fate in Halkirk in 1222. The seat of the Bishopric was thus moved south to the relative safety of Dornoch and in 1224, Bishop Gilbert, the newly appointed Bishop of Caithness, began his great work of founding the cathedral.

Looking out over the well-tended golf links and fertile fields round Dornoch, it is hard to think of these lands as being once an embattled "frontier". The truth is that hardly an inch of soil in this corner of Sutherland is unstained with the blood of some feud or bitter battle. I went in search of the burial place of one of the participants, the Norseman Earl Sigurd the Mighty, who was killed during a fearsome scrap in about AD 900.

Norse domination of the firthlands of Ross and Sutherland was a constant thorn in the flesh of burgeoning Scottish nationhood. According to the *Orkneyinga Saga*, Sigurd was slain by a local earl named Máel Brigte. As was the custom, Máel Brigte cut off his opponent's head and slung it over the saddle of the horse he was riding. In doing so, however, his leg was scratched by one of the unfortunate Sigurd's teeth and this wound caused Máel Brigte's death shortly afterwards.

I drove south west from Dornoch, bordering the calm waters of the firth, to find Cyderhall Farm and the mound under which the Viking warrior lies. Five fine sycamore trees greeted me, a flock of sheep and lambs baa-ing urgently under their leafy branches. The mound is to the left of a farm track on a small hillock, Cnoc Skardie, near the slow-flowing Evelix River. Well, he is reputed to be there. Not having a spade or shovel with me at the time, I can't confirm this truth. But I swear I heard him cough.

Back in Dornoch, I called at the Dornoch Castle Hotel, across the road from the cathedral. This remarkable building was formerly the Bishop's palace and it retains much of its early character. At the foot of a tall semi-circular tower there is a small doorway. A winding stone staircase leads to the reception area on the first floor. The bar is half-panelled in dark wood and there is a huge stone fireplace where the scent of burning peat lingers. Stag's heads glower from the walls below a timbered ceiling.

The walled garden, overlooked by a stone balustrade balcony, is a "secret" garden, almost not of this world in its calm beauty. Stately Yew trees form an avenue, centred by a green verdigris-stained statue on a plinth of the Greek God Pan, busy piping. Inscribed around the base is the name Beatrice Sykes, whose home the castle was before it became a hotel.

The castle, cathedral and town were less peaceful when "visited" by rapacious Caithness and Strathnaver neighbours in 1570. The then Earl of Caithness, George, was determined to annex Sutherland to his lands, by fair means or foul, and he besieged Dornoch to achieve his evil ambitions. His son John, Master of Caithness, was anxious to avoid bloodshed and negotiated the handing over of hostages as a guarantee of Dornoch's future good behaviour.

Earl George was made of sterner stuff. He accepted the hostages, murdered them and then ordered the town to be burned. Much of the cathedral was destroyed, including the entire roof, and it was not until 1616 that the task of rebuilding and repairing was begun by Sir Robert Gordon; continued by Elizabeth, Duchess-Countess of Sutherland, from 1835 to 1837 and the Rev. Charles Bentinck in 1924.

I stood by the tomb of Countess Elizabeth near the communion table in the Chancel of the restored cathedral and pondered these matters. The Countess and her husband, the Duke of Stafford, were the architects of the infamous Sutherland Clearances, when they brutally evicted 16,000 of their tenants to make way for more profitable sheep. No mention of that here. Instead, on the marble slab, the words: "Her attachments to Sutherland and her clansmen were shared by her husband . . . she enjoyed the admiration and love of her family and friends."

I remembered the story of one poor woman, evicted twice during the clearances. When she eventually died, she was buried in Dornoch churchyard. Her relatives said, "Well, the Countess will move you no more, now." Remarkably, the Countess did. The restoration work she began required a number of graves to be "relocated", one being the grave of the unfortunate woman who had been so persecuted.

Another poor, persecuted woman is commemorated by a rounded stone, about 2ft 6in in height, that stands in the garden of the last house in Carnaig Street. It took me a bit to find because there is no signpost to it. The Witches Stone marks the place where Janet Horne was burned in 1722 after being found guilty of witchcraft, the last such judicial execution to be carried out in Scotland.

I left the Witches Stone and drove out to Dornoch Airfield – a grass field with a wind-sock and a wooden shack at one end. The shack was locked and the only sign of business was a notice on the yellow painted door asking aviators to pop flight details in a red letter box. I walked from the terminal building across the saltmarsh dunes between the golf practice area and the sea.

This is a wildlife paradise, alive with the cry of curlew and red-billed oyster-catcher, decked with wildflowers: yellow rattle, grass of parnassus, marsh orchid, frog orchid, mouse-ear hawksweed, Baltic rush and ragged robin, some of which are rare in Scotland. From the dunes, I looked down onto a vast crescent of spotless golden sands that stretched north as far as the white-painted edifice of Dunrobin Castle near Golspie.

Before leaving, I returned to the cathedral to make my farewells to Bishop Gilbert. Afternoon sunlight slanted in through the splendid stained-glass windows and splashed at my feet. I said a prayer for all those who had laboured so hard to preserve this glorious building which so enhances our understanding of the importance of humility in modern times. And to ask for some help also in burnishing up my entirely hopeless golf swing.

For further details, contact: Tourist Information Centre, The Square, Dornoch, Sutherland IV25 3SD. Tel: 01862 810400.

19.
Discovering Shetland

The Shetland Island accent makes music out of words. When Ann and I were there in June 2009, a friend gave us a copy of *The Shetland Dictionary*, inscribed, "Aa du needs ta ken aboot kabes and humlibands." Meaning, "All you need to know about how to row Shetland boats." Ann and I are anglers. Shetland people are proud of their pristine environment and work hard to keep it that way. For instance, visitors are advised, "Dunna chuck bruck," don't scatter litter.

My ancestors come from Shetland and the islanders are an independent race. I remember discussing the question of Home Rule for Scotland with a friend in Lerwick, the largest town in Shetland. He was less than impressed. "It would make little difference to us, Bruce," he said, "being ruled from Edinburgh or from London. The one would be just as bad as the other." Indeed, Lerwick is nearer to Bergen in Norway than it is to Edinburgh, Scotland's capital city.

Shetland comprises 100 islands covering an area of more than 1,295 square kilometres. The principal isles are Mainland, Bressay, Whalsay, Fetlar, Yell and Unst. From AD 875 until 1468, they belonged to Norway. Then they were pledged to Scotland as part of the dowry when King James III married Margaret, daughter of King Christian I of Norway. This Norse influence is still evident in the characteristic design of Shetland boats, the domestic architecture and in Shetland place names.

There is no "best" time to visit these magical northern isles. They lie beyond Orkney, 110 miles north from mainland Scotland, and are always welcoming. Their overwhelming beauty instantly ensnares the soul. But June is a captivating month. As the islands awaken from the grip of winter to embrace summer, midnight is as bright as dawn during the long twilight of Shetland evenings, the "simmer dim". This is the ideal moment to launch a boat and fish for your supper on Shetland trout lochs.

The largest freshwater loch is Loch of Spiggie, near Sumburgh Airport on South Mainland. It is owned by the Royal Society for the Protection of Birds and is an important nature reserve. We had a wonderful evening's trout fishing there, serenaded by curlew and whimbrel. On the west shore, by Littleness, in times past, non-anglers used to splash and splutter in Hallelujah Bay – adherents of the Baptist faith were "ducked" there into membership of their church.

We stayed near Ocraquoy, a few miles south from Lerwick. There were splendid walks from our front door and we rarely needed the car. One morning, we tramped north to Coall Head (64m). At Bay of Ocraquoy, we were greeted by a symphony orchestra of be-whiskered barking seals, eyeing us cautiously, paralleling our passage along the shore.

A headland was decked overall in a carpet of blue squill. Yellow flag nodded by tiny ochre-coloured burns. In one small corner we found more squill, along with tormentil, marsh orchid, spotted orchid, lousewort, lesser celandine, white and lilac cuckoo flower, sorrel, red campion, sea rocket, silverweed and milkwort all growing together in happy unison. We beach-combed Bay of Fladdabister and climbed to the ruins of old limekilns, still in use in the 1930s, to have lunch. They made the perfect dining room: grass-lined hollows, sheltered from the wind with a place to rest tired backs. Sea sound and gull cry eased our spirits.

Lerwick is the bustling commercial centre of Shetland. The harbour is invariably packed with ships of all nations. During our visit, we watched the arrival of the graceful sailing boats taking part in the Bergen to Shetland race. The main street is flagstone-paved and many houses have direct access to the sea. A replica of a Viking longship, the *Dim Riv*, rides at anchor and during summer months, visitors can enjoy trips round the bay with a difference: they have to row the boat themselves. On one occasion, two less-than-experienced American lady oarswomen came ashore after never once having managed to get their oars into the water, but delighted nevertheless with the experience.

Other unforgettable visitor experiences are the ancient monuments that abound in Shetland. Just outside Lerwick is a settlement site and broch on Loch of Clickimin, occupied from 700 BC to the fifth or sixth century AD. Close to Loch of Spiggie is Jarlshof, a settlement that was used by successive cultures for 3,000 years. On Mousa Island, off the east coast of South Mainland, is Europe's best preserved broch, built around the time of the birth of Christ. By the Loch of Asta, close to the first tee of a delightful little 9-hole golf course, there is a 4,000-year-old Neolithic standing stone. Touch these ancient stones. Listen. Hear the sound of children laughing. Smell peat smoke rising from cooking fires.

During our Shetland sojourn we paid our respects to Shetland's old "capital", Scalloway, on the west coast. The town is dominated by the gaunt ruins of Scalloway Castle, built by Earl Patrick Stewart, a monster, renowned for his brutality. Dinner with Patrick, if he became angry, could be a dangerous affair. We found nearby Scalloway College restaurant much more user-friendly and a must when you are in Shetland. They serve the finest seafood imaginable in an informal, relaxed atmosphere. Shetland wool garments are also enticing, vibrant with natural colours and remarkably inexpensive. Shetland sheep are not clipped; the wool is gently pulled out by hand.

Another must is a visit to Ireland, a cluster of houses overlooking St Ninian's Isle south from Scalloway. We arrived on a sparkling morning with the distant island of Foula clearly visible on the horizon. The sheer cliffs guarding Foula are 366m in height and the Vikings called the island *Flugloy*, "The Island of the Birds". On the shore of Ireland Wick ("wick" is the Norse name for a bay) lay a classic Shetland-style boat, pointed at both ends, broad-beamed and utterly beautiful. They say in Shetland that you may do as you please with another man's wife but you must never lay hands on his boat. Nobody was looking, so I risked stroking the vessel.

St Ninian's Isle is joined to the mainland by a 656-yard-long golden sandbank. A church, dedicated to St Ninian, was built on the island in the sixth or seventh century, but the island is most famous for a hoard of treasure found in 1958. A fifteen-year-old schoolboy, Douglas Coutts, who had volunteered to help excavate the site, made the find. Douglas recalled the moment: "I got down to a stone slab marked with a Celtic cross. Beneath this stone was a box, which contained the collection of silverware which has been dated back to 800 AD. The cache included twelve brooches of Celtic design, many inset with semi-precious stones, numerous bowls and a hanging lamp and other objects."

On the island of Yell, a bumpy boat ride across a narrow stretch of sea appropriately named the "buttocks", we parked by the ruins of Windhouse, which is haunted by a family of ghosts: the Lady in Silk, whose broken-necked skeleton was discovered under floorboards at the foot of the staircase; the Man in Black, a tall spectre, dressed in a black cloak and noted for his ability to walk through walls; the Child, whose remains were found built into the kitchen wall; and a black dog to keep them company.

Nobody was home when we called, so we tramped out to explore the deserted village of Vollister. A track leads north from Windhouse above Whale Firth, crossing Brocken Burn on the slopes of Muckle Swart Houll (110m). After about a mile, you will see the ruins of the village ahead on a promontory overlooking the firth. Vollister was cleared of its people in the latter years of the nineteenth century. All that remains to mark their passing are broken buildings and a rusty boat-mooring ring in a rock by the shore.

Further north, on the Island of Unst, another ghost is commemorated in the name of ale brewed in Scotland's most northerly brewery, the Valhalla Brewery at Baltasound. It is called "White Wife". This woman appears in cars, generally being driven by lone men. She was last seen by Steven Spence in 1996 whilst he was driving along the road two miles south from Baltasound. The ale is pretty stunning, too – dry and refreshing, bitter with a characteristically fruity after-taste.

Unst has "the most northerly" everything in UK: golf course, rugby ground, post office, castle (Muness), church and, of course, the famous lighthouse of Muckle Flugga. The lighthouse was built in 1858 by Thomas

Stevenson. As a young man, his son, the author Robert Louis Stevenson, stayed on the island. He is said to have based the shape of the island in his famous adventure story, *Treasure Island*, on the shape of Unst.

More tangible treasure has been accrued in Shetland by wise investment of the revenue gathered from the oil industry, which arrived in Shetland during the 1970s. The value of these funds has now reached £705 million, making Shetland the richest local authority in Britain. The money currently equates to a tidy £30,653 for each of the islands' 23,000 inhabitants. Whilst the oil-boom may have made Shetland rich, it has not altered the character of the people, or their deep commitment to and love of their sea-girt homeland. Just remember, avoid touching their kabes, humlibands or boats – and dunna chuck bruck.

For further information about Shetland, contact: Shetland Tourist Office, Market Cross, Lerwick, Shetland ZE1 0LU; Tel: 01595 693434; Fax: 01595 695807; Email: info@visitshetland.com; Website: www.visitshetland.com

For books about Shetland, contact: The Shetland Times Bookshop, 71–79 Commercial Street, Lerwick, Shetland ZE1 OAJ; Tel: 01595 695531; Fax: 01595 692897; Email: bookshop@shetland-times.co.uk; Website: http://www. shetlandtimes.co.uk/shop/

20.
Highland White Dream

Skerray is a scatter of crofts and houses clinging to the skirts of a cliff-girt headland in North Sutherland. It is pronounced "Skera". The yellow sands of Tongue Bay guard the headland to the west. In the east, Icelandic waves sweep the shores of Torrisdale Bay. The Gaelic for Skerray is "Sgeireadh" and the name means "between the rocks and seas".

Eleven crofting townships here have survived the test of time: Strathan, Modsarie, Achnabat, Skerray, Tubeg, Clashbuie, Clashaidy, Achtoty, Aird, Torrisdale and Borgie. This is the land of Clan Mackay and the predominant surname is of that ilk. At a recent children's Christmas pantomime, half of the little ones taking part in the production had the surname "Mackay". The population of Skerray – men, women and children – amounts to some eighty souls.

If you are traveling between John O'Groats and Durness in the west you can easily miss Skerray. The main road bypasses the community. To explore this magical enclave, turn right from the A836 after the stone bridge where the Borgie River tumbles seawards. A narrow, single-track route winds tortuously north to Torrisdale beach, past the tomb-stoned graveyard on the shore and through the principal townships, before rejoining highway A836 after a semi-circular journey of five miles.

But Skerray is more than just scenically magnificent. It is a thriving community, as fully engaged in the new millennium as it is proud and mindful of its Highland history and heritage. It is also a community that has successfully integrated both local and newcomer into the complex fabric of daily life. The population of Skerray is highly cosmopolitan, with a wide range of externally acquired skills mixed with local knowledge and experience.

Andrew Fraser, the Free Church minister who served his Skerray "flock" for fifteen years, puts the matter simply. He says, "The people here are amongst the most welcoming that I have ever known." Pat Rodlin, a noted horticulturist, told me: "Perhaps we get on together because we need each other. New arrivals often have little or no idea whatsoever of how to work a croft. The only way they can learn is by seeking help from those whose families have worked this land for generations."

Elizabeth "Babe" Mackay is of that line of families. She and her husband, Sinclair, live at Clashaidy, close to the harbour where Sinclair keeps his fishing boat. Babe was born in the old post office in Skerray where her father was postmaster. Babe acquired her nickname because of her childhood love of animals. Whenever one asked where she was, the response invariably was, "Oh, the babe will be up the hill with the animals."

Babe and her sisters, Catherine, Mary and Annie, followed their father's post office footsteps and the family looked after the Royal Mail in Skerray for seventy years. Babe has been a member of the Skerray Public Hall Committee ever since she left school, but she won't say exactly when that was. She is also involved in the Skerray/Borgie Community Club, Age Concern and a host of other local activities.

The present post office is in Jimson's (tel: 01641 521445), an eclectic shop in a wonderfully restored thatched croft adjacent to the most northerly garden centre on mainland Britain. Until recently, Postmistress Marilyn Macfadyen, like most other Skerray residents, played an important part in the affairs of the community. Marilyn is multitalented. She hails from Glasgow where she worked in the Scottish Civil Service. Marilyn also trained as a ballerina. She recently wrote and directed a hilarious production of *Cinderella*, performed to great acclaim before a capacity audience in the village hall. Her daughter is now the sub-postmistress.

The mainstay of horticultural activity is, however, Pat Rodlin, a native of the Orkney Islands. Pat worked extensively in Finland, Holland and Switzerland before coming to live in Skerray in 1984. She brought with her a unique chrysanthemum, the Highland White Dream, which has gained international fame and recognition. Over the past five years, approximately a quarter of a million examples of this beautiful flower have been grown at Skerray and sent all over the world.

The garden centre specialises in silver birch trees grown from locally collected seeds, as well as holly, yew, elderberry, rowan, alder, aspen and sycamore. Although the centre is small, it hosts an astonishing array of plants, all raised and cared for with loads of TLC. As well as trees, the centre has splendidly strong heather plants, alpine species, gorse and whin, all well accustomed to thriving in the harshest of climes.

Much of this enterprise is promoted through NORC-CELT (North Coast Community Enterprise Limited), set up by Skerray people to address the needs of the townships. NORC-CELT has been supported famously by funding from local government organisations as well as by generous donations from residents. Adjacent to Jimson's shop and the garden centre are the offices of "An Comann Eachdraidh Sgeireadh", the Skerray Historical Society. An absorbing archive, open to visitors, is being built up depicting the life and work of the community, based upon personal letters, documents, photographs and reminiscences.

Another mainstay of the local community is Meg Telfer, who devotes a huge amount of time and energy to promoting Skerray and its environs. But it is her work as an artist that commands most instant admiration: wide, bold, sweeping landscapes, which capture the spirit of the north far more vividly than any spoken or written words could ever hope to do. Until she retired, Meg was a visiting art teacher in local primary schools. She told me, "Teaching children art is the best job in the world."

Meg also teaches at the Skerray Studio, another string in the NORC-CELT bow. Drop-in art courses are a feature of the annual calendar where expert tuition can be arranged. All you are required to bring is enthusiasm and the desire to learn. Frances Bowman, from Skerray Mains, is also an artist. Frances specialises in watercolours. Her classes are well attended by young and not so young alike. Mike Roper runs practical courses in photography.

When Marilyn Macfadyen's production of *Cinderella* hit the Skerray boards in March, your correspondent was an unlikely Ugly Sister. His companion, affectionately known as UGS 2, was David Illingworth, a recycled teenager in his eighth decade who lives in a small cottage at Tubeg. David is a clockmaker who learned his trade during the Second World War when he worked on the Type X cypher machine, the British answer to the German Enigma encoder.

David's cottage is loud with the tick and tock of his business: fob watches, pocket-watches, wristwatches, mantel clocks, ormolu clocks, carriage clocks and longcase clocks of various sizes. The walls are adorned with his paintings, the floor with tiles designed and made by his Danish-born wife, Lotte Glob, an internationally renowned ceramicist. In spite of being eternally busy, David was, until recently, treasurer of the historical society. David says, "Living in Skerray is easy on the spirit."

Known universally as "Doc", Betty Mackenzie, a retired medical practitioner, has lived in Torrisdale for, well, quite a few years. She is a powerhouse of ideas and an active member of most of the local organisations, including being clerk to the Skerray Grazings committee who manage the communal community land. Doc's latest project is centred upon using whin and gorse chippings to prevent mice and other pests from eating prized garden plants.

She heard a report on the radio about the chippings whilst she was looking out of her window – onto a large expanse of whins: "There's a great idea, we could market gorse chippings as mulch." Wheels are already in motion and the idea is gathering speed, as do most ideas in Skerray. Doc played an important part in another highly successful Skerray idea, this time from Meg Telfer and Marilyn Macfadyen. Wool taken from individual sheep was knitted into hats, complemented with a picture of the sheep which provided the wool. Doc did the knitting.

At a time when so much is heard about depopulation and stagnant Highland communities, Skerray is an outstanding example of what can be achieved when people care about their environment and care about those who live and work in that environment. This is perhaps exemplified by a poignant plaque attached to a cattle-grid on the A836 road to the north of Skerray. It says, simply, "Willie John's Grid, 7/9/1914–13/12/1996".

Willie John Mackay was a Skerray man who fought tirelessly to have cattle-grids placed in roads to prevent wandering cattle from entering and damaging gardens. In a crofting community, traditionally, sheep and cattle are free to roam and this can sometimes cause angst and ill feeling. Finding the money to construct the grids was the problem, a problem that Willie John addressed with customary diligence. He won his battle but never lived to see the grid built. The plaque is his small memorial.

Since this piece was written, many of those featured in it have since "moved on" to the great croft in the sky. But their spirit still lives and still burns brightly in my mind and heart.

21.
Caithness Memories

Of all the airs the wind can blow, I love those from Caithness best, Scotland's Lowlands up beyond the Highlands and the home of my paternal grandfather. He was born in the fishing village of Staxigoe to the north of Wick, where his brother had a farm overlooking the cold waters of the Moray Firth. My father, John Sandison, as a young man used to spend his holidays working with his uncle and it was here that one of the most notable Caithness brawls of the 1920s was arranged. The local "Wheeper-in", the school truant officer, was also named John Sandison and had the reputation of being a useful boxer. My father was skillful in fisticuffs as well, so the town worthies determined that it would be a good idea to find out which John Sandison was the better man in the ring. The match was to be fought in a barn near Staxigoe Harbour.

A date was set and speculation on the outcome sharpened. Age and experience were on the side of the Wheeper-in but my father had the asset of youth. At the appointed hour, bales of hay were dragged into the barn to form a ring. Wagers were placed and strong drink taken. It is alleged that those who supported my father plied the Wheeper-in with copious amounts in an attempt to blur his defenses but this is pure hearsay. Stripped to the waist, the men stepped up to scratch and after half an hour of hard work, the Wheeper-in acknowledged defeat. "Lad," he said, "if I was half my age and twice as sober, it might have been a different story, but you won fair and square." They remained the best of friends.

Staxigoe is less boisterous today but it used to boast upwards of sixty vessels, bobbing in the bay: herring boats, sailing ships discharging timber from Scandinavia, the bustle of fish-curing stations on the shore – a vibrant community which lived by and from the sea. However, during the early years of the nineteenth century, Wick became the principal herring port. At its height, this fishery supported more than 1,000 boats and it is said that when they were all in port together, a man could walk dry-shod from one side of Wick Harbour to the other. The herring, "the silver darlings", made the town rich.

The small villages along the ragged coast prospered as well – Latheron, Lybster, Dunbeath and Berriedale – but perhaps the most dramatic fishing station was at Whaligoe, a few miles south from Wick. There, the harbour is situated at the base of fifty-four-metre cliffs and to reach the bottom, steps were cut into the sheer sides, descending precipitously to the sea. The catch was loaded into creels, which fishwives carried on their heads to the top of the steps to be taken from there to the gutting tubs at Wick.

After the collapse of the herring fishery, Whaligoe was deserted. However, until the 1970s, the harbour steps were cared for by Mrs Juhle, a local lady who was concerned that they may fall into disrepair. She reasoned that since Jesus had been a fisherman, then, "at the second coming", He could arrive at Whaligoe. She would make certain that the steps were in a fit state to receive Him. The steps are now cared for by the Wick Heritage Society.

The prosperity engendered by the herring fishery embraced much of the north of Scotland. As people were driven from their homes during the Highland Clearances so that the lairds could rent the land they had stolen to Lowland sheep farmers, the dispossessed trekked to Wick in search of work – men to sign on as fishermen, women and children as fish-gutters. Whole families made the journey and they followed the herring shoals down the east coast seeking employment where and when they could, then making the long journey back to the hovels that had replaced the homes out of which they had been burned by rapacious landowners.

Wick boasted the largest Gaelic-speaking congregation in the world,

The heart of King Robert the Bruce lies buried beneath this marker at Melrose Abbey in the Borders

Loch Katrine from the summit of Ben Venue, Trossachs

Helmsdale Harbour, East Sutherland

Traigh Allt
Chailgeag, North
Sutherland

Kyle of Durness
looking south
to Foinaven,
Sutherland

Neidpath
Castle by the
River Tweed,
Peebles

The Kyle of
Tongue and
Ben Hope from
Island Roan

Poca Buidhe Flowerdale
Forrest Wester Ross

The Lone Pine – a Scots
Pine tree estimated to
be more than 300 years
old. Beinn Eighe Nature
Reserve, Wester Ross

Dunkeld Cathedral,
Perthshire

Scottish Youth Hostel croft
cottage, Howmore, Isle of
South Uist, Western Isles

Sandwood Bay, North West Sutherland

Skerray Township, Sutherland

Torrisdale Bay and mouths of the rivers Borgie and Naver, Sutherland

Whaligoe Steps, Caithness

Windhouse: the haunted house on the Island of Yell, Shetland

Eilean Donan Castle, Loch Duich along the Road to the Isles

Coldbackie
Beach looking
towards Island
Roan in North
Sutherland

Castle Varrich
and Ben
Hope, Tongue,
Sutherland

Stromness,
Orkney Islands

Urquhart Castle,
Loch Ness,
Inverness-shire

Hugh Miller's fossil beds, The Black Isle

Crichton Castle, Midlothian

where 5,000 souls would gather on the Green by the Wick River to hear their ministers preach on Sunday mornings. And the ministers had plenty to say. Herring fishing was thirsty work. More than 800 gallons of whisky were drunk each week. Ministers complained bitterly that whilst it was hard to get people in for evening service, "for a wedding you could get six pipers at a stroke, and not a teetotaller amongst them".

The Wick herring industry reached its peak during the 1860s, when, due to the introduction of cotton nets, the catching capacity of the fleet vastly increased. In a few days in the 1860 season, unprecedented numbers of fish were caught: 50,160 crans containing fifty million herring. The town bustled. One man, above all, helped achieve this: James Bremner, born in the village of Keiss a few miles north from Wick.

Bremner was the most successful fish curer and an inventor of extraordinary talent. He raised 200 sunken and stranded vessels, including the world's largest steamship, Brunel's *SS Great Britain*. He designed and built sailing vessels of up to 500 tons in weight, advised Brunel on repairs to the Blackwall Tunnel under the River Thames in London when it began to leak, built more than twenty harbours, and invented a suspension crane with an expandable jib and floating work platforms.

Bremner was loved and admired by all. When he died, shops closed their shutters and window blinds were drawn. I often visit Wick Town Hall, where there is a wonderful portrait of the great man, to pay my respects, and the graceful, slim monument to him that stands on a hill on the south shore of Wick Bay overlooking the scene of so many of his labours.

Earlier rapacious visitors, the Vikings, made Caithness their home, their "Land of Cat". The Norsemen arrived toward the end of the ninth century from Orkney and tried to impress their will upon the people, not so much as invaders as settlers. But these fertile lands were also coveted by the Kings of Scotland, who were determined that they should remain in their hands and not those of the Viking Earls of Orkney. The Norse influence in Caithness ended soon after the King's bishop, Adam, was outrageously murdered. When Adam imposed a tax on butter, the tenants complained to Earl John of Orkney, who replied: "The devil take the bishop and his butter; you may roast him, if you please." Which the tenants promptly did. King Alexander II (1198–1249) was not amused and marched north to restore order.

But order was never much in evidence in Caithness during the Middle Ages. A local rhyme succinctly tells the story: "Sinclair, Keith, Sutherland and Clan Gunn, there seldom was peace where these four were in." Clan Gunn was the dominant force then, descended from Svein Asleifarson who was alive and kicking all and sundry out of his way during the twelfth century. The ruins of Svein's Caithness home may still be seen at Freswick, a few miles from the Stacks of Duncansby near John O'Groats. The site is to the south of the present fortified tower house, built by the Sinclairs of Freswick in the seventeenth century.

As Clan Gunn lost its authority and much of its land, various septs were established: the Hendersons, Williamsons and Wilsons. Other sept names included Georgeson, Jameson, Johnson, MacComas, MacCorkill, MacIan, MacKeamish, Manson, Nelson and my own bunch, Sandison. One of the most famous of the clan, Sir James Gunn, is said to have accompanied Sir Henry Sinclair, Earl of Orkney, on his voyage of discovery to the New World in 1398, almost a century before Columbus made a similar, better-known journey. Sir William Gunn, knighted by King Charles I in 1639, was a soldier of fortune who became a General and a Baron of the Holy Roman Empire. Another member of the clan named Lake Gunn in the south island of New Zealand. Perhaps the most notable, however, is Neil Gunn (1891–1973) one of Scotland's best-loved authors who was born at Dunbeath and wrote emotively about his native land in such enduring books as *The Silver Darlings* and *Highland River*.

Another important industry that was unique to Caithness was the quarrying of flagstone. In a county virtually devoid of trees, flagstone was used for fencing, for roof tiles and for floors. During the nineteenth century, when railway-building fever swept Britain, the preferred stone for platforms was Caithness flag. The Strand, in London, was paved with

Caithness flagstone and 20,000 tons were quarried each year and exported all over the world. The industry "died" with the invention of concrete, but it has revived spectacularly and Caithness flagstone is as much in demand today as it was 150 years ago.

Although quarrying is automated now, one man, the late Jack Green, still worked his quarry in the old way, by hand: raising the slabs by levers, carefully splitting and dressing the flagstones with hammer and chisel. Jack Green was still working at the age of eighty-six years and would work in his quarry from dawn to dusk. When I last called to say hello to Jack he was training up two apprentices, both men in their mid-sixties.

But the story of Caithness is as much about land as it is about people. Behind the fertile coastal fringe and the farms and fields between Wick and Thurso, lies one of the great natural wonders of the world: the Flow Country, the largest remaining example of blanket peat bog on planet Earth; a vast uninhabited area of interconnected lochs, lochans and bog pools, filled with the cry of curlew, golden plover, dunlin and greenshank; home to rare black-throated and red-throated divers, golden eagle, hen harrier, peregrine and buzzard; where red deer roam and otters play and fierce-eyed wildcat mark your passing on the purple heather moor.

This was also our family playground when we lived in Caithness. Our children learned to fish for brown trout in the Flow Country; tramped for miles with us to remote sparkling blue waters beneath cathedral skies; discovered the simple joy to be found in myriad wildflowers which grow there: bog asphodel, tormentil, wild violet, sundew, butterwort, yellow flag and red-tinged sphagnum moss. On warm summer days, we swam from silent sandy shores and, invariably, a basket of beautiful trout accompanied us home.

Caithness is a land for all seasons, as welcoming in the depths of winter as it is during the long summer nights of the "simmer dim" (summer dimness), when it never really gets dark. There are a host of things to keep you and all your tribe busy: outstanding archaeological sites such as the dramatic 4,500-year-old Neolithic burial chambers at Camster; the ruined castles of Sinclair and Girnigoe, still the official residence of the Earl of Caithness; gaunt Ackergill Tower, where Oliver Cromwell's officers were billeted during the terrible religious wars of the seventeenth century.

There are splendid links golf courses; salmon and trout fishing of angling dreams; empty golden sand beaches at Dunnet in the north and Sinclair Bay to the east; and the delights of downtown Wick and Thurso, where you will meet the kindest people in the world. However, if you're ever invited into a boxing ring up here, just remember the fate of the Wheeper-in and abjure the consumption of too much *uisge beatha*, the Water of Life.

22.
Edinburgh, "Auld Reekie"

I was born in Edinburgh and wear the old grey city like a warm blanket round my soul. I discovered the worth of the nation I love whilst growing up in "Auld Reekie"; in the closes and wynds of the Royal Mile; on monument-bedecked Calton Hill and proud Princes Street; in the calm of Holyrood Park and amidst the ancient woodlands of Cramond.

Edinburgh is above all a city of culture, and I was delighted when the United Nations Educational, Scientific and Cultural Organization (UNESCO) embraced this view. Meeting in Paris, France, in 2004, UN chiefs announced that the Scottish capital would become the world's first "City of Literature".

In the 1760s, an English visitor, John Amyat, the King's Chemist, famously declared: "Here I stand at what is called the Cross of Edinburgh, and can, in a few minutes, take fifty men of genius by the hand." This was the high point of what has become known as "The Enlightenment", when Edinburgh was the world centre of inspired thought.

These men of genius included the poet Allan Ramsay, "The Gentle Shepherd"; his son, also Allan Ramsay, portrait painter to George III; David Hume, philosopher and historian; Alexander "Jupiter" Carlyle, minister and political pamphleteer; the Reverend John Home, whose play, *Douglas*, outraged his fellow clergymen and inspired a member of the audience to call out: "Whaur's yer Wullie Shakspeare noo!"; the great architect, Robert Adam; Adam Smith, political economist and author of *The Wealth of Nations*, and many more.

The spirits of these men haunt Auld Reekie. When I walk down the Royal Mile, I think that I see them clearly, as if they were still there today:

Robert Burns, sharing a drink with friends in John Downie's pub in Libberton's Wynd; Allan Ramsay, busy with customers in his bookshop in Carrubber's Close; Old Playhouse Close and the bustle of the audience gathering for the first night of the scandalous play, *Douglas*; the painter Henry Raeburn, relaxing at the Isle of Man Tavern in Craig's Close off Cockburn Street.

Most of these men were educated at the Royal High School of Edinburgh, known as the "Tounis Scule". The story of Edinburgh is inextricably intertwined with that of the school, which traces its beginnings back to AD 1128 when King David I established the Abbey of Holyrood. I arrived at the school somewhat later, in 1943, and was a pupil there until 1954. My academic light shone less than brightly but I learned to love history, literature, art and music, and these joys have stayed with me throughout my life.

Whilst at Royal High, I also discovered the poetry of Robert Burns. There is a monument to him across the road from the old school on Calton Hill and each year on the anniversary of his birth, 25 January, senior pupils laid a wreath at this memorial. I won my only academic honour – well, nearly – by coming third in the annual competition for an essay on one of Burns' poems. From then on, I was determined to become a poet when I grew up. Still mean to when I grow up.

Burns arrived in Edinburgh in December 1786 with a "sair heed", caused by the generous hospitality he received from admirers along the way. He lodged with John Richmond, a friend from Mauchline who worked in the city, in a flat in Baxter's Close. The house has long since been demolished but the poet's residence there is commemorated in a plaque above the Lawnmarket entrance to Lady Stair's Close. Burns later lodged in Buccleuch Street with Willie Nicoll, a master at the High School, and he immortalized his friend in the lines:

> Willie brew'd a peck o' maut'
> And Rob and Allan cam to pree;

Three blyther hearts, that lee-lang night,
Ye wid na found in Christendie.

Burns was also a companion of the Crochallan Fencibles, a drinking club that met in Dawney Douglas's tavern in Anchor's Close. A product of these meetings was Burns' bawdy poems, later published as *The Merry Muses of Caledonia*, a copy of which is by my side as I write. It was during this visit that the poet met the young Walter Scott in a house in Braid Place, Sciennes, on the south side of the city. There is a plaque on the wall commemorating the meeting and I always used to make a detour, walking home from the Old Town to Newington where my parents lived, to read it.

Scott, a boy of fifteen at the time, later recalled: "There was a strong expression of sense and shrewdness in all his [Burns'] lineaments; the eye alone, I think, indicated the poetical character and temperament. It was large and of a dark cast, and glowed (I say literally glowed) when he spoke with feeling or interest. I never saw such another eye in a human head, though I have seen the most distinguished men of my time. His conversation expressed perfect self-confidence, without the slightest presumption."

On his second visit to Edinburgh in 1788, Burns lodged with another High School master, William Cruikshank, in St James's Square. St James's Square was wantonly demolished in the 1960s to make way for a shopping mall. On this visit, Burns began his ultimately fruitless relationship with his "Clarinda", Mrs James (Nancy) Maclehose. As an old woman, Nancy is said to have "spoke o' her love for the poet like a hellcat bit lassie in her teens. Whilst exhibiting to her cronies the faded letters from her Robbie, she would greet (cry) just like a bairn".

The best way to discover Edinburgh is on foot. As a boy, I used to roam the streets of the city. I haunted the Royal Mile, peering in windows, exploring the narrow wynds, climbing Arthur's Seat and Calton Hill to view the town and the surrounding hills, the broad blue sweep of the Firth of Forth, the distant mountains to the north. Time was a friend then, just the space between my dreams and dinner.

In my wanderings, I discovered the house in York Place where Henry Raeburn had his studio and I thought of him there, hard at work on his famous portrait of the Reverend Robert Walker skating on Duddingston Loch; the house where Robert Louis Stevenson stayed, 17 Heriot Row, and their family cottage in the village of Swanson on the edge of the Pentland Hills.

The walk from Cramond along the shore of the Firth of Forth to South Queensferry led me to the Hawes Inn, crouched below the massive bulk of the Forth Railway Bridge. Stevenson was a frequent visitor and he devised the plot of his book *Kidnapped* whilst staying in Room 13. Not so many years ago, I found myself in the same room, warmed by an open fire as Stevenson must have been. In his memory, I recited lines from one of his *Songs of Travel*:

Spring shall come, come again, calling up the moor-fowl,
Spring shall bring the sun and rain, bring the bees and flowers;
Red shall the heather bloom over hill and valley,
Soft flow the stream through the even-flowing hours;
Fair the day shine as it shone on my childhood –
Fair shine the day on the house with open door;
Birds come and cry there and twitter in the chimney –
But I go forever and come this way no more.

Another of my Edinburgh literary heroes is the poet Norman MacCaig who died in Edinburgh in 1996. My greatest regret is that I never worked up sufficient courage to go and meet him. We had much in common, both having been educated at the Royal High School, and both with a shared love of the broken lands of Assynt in Sutherland, stalking the hills there, fishing for wild brown trout. MacCaig's poetry echoes this love in its directness and does the work of Robert Burns, yet points the way forward to an as yet unseen, better world. Here is his poem, "Bell Heather":

People make songs about your big cousin,
Extravagantly sprawled over mountain after mountain.
They tear him up and he goes off to England
On the bumpers of cars, on shiny radiators.
But you are more beautiful and you blossom first,
In square feet and raggedy circles.
Your blue travels a hundred yards
That are the main road for bees.
If I were an adder, I'd choose you
For my royal palace. My sliding tongue
Would savour the thin scent
Of your boudoirs and banqueting halls.
A modest immodesty is a good thing,
Little blaze of blue on a rock face.
I'll try it myself. Will the bees come,
The wild bees with their white noses?

Edinburgh, "The City of Literature", is as vibrant and vital today as it was in the time of Scott and Burns. Find its magic, as the poet William Ernest Henley did when he visited the "Athens of the North":

A late lark twitters from the quiet skies;
And from the west,
There the sun, his day's work ended,
Lingers as in content,
There falls on the old, gray city
An influence luminous and serene,
A shining peace.

23.
The Story of Windhouse on the Island of Yell, Shetland

I believe in ghosties and ghoulies and things that go bump in the night; in hobgoblins, water sprites, witches and warlocks and the whole bang-shoot of the unexplored, mysterious nether regions of this mortal coil. This is why the ruins of Windhouse on the Island of Yell in Shetland made me uneasy.

Tattered walls, once pitch-pine and lath-and-plaster clad, seep dampness. Broken roof beams spear-point the gloom. Empty window frames gape like missing teeth. The staircase hung crookedly. Most of its steps are missing. My spine tingled. I turned to speak to my wife, Ann, to ask her if she felt uncomfortable. She was nowhere to be seen. Then I heard her call from outside, "Come on, Bruce, let's get on with our walk."

This was my introduction to Windhouse and I had no idea then that the house was haunted by not one, but by a whole family of spirits; the Lady in Silk, the ghost of a woman whose skeleton, with a broken neck, was found under floorboards at the foot of the staircase; the Man in Black, a tall spectre in a black cloak most frequently seen outside the kitchen window; the ghost of a child whose remains were discovered built into the kitchen wall; and, to keep them company, the ghost of a black dog.

In 1995, the Shetland writer and author Johnathan Wills spoke to Greta Manson, whose mother, Ruby, had worked as a maid at Windhouse in the 1920s when the estate was owned by Mr James Gordon. She remembered being there. "I was once in the house as a child and I was not very happy about it. There was what they call 'The Lady in Silk' who shuffles round you three times before disappearing."

Greta recalled, "One night my mother was sitting in the kitchen when she heard a child wailing. She thought it was the other maids trying to frighten her but then she heard it again, closer. When it cried a third time and she felt the touch of a little hand on her cheek, she ran out. Later they found the remains of a baby, walled up next to where she'd been sitting."

I know about these things. I have spoken to a ghost. In 1968, we bought an old farmhouse, Hardriding, near the Roman Wall in Northumberland. Mrs Smith, the previous owner, died peacefully one evening after supper in the Morning Room. In the middle of the night, I think it was May, I got up and went downstairs. I don't know why.

A woman swept past me and I followed her into the drawing room. It seemed to be the natural thing to do. "Now," she said, sitting down in a chair before the fire, "tell me about yourself and your family." We talked. She was kind. She said she was glad that we lived in her house.

I discovered later that it was the first anniversary of Mrs Smith's death and I described her perfectly to neighbours who had known her for years. But I was never uncomfortable with that experience. We lived at Hardriding for a long time with our wonderful, supportive friend. How would I have reacted to being confronted with the most widely reported ghostly appearances at Windhouse? I don't know. Andrew Mathewson, the schoolmaster at East Yell, wrote about it in 1863:

"It so happened that a vessel of much importance got embayed on the north west of Shetland on a Christmas evening [in the early 1800s] and was wrecked at the Dall of Lumbister. The Master escaped safe to land with nothing but his sheaf knife strapped firm and his poleaxe in his hand.

"On his recovery from being almost drowned, he wandered inland in search of relief, which brought him in full view of Windhouse. Hither he hastened forward as the day was drawing to its close and on reaching the mansion he was welcomed as a friend and refreshed as a brother."

The account then relates how the seaman was surprised to find everyone at Windhouse busy packing and preparing for departure. He asked his host, Mr Neven, where they were going.

"To this request he received for answer that for this night of the year, namely Yule E'en or the 24th of every December, that he would have to seek lodgings for himself, as no mortal who had ever attempted to sleep in the house that night was ever found alive in the morning but was destroyed and slain by some evil spirit from the sea called Trows," the Shetland name for goblins.

The ship's captain persuaded Mr Neven to let him remain at Windhouse so that he could confront the demon. Our hero fortified himself in the library, where he drank a lot of Neven's wine, and ate a lot of the food his considerate host had prepared for his coming ordeal. The captain slept a little. Drank more wine, read a book and composed himself.

"At one o'clock a sound arose as of rolling thunder and the whole fabric of the house shook and trembled as if going to ruins ... to sit still and die so ignominiously was not his desire. In the name and strength of the Blessed he made ready, felt his dagger and grasped his axe, tore down the barricades from the door and threw back the bar."

A dark shape fled from him and he pursued it towards Mid Yell Voe. Just before the creature reached the sea, the Captain hurled his axe, striking it in the head. When he examined the body, all that he could make out was a "shapeless mass". He disposed of the creature in a large hole, covered it with earth and then formed the fence around it, which still remains.

The Windhouse ghosts are a mystery. Why do they persistently haunt the dwelling? The deeds of a previous owner, Ninian Neven, might provide a clue. Ninian was a notary public, a latter-day lawyer and a rogue. When John Swanieson, the master of Windhouse in 1614, died, Ninian was asked to attend to the transfer of the estate to John's son and heir, James.

Ninian contrived, through duplicity and manipulation of the law, to oust Swanieson and acquire the estate for himself. James was no match for the glib-tongued lawyer and eight years after the death of John, Ninian was master of Windhouse. In succeeding years, he bought land throughout Yell and soon became the island's most important and feared landowner. Perhaps the Windhouse ghosts are the souls of those he persecuted.

Ruby Manson claimed that an old woman put a curse on the Neven family when they evicted people to make way for sheep: "She told the laird that neither he nor his progeny would ever prosper and that one day sheep would wander through his house, as indeed they do today." When Ann and I were there we found evidence of sheep aplenty.

The Neven family was eventually forced to sell the estate in 1884 when John Harrison, an up-and-coming Lerwick fish merchant, bought it. John had grandiose ideas about his status in the community and it was he who added the crenellated abutments and entrance porch to Windhouse. Nevertheless, he was no more fortunate in his property than the Nevens had been and was declared bankrupt within ten years.

The next owner, William Gordon, was a soldier and when he died in 1919 in the Middle East, his nephew, James, inherited Windhouse and lived there into the 1930s. James was the last person to occupy the famously haunted dwelling and it was during that time that the estate farm was let to an eminent local family, the Johnsons. But the eminently sensible Johnsons chose to settle at Setter, a step south from dreaded Windhouse.

Windhouse began to die. The body deteriorated and the garden became a wilderness. Winter storms ravaged the once-bold abutments and surrounding walls. They crumbled and collapsed. Only the stark uprights of the entrance pillars are left to guard the way in. Above the front door is the Neven family coat of arms, a fading affair of shields and plumes surmounted by barely discernable words carved in stone: "Faithful," and, perhaps, "doing good to all"?

I turned from the somber ruin and joined Ann on the hill. Together, we tramped the golden moor to the deserted village of Vollister on the east shore of Whale Firth, near to where the slayer of the Windhouse trow was wrecked. But unlike Windhouse, the tumbled ruins here greeted us happily and, borne about the soft wind, I heard the sound of dogs barking and children's laughter echoing amidst the grey stones.

24.
Dornie to Durness

Laughter from the bar of the Dornie Hotel mingled with curlew call from the shores of Loch Duich. I looked towards Eilean Donan Castle, the ancient home of Clan Macrae. The clan paid a heavy price for joining the 1719 uprising in support of the Old Pretender, son of the deposed King James II. In order to dislodge a contingent of Spanish soldiers sheltering there, the castle was reduced to rubble by the British frigate, *HMS Worcester*.

I was at the start point of a fantastic journey, from Dornie in Inverness-shire, through the North West Highlands to Durness in Sutherland. I nodded goodbye to Eilean Donan, wondering if Clan Macrae and Spanish ghosts still haunted its elegantly refurbished halls. Half an hour later, humour restored, I was in Plockton, on the shores of Loch Carron. A boisterous Labrador dashed in and out of the shallow waters of the bay. Visitors luxuriated in warm sunlight.

But most residents were preparing for church. I remembered another Sunday morning, many years ago, when, as children, we spent a holiday there. My father was an angler and, thinking that with everyone in church it would be safe, he decided to go fishing. Sunday fishing was much frowned upon then. When church came out, my father hid from sight by lying in the bottom of the boat. How an empty boat came to be there, or how it managed to moor itself again, remained a mystery.

Plockton is an artists' paradise. Miriam Drysdale runs painting holidays from her home in an old manse overlooking the loch: "I managed to rent the Plockton Small Boat Sailing Clubhouse as studios, just beside the little jetty. It's great! Warm, big sink and good light and ideal for all painter-persons," she said. As well as artists, you may also meet cattle tramping the main street, for this is still a working crofting community.

A wondrous road winds along the shore of Loch Carron, passing a tiny, lighthouse-pricked island. The view north into the Applecross Forest is unforgettable: Beinn Bhan (896m) and the peaks of Sgurr a'Chaorachain (792m) and Meall Gorm (949m) enfolding the tortuous track over Bealach na Ba (626m), "The Pass of the Cattle". Within six miles from Tornapress at the mouth of the River Kishorn, the road rises to over 610 metres. The view from the top is magnificent: westwards to the Cuillin on Skye and, in the distance, a glimpse of the "Heather Isles" of the Outer Hebrides.

Back on the main road, descending into Torridon, I admired three of Scotland's best-loved mountains: Beinn Alligin (The Jeweled Hill), Liathach (The Grey One) and Beinn Eighe (The Big Red Peak). Beyond these is a Scottish gem, Poca Bhuidhe (the yellow stone), a bothy at the head of Loch na h-Oidhche (The Loch of the Night). Ann and I hiked the four miles out to the bothy a few years ago and spent happy days enjoying the "large religion of the hills".

Many West Highland mountains are composed of red Torridonian sandstone and are often surrounded, in their lower levels, by evidence of retreating ice flows, 10,000 years ago; small, rounded hillocks show where heavier rocks and other debris dropped through the ice sheet, forming distinctive features known as "hummocky moraines".

North from Gairloch (The Long Loch), I paid my respects to Osgood Mackenzie's famous Inverewe Garden where 2,500 different species of trees and plants cover fifty acres. It was raining but this did not stop visitors from enjoying themselves. Osgood was famous for his prowess with gun and fishing rod, described in his book *A Hundred Years of Sport in the Highlands*, and has the dubious reputation of shooting the last osprey in Wester Ross.

From Inverewe, before the tiny township of Laide, is a hill with a view. The panorama from the roadside at Cnoc nan Colunnan is stunning. To the south, the majesty of the peaks and ridges you have driven round is laid out in a panorama of sheer delight. The road ahead margins Little Loch Broom.

Beyond Dundonnell, stop and look back to An Teallach (1,062m), "The Forge". Tradition has it that the mountain is named thus because the sunset glow from An Teallach's red sandstone corries resembled embers in a blacksmith's forge.

This road, from Dundonnell to Braemore Junction, is known as "Destitution Road". It was built in the aftermath of the 1851 potato famine, when Highland people starved. But the authorities considered that giving the populace food would encourage them in idleness. Therefore, to alleviate hardship, whilst Lowland granaries bulged with corn, the local lairds, ministers and the powers that be decided that the people should work for their relief. The "Destitution Road" is their memorial.

Ullapool is bright and bustling. A dozen different languages may be heard as you walk the harbour front. Fishing boats bob by the pier and hotels and restaurants have an almost Mediterranean feel. Visitors linger over al fresco meals whilst the inevitable cat begs for scraps. The town is "new" in Highland terms, built by the British Fisheries Association in 1788 to exploit the herring fishing industry. Ullapool is still a busy fishing port today and one of the main ferry terminals for a magical journey over the broken waters of the Minch to the Western Isles.

It is also a jumping-off point for the Summer Isles, where I next stopped to examine a more modern construction, the temperature-controlled domain of the Hydroponicum at Achiltibuie. Hydroponics is the art of growing plants without soil. Water does the work of transporting all of the plant's nutrient requirements to the roots. Mark Irvine, former owner of the Summer Isles Hotel, set up the Hydroponicum to ensure a regular supply of fresh vegetables for his internationally renowned restaurant. I relaxed in semi-tropical warmth with a cup of coffee and a Highland banana.

A narrow road leads north round the coast from Achiltibuie into Assynt, "the broken lands". To the east, the mountains of the Inverpolly National Nature Reserve dominate the horizon: Stac Pollaidh (612m), Cul Mor (849m), Cul Beag (769m), and the dramatic thrust of Suilven (731m), the peak the Vikings called their pillar mountain, "Sul-val". Entering Assynt is like coming home for Ann and me. We have spent some of our happiest moments here, hill-walking, fishing, watching birds, discovering wildflowers, bickering over map references, being together.

We also bought a lot of books at Achins Bookshop, the most remote bookshop in Europe. Achins is just in Sutherland. The boundary between Ross-shire and Sutherland is the centre-line of the River Kirkaig and Achins is hidden amidst the trees above this rocky stream. When I called, in the absence of her mum and dad, young Kathleen Dickson was holding fort. It had been a busy day but she greeted me with a captivating Highland smile.

After driving through Assynt to Kylesku, I swept importantly across the graceful bridge over Loch a'Chairn Bhain and on to Scourie, the land of Clan Mackay. Ann and I first visited Scourie in, well, a lot of years ago. We stayed at the Scourie Hotel and spent our time trout fishing. Our principal objective was a tiny, unnamed lochan in the hills to the south of Ben Stack. It contained a wise old trout known as "Granddad", desired by every angler who knew the location of his home. Granddad eluded all our efforts and, indeed, everyone else's.

To the best of my knowledge, Granddad died of old age.

Beyond Scourie, by Tarbet, you will find "the restaurant at the edge of the world", specialising in fantastic seafood. Big it is not. It is an extension to the front of a traditional croft cottage, built by Julian Pearce when he was a youth of sixteen years. The restaurant is not licensed but what it does provide is miraculous cooking – prawns, crab and lobster that are often served within hours of being caught. Arm yourself with a bottle of Chablis before setting out.

Julian's wife, Jackie, who does the cooking, believes seafood should be served unadorned. Jackie's daughters, Rebecca and Lucy, do the work behind the scenes. I asked Jackie what her most memorable moment had been.

She pondered. "After a guest finished eating, he asked me to marry him."

"Julian?" I inquired.

"No, not Julian," Jackie said, "the guest. He had really enjoyed his meal!"

As I approached journey's end, driving over the watershed north of

Rhiconich in the shadow of Foinaven (914m), the underlying rock structure changed again. Here, a limestone outcrop surfaces and blesses the landscape with an amazing array of wildflowers. Across the sands of the Kyle of Durness, Grudie Cottage glistened. Also glistening, but for entirely different reasons, were the group of people I found waiting to cross to Cape Wrath. The ferryman was there but the bus driver was not. A few "Highland minutes" later, he arrived.

Close to the Cape Wrath Hotel, an imposing whitewashed building that guards the narrows of the Kyle and is now a private dwelling, I discovered one of Scotland's most important sheepdog trials. Jock Sutherland from Sangomore, who travels to trials throughout the UK, told me that some of Britain's top dog-handlers were taking part. His bright-eyed, tongue-lolling, happy sheepdogs, Maid and Nell, eager for action, nodded in agreement.

At the end of my journey, I said hello to another important person, John Lennon of The Beatles fame. As a youth, John often visited relatives at Durness and a memorial garden at the newly built village hall commemorates this connection. I looked out over Sango Bay. How long had it been since I set off? A curlew poked and probed along the margins of the tide and I remembered the sound of curlew at Eilean Donan. A haunting call, "as desolate, as beautiful as your loved places, mountainy marshes and glistening mud-flats by the stealthy sea."

25.
Highland Museum, Kingussie and Newtonmore

I looked at the ink-spattered paper on my desk and shuffled uncomfortably. It wasn't my fault. The steel nib of the wooden-shafted pen seemed to have a life of its own. Pupils behind me giggled at my discomfiture. The thumb and forefinger of my right hand were stained black. There was a spot of ink on my shirt. Mrs Brownlee loomed over me. "Please, Miss, I didn't mean to do it, honest," I pleaded.

"That's just not good enough, Bruce," she said. "You must try harder, otherwise you will have to pay the penalty." Mrs Brownlee glared crossly and flexed the thick leather strap she was holding.

Thankfully, it was all "pretend". I was not a child again, only an adult visitor to the splendid Newtonmore Highland Folk Museum (HFM) schoolroom a few miles south from Inverness. But it had been a close-run thing because the reality of the experience had brought childhood memories flooding back. The classroom was an exact replica of the one where I had struggled in vain so many years ago with pen and ink at same unforgiving wooden desk. With the familiar hollow for holding the pencils I never remembered to bring to school and the same intimidating white ceramic inkwell.

Anna Brownlee is in fact a wonderful communicator, humorous and kindly, and with the sort of personality that brightens the dullest of days. The classroom once housed destitute Glasgow children whose fathers had been killed during the First World War. Its original location was near Kirkhill, north of Inverness, where it was intended to be temporary. The school closed in 1987 and HFM acquired the property, dismantled it and reconstructed it at Newtonmore. The walls are covered with 1930s maps. There is a "nature table", blackboard, writing slates, games cupboard, children's paintings on the walls, coat-hanging pegs and, dominating all, the teacher's majestic desk.

The HFM Newtonmore site covers an area of eighty acres and is one and a half kilometres in length. Everything about this vibrant open-air museum inspires. The care, attention to detail and the meticulous planning and veracity of the exhibits demonstrates the highest standards of excellence. Clearly, this is a labour of love for those involved, from Ross Noble, the curator, and his staff, to each of his forty-strong, part-time team of helpers. Their most notable characteristics are unwavering courtesy and patience, fortified with a thorough knowledge of the exhibits they attend. From start to finish, everyone I met was welcoming.

The original museum, Am Fasgadh, "The Shelter", was established in 1944 in Kingussie and was the inspirational dream of a remarkable woman, Dr Isabel Frances Grant (1887–1983). Dr Grant visited Scandinavia during the 1920s and was impressed by the importance placed there upon folk museums – museums that captured the culture of the people and how they lived and worked and played. Dr Grant was determined to replicate that philosophy in the Highlands of Scotland, initially by opening a museum on Iona in 1936 and then, when the collection outgrew the space available, by moving to Kingussie.

In a time when government subsidies and grants for small museums were unheard of, Dr Grant used her own money to further the development of her invention. When she retired in 1954, she arranged for the museum to be taken into the care of a trust controlled by Scotland's primary universities: St Andrews, Edinburgh, Glasgow and Aberdeen. But as the museum continued to expand, they too found it hard to appropriately finance Am Fasgadh. Consequently, in 1975 and largely due to the support of Councillor Sandy Russell of Newtonmore, the leisure and recreation committee of the Highland Regional Council agreed to take over responsibility for the museum.

There are tens of thousands of items and artefacts in the collection and, due to limitations of space, only a small part of them can de displayed at any one time. What is on show, however, is utterly absorbing. I spent one day at the Kingussie site and the following day at Newtonmore. In order to do so, I had to stay overnight in Kingussie and chose the Columba House Hotel as my base. This was a happy choice, not only because it is one of the most comfortable and friendly places in which I have ever stayed, but also because I heard about the mystery of "the lost priory".

Myra Shearer had owned the hotel for sixteen years and as we chatted over pre-dinner drinks, she explained: "I was working in the garden one afternoon when, suddenly, the earth simply fell away to expose a flight of stairs. I followed them down and found myself in an underground room measuring approximately ten feet by eight feet. There were bits of dishes and plates lying about, but what really fascinated me was a stone lintel, at floor level, which suggested that there might be more rooms at a lower level." Could Myra have stumbled on the thirteenth-century priory that tradition says was located in the vicinity?

I walked from the hotel to the HFM Kingussie site and fell in with a bearded crofter crouching over a peat fire on the floor of a Black House. Men from the Island of Lewis in the Outer Hebrides had erected the building. I stooped low to enter: "Is it all right to come in?" I called. A kettle was suspended over glowing embers.

"Good morning! Yes, in you come to the fire." Peter Bruce, an HFM part-timer and dressed for the role he played, explained how the Black House was built, why it took the shape and form it did, and how it was used. Peter, a retired art teacher from Shetland, was captivating.

Pitman Lodge, a Georgian town house, hosts the HFM reception area, where young Eilidh Macpherson greeted me with a mile-high smile. Eilidh's mother, Gail, helps out here with demonstrations of spinning and weaving. Her grandmother, Iris Robertson, a splendidly happy woman, also works with the HFM. I could have spent a week at Pitman Lodge. It contains a treasure trove of magnificent objects: snuff boxes, delicate china, musical instruments, kitchen utensils, portable baths with their own internal water-heating systems, costumes, quaichs, wooden plates and bowls. There is a farming museum, complete with stables, harness pack saddles, ploughs, harrows and threshing machines, and a dairy with butter churns and cheese presses.

Adjacent to Pitman Lodge is the MacRobert House with its textile crafts room, where you can find out about wool spinning – from using a simple spindle, then the "muckle wheel", turned by hand, to the seventeenth-century treadle spinning wheel. But for me, the MacRobert House Furniture Gallery was most spectacular. There is something unique about the strong smell of well-polished wood and the collection on display here is illustrious. There is an amazing two-tier box-bed, built in 1702, part of a double unit that probably had two lower and two upper beds providing sleeping quarters for a whole family. I tiptoed past. Who might still be asleep there?

Down at the Newtonmore HFM site, I caught a courtesy bus to visit Baile Gean. Geoff Pittard, the driver, proudly showed off his vehicle, a masterpiece sit-up-and-beg replica of 1930s public transport. The green leather-clad seats were supremely comfortable. Baile Gean means "The Township of Goodwill" and arriving there is like stepping back into another age. It is a recreation of an early-eighteenth-century Highland community, complete with houses, barns, corn kiln and shieling huts, based upon current archaeological research. The township is surrounded by mature trees, loud with birdcall and enchanting glimpses of native red squirrels amidst the old branches.

I expected at any moment to see residents going about their daily tasks. And I did. HFM helpers, in period costumes, invited me into their lives. Wendy Smith was busy woodturning but stopped to introduce me to her friend, Gerry Smith. We wandered down to the duck pond to inspect a newly arrived red-brown pig. Clutching a bundle of thatch, Gerry chatted with Wendy whilst she fed the ducks. Before I left, I peeked into Wendy's "home". She was sitting before a cooking pot. A beam of light slanted down from the roof to give her an almost ethereal presence, a "solitary Highland lass".

The animals at Netwonmore are in the care of Eric Stewart, previously a farmer from the Glens of Angus, now working for HFM. He has a fine flock of Blackface sheep that were busy cropping grass fields bounded by drystone built walls. The walls themselves are fascinating, demonstrating different dyking techniques from various areas of the Highlands. Bob Powell, HFM Assistant Curator, agricultural historian and registered farmer, introduced me to the latest arrival: Jubilee, a Clydesdale foal snuggled up to his mother, Rosie, and born on 4 June, the date of HM The Queen's Jubilee.

At the farm steading, I caught up with another HFM character, Billy Kirk, whose father had farmed the Newtonmore site before it was acquired by the museum. Billy took me to a small corrugated-iron clad house. He explained: "When visitors came here during the summer months, the family would rent their big house to them, to make some money, and move in here." The little house was simply but comfortably furnished in the 1930s style. Billy lit the fire and put the kettle on for tea.

As I nursed my cup and the dreams my visit had evoked, I thought of these long-gone Highland people – the clamour of the school bell, calling children to their studies; the warm smell of animals lying together in a hay-filled byre; the busy clatter of a butter churn; spluttering fir candles lighting an evening entertainment. I remembered, also, words written by the founder of the HFM, Isabel Grant: "I hope and dare to believe that in this little museum there does exist some sense of the spirit of the people of the Highlands, the race from which I am so proud to have sprung."

The Highland Folk Museum has two complementary venues, Kingussie and Newtonmore, two and a half miles apart. They are located on the A86 and are easily found by following signposts off the A9. There is free parking at both sites. Allow at least two hours for a visit to the Kingussie site and four hours to visit Newtonmore.

For further information, contact: Highland Folk Museum, Kingussie Road, Newtonmore, Scotland PH20 1AY; Tel: 01540 673551; Fax: 01540 673693; Website: www.highlandfolk.com

26.
Nothing to Do and Not Enough Time to Do It

An acquaintance in London once asked me where I lived. "Tongue," I said, "in North Sutherland."

He seemed puzzled. "All year round?" he asked.

I glanced from his skyscraper office window, twenty levels up. The street below was nose-to-tail packed with cars. The pavements were crowded. "Yup," I replied happily, "all year round."

Our cottage overlooks Castle Varrich, a sixteenth-century Clan Mackay fortress guarding the shallow waters of the Kyle of Tongue. Our previous home was near Loch Watten in Caithness. Across the loch, Caithness mountains Scaraben, Smean and graceful Morven lined our horizon.

Our children thrived in the freedom and security of the far north. They explored with us the wilderness of the peat lands of the Flow Country; learned from us the friendly names of its flora and fauna; enjoyed with us the sharp bite of winter storms and the precious calm of long summer evenings.

There was always so much to do. I was the Secretary of the Wick Arts Club for a number of years when we welcomed performers of international repute to play for us – pianists, string quartets, ballet and opera, et al. Caithness also hosts a major summer arts festival, Northlands, celebrating the finest in Highland and Celtic culture.

The longest day, 21 June, is busy with midnight bowls tournaments, trout fishing outings, golf matches and midsummer parties. Visitors from all over the world brighten these gatherings, mingling and making friends with local people. Scotland's two most northerly counties provided for our every need, spiritual and physical. They will do the same for you.

Here are some of my favorite Caithness and Sutherland expeditions. The list is not exhaustive and is, of necessity, limited. But I hope that it will encourage you to join us. Come and explore the solitude of our ragged cliffs and silent beaches. Climb our mountains. Listen to the echo of time amidst sentinel tumbled stones that were alive with the sound of laughter 5,000 years ago.

SLETELL VILLAGE AND SKERRAY TOWNSHIP, SUTHERLAND (Open all year)

The deserted village of Sletell graces green pastures looking across the sea to Island Roan. North Country sheep and handsome cattle graze contentedly. The sense of peace is a tangible presence. When Ann and I last walked there, we lunched in the lee of one of the ruined cottages. By the shores of a cliff-top lochan, an otter played with her cubs.

Begin your adventure at the croft museum in Skerray. A summer exhibition features the life and times of Sletell and you will be given directions to the start of the Sletell track; an easy walk, there and back in three hours including plenty of time to explore the village and enjoy its wonderful setting.

Also explore the Millennium Memorial Forest at Borgie, ten minutes drive from Skerray Post Office. Native trees were planted here in a Celtic circle, their names following the order of the old Gaelic tree alphabet. A path leads to the centre where stones from houses burned during the eighteenth-century Sutherland Clearances are shaped in the form a magical leaf.

WORLD KNOTTY CHAMPIONSHIPS, LYBSTER, CAITHNESS (August)

During the Caithness herring fishings of the nineteenth century, Lybster was an important centre of the industry and Lybster fishermen, to entertain themselves when not fishing for herring, invented "Knotty". Bert Mowat, a proprietor of the Portland Arms Hotel in Lybster, a few miles south from

Wick, is said to have discovered the rules for the game in an old Gaelic Bible.

The game is a cross between shinty and hockey, played using a cork float from a herring net as a ball. Wooden staves from herring barrels were used to hit the ball. Hazel twigs stuck in the ground formed goal posts. When a goal was scored, to keep the score, a knot was tied in a length of fishing line.

Marshall Bowman, a local schoolteacher who acts as referee, explained: "There are seven-a-side teams. Last year, fifteen teams competed, including 'Gunn's Guzzlers', 'Gunettes' and 'Rita's Boys', named after local businesses. Men compete for a cup, ladies' teams compete for a Shield."

George Carter, another Knotty aficionado, told me it was a vigorous day out and that the game was played with a lot of spirit, some of it taken from straw-coloured bottles. "Bruised shins, lumps and knocks are taken as well," he added, "but everyone enjoys themselves."

CAITHNESS COUNTY SHOW AND WICK GALA WEEK
(July and August)

One of my Caithness farmer friends was to be presented to Princess Anne, the Princess Royal, at the County Show. He told me he was not the slightest bit awed by the prospect. In the event, he confessed, when Princess Anne asked him a simple question about farming, he was overwhelmed and speechless. You will be also, by the beauty and quality of the stock on display at the show.

A week after the County Show, the Royal Burgh of Wick bursts into bloom during Gala Week. Every day is interest-packed: decorated floats tour the town; the Gala Queen is crowned; there are children's talent competitions, horse racing and cycle races; Scottish concerts and pipe bands get toes tapping; and there are tennis competitions, vintage car exhibitions, football matches and old-time dancing.

The highlight of the week is the final evening when there is a huge bonfire and firework display on the banks of the Wick River. We always took our family along. I rarely saw much of the fireworks. My younger daughter,

Jean, insisted on being perched upon my shoulders to get a better view. In her excitement, she invariably clasped her hands tightly over my eyes. Fireworks? What fireworks?

DURNESS, SUTHERLAND

Durness, in North West Sutherland, is an essential venue for a family day out. It offers something for everyone. I know, because Clan Sandison has been enjoying the delights of this happy Highland community for more years than I care to remember.

I love game fishing. Durness has four of the most exciting trout lochs in Europe: Caladail, Borralie, Croispol and Lanlish. There is a wonderful little 9-hole golf course, ideal for the pleasure of those so afflicted. My wife, Ann, studies wild flowers. The lime rich soil here hosts an amazing array of plants, including several species of orchid, mountain everlasting and mountain aven.

Balnakeil Beach is an irresistible attraction for children, a wide sweep of golden sand backed by tall dunes. The shallow waters are safe for splashing, whilst older children can surfboard and fall off sailboards to their hearts' content. There are walks from the beach out to Faraid Head, a round trip of six miles, where the cliffs abound with seabirds including, during spring months, firework-beaked puffins.

The great caves at Smoo to the east of Durness also demand inspection. The Scottish novelist Sir Walter Scott, the wizard of the north, is just one of many famous visitors to these spectacular limestone caves. The principal cave is 61m in length, 15m in height, and close by, another cave contains a 24m high waterfall that is a thunderous roar after heavy rain.

For rest and recuperation, call at Balnakeil Craft Village, where crafts-persons and artists work and display the results of their talents. Best of all, stop at my favorite bookshop, the Loch Croispol Bookshop, the most northerly bookshop on mainland Scotland. They offer first-class food, a wide range of teas and real coffee, all served with grace and charm. There is a children's section complete with toys to keep curious minds active. Browse the shelves and plan your next adventure.

WICK HARBOUR EVENING, CAITHNESS (July)

The Royal National Lifeboat Institution is entirely supported by voluntary contributions from the public and has been saving lives at sea for 178 years. The Wick Harbour Evening is a fund-raising event organized by the RNLI and it has become a "must" for visitors and locals alike.

Sales stalls are set out, there is music and line dancing, and activities to keep everyone happy and busy. The airport and Highland Council fire engines and an ambulance are available for supervised inspection by children of all ages, but the highlight of the event is a harbour raft race.

Teams, including the police force, fire brigade and the RNLI, compete in this less than serious maritime escapade. The result is always unpredictable and always incident-packed. In 2003, much to the hilarity of the assembled crowd, the RNLI raft sank having covered no more than six metres of the course, requiring the crew to be ignominiously "rescued" by their colleagues.

SANDWOOD BAY, SUTHERLAND

Ann and I sat on black basalt rocks that centre Sandwood Bay in North West Sutherland. A figure splashing in the surf caught our eye. Could this be the famous Sandwood mermaid? I grabbed my camera. In the eighteenth century, a local shepherd, Sandy Gunn, reported seeing a mermaid at Sandwood sitting on a rock gazing wistfully out to sea. Three learned lawyers from Edinburgh, and lawyers don't come much more "learned" than those from Auld Reekie, could not fault his story.

As we watched, a grey seal, rather than a mermaid, emerged from the waves and laboriously hauled itself onto the deserted yellow sands. Not as spectacular as a mermaid, perhaps, but just as magical and enthralling. We relaxed, refilled our coffee cups and watched the graceful creature as we finished our picnic lunch.

Sandwood is one of the loveliest bays in the world, home for 3,000-mile-old azure and white Atlantic waves. Dark cliffs march northwards to Cape Wrath, the Vikings' "turning point" on their annual journey from Denmark to visit their Scottish domains. The gaunt stack of Am Buachaille, "The Herdsman", guards the southern entrance to the bay. Sandwood Loch sparkles in summer sunlight behind steep dunes.

The track to Sandwood Bay starts a few miles to the west of Oldshoremore where there is room to park your car. There and back is a comfortable eight miles along a good track. Nevertheless, wear stout walking boots and carry Ordnance Survey Sheet 9, Cape Wrath, Second Series, Scale 1:50,000. Just how long your journey takes depends entirely on how long you choose to stand or sit and stare. But be warned. It is so captivating that you could be there forever.

HIGHLAND GAMES (July onwards)

Charlie Simpson from Wick was one of the leading "heavies" in the north Highland Games circuit. He is still a formidable presence. Less well-known is his remarkable memory, particularly when it comes to reciting the poetry of Robert Burns. Charlie is always in demand for Burns Supper engagements. I asked him to give me the dates for the Caithness and Sutherland games and he reeled them off faster than I could write them down.

During the summer season, no matter where you are, you will generally find a Highland Games event "just around the corner": the Assynt Games at Lochinver, Halkirk Games, and the principal Caithness event at John O'Groats; games at Dunrobin Castle, Dornoch, Durness, Dunbeath and Helmsdale. Watching the games is almost as exhausting as taking part. The sheer energy and enthusiasm engendered is a living, vibrant presence. Whichever venue you choose, believe me, you and all your "clan" will have a memorable day out.

Now, you will have to excuse me, things to do. Meg Telfer, a local artist, has a pottery class starting at Skerray this evening. And I have to sort out my fishing tackle for a sea-trout fishing expedition on Loch Hope. Then there is a sailing regatta on Loch Shin at Lairg. Iain Sutherland from the Wick Heritage Society is screening, for one night only, archive films from days of the Caithness herring fishings. Will I be able to fit in the céilidh on Saturday night? Perhaps I should ask my London acquaintance for advice?

27.
Highland Railway

James Hamish Mackay stood on the railway platform at Kinbrace in Sutherland. It was winter 1955, one of the fiercest anyone could remember. Huge snowdrifts blocked the line north. As he watched, five hissing steam engines were linked together, ready to "charge" the drifts in an attempt to clear the blockage.

Hamish was ten years old and he should have been in school, but the sound and smell of impending battle transfixed him. The engines reversed slowly south, out of sight. A few minutes later they reappeared, gathering speed, red coal fragments spitting from their funnels, sparks flying from their wheels.

The noise was tremendous. The ground shook. As the convoy raced through the tiny hamlet, house windows shattered. But the line was cleared. From that moment, Hamish knew exactly what he wanted to be when he left school. When he did, he worked on north railway lines for twenty years, reaching the rank of Inspector.

Hamish now runs the famous Craggan Hotel in Melness, overlooking the Kyle of Tongue in North Sutherland. But he has never forgotten these days, which were amongst the happiest of his life. When I talked to him recently, I asked how he got his first job. "I was told to stand on Kinbrace Station and wait for the Inverness train. The chief would meet me there and interview me.

"The train just went straight through. I didn't know what to do, so I went to the office to ask what had happened. The telephone was ringing when I went in and the call was for me. 'Hamish, this is the chief. You are big enough, you'll do!' The chief had been on the footplate of the engine and had seen me standing on the platform and was phoning from Forsinard, the next station up the line."

If you love railways and viewing wide-open spaces in relative comfort, buy a ticket for one of the last and least-known great railway journeys of the world, from Inverness to Wick/Thurso in Caithness. Along the way, surrounded by outstanding scenery, you will be presented with a succession of memorable cameos of Scottish history.

Wick and Thurso are the most northerly railway stations on mainland Britain, eighty miles north from Inverness as the crow flies. By car the journey takes two hours, by bus just under three. But by train the travelling time is four hours.

The railway covers a distance of 160 miles; wandering round indented sea-blue firths, following fertile straths and peat-stained rivers, stopping at small Highland towns and villages en route before striking north east across the magnificent wilderness of the Flow Country.

When winter storms batter our northern senses and blizzards block the steep cliff-top road, the railway line is often the only way either into or out of Caithness. Although passengers may shiver a bit during winter journeys, at least they know that they will get there, eventually.

Work on the line began in Inverness on 19 September 1860 when Lady Matheson, wife of Sir Alexander Matheson, the principal promoter of the project, cut the first turf. By June 1862, the sweating gangs of navvies had taken the track to Dingwall, the old Viking settlement of Thing Vall, their place of justice.

Work progressed more or less smoothly, apart from a serious delay caused by a recalcitrant laird, Mackenzie of Findon, who insisted upon a bridge rather than a level crossing at one point, to protect his tenants from the danger of rampaging locomotives.

In 1868, the line reached Golspie, where the company ran out of money. Golspie was the home of the Duke of Sutherland, one of the richest men in Europe and the largest shareholder in the enterprise.

The Duke financed the section of line between Golspie and Helmsdale, where he proposed to link it to the line being driven south by the Sutherland & Caithness Railway Company, in which he was also largest shareholder. The route, from a new exchange platform in Caithness at Georgemas Junction, was opened on 28 July 1874.

In September 1872, Queen Victoria travelled from Inverness to visit the Duke at Dunrobin Castle. In an extract from her diary, she recounts:

As our train proceeded, the scenery was lovely. Near the ruins of the old priory of Beauly, the river of the same name flows into the Beauly Firth and the firth looks like an enormous lake with hills rising above it, which were reflected on the perfectly still water.

At twenty minutes to four we reached Dingwall where there were Volunteers, as indeed there were everywhere, and where another address was presented and also flowers. Sir J. Matheson, Lord Lieutenant of the county, was named to me, also the Vice-Lieutenant, and some young ladies gave Beatrice nosegays.

After this and passing slowly through Tain and St Duthus (called after the Cathedral there), we thought that we would take our tea and coffee – which kept quite hot in the Norwegian kitchen – when suddenly, before we had finished, we stopped at Bonar Bridge and the Duke of Sutherland came up to the door.

He had been driving the engine (!) all the way from Inverness but only appeared now on account of this being the boundary of his territory, and the commencement of the Sutherland railroad. He expressed the honour it was to him that I was coming to Dunrobin.

The duchess took me to my rooms [in Dunrobin Castle], which had been purposely arranged and handsomely furnished by the dear late Duke and Duchess for us both . . . I went to see Beatrice's room, which is close by, down three steps in the same passage. Fraulein Bauer, and Morgan, her dresser, are near her. Brown lives just opposite in the room intended for Albert's valet . . . Dined at half-past eight alone in my sitting-room with Beatrice and Leopold, Brown waiting [her friend and gillie].

Today, board the train in Inverness. As you rumble north over Thomas Telford's Caledonian Canal, the next bridge crosses the River Beauly. Beaufort Castle, erstwhile home of Clan Fraser, is on your left. Beaufort was built on the ruins of Castle Downie, burned down in 1746 after the Battle of Culloden when the King's son, "Butcher Cumberland", ordered his soldiers to ravage the Highlands in reprisal for their support of Bonnie Prince Charlie's rebellion.

First stop is Muir of Ord, "The Moor of the Hammer", an old Highland cattle trading centre, where there used to be a branch line heading eastwards into the Black Isle and Fortrose. Ben Wyvis, a Munro (Scottish mountains over 914.4m in height), towers ahead, a graceful, rounded slope guarding the market town of Dingwall. Dingwall was the junction for Strathpeffer, a "spa" town in the nineteenth century famous for the healing quality of its water and still a popular holiday centre today.

North from Dingwall on Fyrish Hill is a monument erected by General Sir Hector Munro of Novar (1727–1805). Sir Hector distinguished himself at the Battle of Negapatam in India in 1781. When he returned home, to provide work for his impoverished tenants, he ordered a replica of the Gates of Negatapam to be built on the hill. The Gates are as much a memorial to the hardiness of the men who raised the massive stones as they are to Sir Hector.

The train ambles through Alness to Invergordon, the site of the last mutiny in the British Navy in 1931, now a centre for the repair of North Sea oil-drilling platforms and the Beatrice Oil Field Terminal. The line then passes Balnagown Castle, once the home of the powerful Ross family, now home to the controversial Al Fayed family who owned the London department store, Harrods.

Across the Dornoch Firth lies Skibo Castle, the Scottish home of Andrew Carnegie (1835–1918), the Dunfermline-born multimillionaire who built up the largest iron and steel business in America. Carnegie gifted more than £70 million to charitable works, including the building of libraries throughout the USA and in Scotland. Skibo is now the home of another multimillionaire, Peter de Savary, who runs it as an exclusive "retreat" for the world's rich and famous.

The track turns west at Tain to reach the Kyle of Sutherland and Strathcarron. This circuitous route was greatly influenced by the Duke of Sutherland. Since much of the line was to run through his land and because he was footing a large part of the bill, the route was designed to serve a two-fold purpose: communication with his sheep farms and ease of access to his sporting estates.

The Duke also insisted on a private station close to the gates of his Scottish residence, magnificent Dunrobin Castle. The Duke was determined to "improve" his estates. His tenants had to be taught the virtue of the Victorian work ethos, even if to do so meant evicting 16,000 of them from their farms and replacing them with sheep – the infamous Sutherland Clearances.

From Golspie through Brora to Helmsdale, the railway hugs the rugged Moray Firth coastline. It then turns north west up the Strath of Kildonan by the banks of the Helmsdale River, one of the most exclusive salmon streams in Scotland, much enjoyed by HRH Prince Charles and, in her earlier years, by his grandmother, HM The Queen Mother.

In the same year that the railway reached Golspie, Robert Gilchrist found gold in Helmsdale streams. Gilchrist had returned from the Australian gold fields and was convinced there was gold in his homeland hills. Thousands of people flocked north to seek their fortune.

Few found it, apart from the Duke. He owned the river and land and rented out forty-square-feet plots at a fee of £1 per month to prospectors. In the end, he made more money than most of the diggers. But when the presence of so many people began to affect his salmon fishing and deer stalking in 1870, the Duke closed the operation.

Midway up the strath, at Forsinard, the north line turns towards Caithness. There it crosses the Flow Country, one of the last great wilderness areas of Britain. This is a land of wide-open moors largely untouched by the hand of man for 7,000 years – until 1979. During a devastating decade,

200,000 acres of virgin moorland were planted with foreign conifers, simply so that those who did so could benefit financially from a tax loophole.

After what became known as "The Battle of the Flows", when conservationists fought the tax-dodgers, the madness ended. The Royal Society for the Protection of Birds (RSPB) purchased 30,000 acres of Flow Country and is working hard to undo the damage. The station building at Forsinard is their operational base, where there is an exhibition centre and RSPB staff lead guided walks into this magical land.

As the train leaves the Flow Country and enters Caithness, passengers stretch and sigh, collecting luggage and calming overexcited offspring. At Georgemas Junction, the train divides, one carriage going to Thurso, the other heading east by Loch Watten to Wick; the end of a long journey and, like my friend James Hamish Mackay, one that you will never forget.

28.
Unst Revisited

It was a good-to-be-alive morning. The Shetland sun shone on a sparkling bay as snow-white gulls wheeled and cried plaintively overhead. The sea was clear and calm, shaded silver, green and blue. Foam-tipped wavelets gently caressed the black rocks guarding the ruins of St Olaf's Church, built in the twelfth century on the foundations of an even earlier place of worship. St Olaf's sits on the cliff edge by the shore of Lunda Wick on the Island of Unst. Ann and I parked our car by the gaunt remains of Lund Hall and walked across the golden moor to have a few words with my ancestors.

Sandison has always been a pre-eminent name in the island and it is my belief that my people came from Unst, initially to Caithness, where my grandfather was born, and thence to Edinburgh where I was born. As ever in these northern climes, the force that drove many to move was the search for work. However, on the ferry over Bluemull Sound from Yell to Unst, the ticket-collector noted my name and remarked, "Well, be careful who you tell, that's all I'm saying." Clan Sandison must have gained a serious reputation, the cause of which remains unbeknown to me, but Sandisons still run one of Unst's longest-established businesses: Alexander Sandison & Sons, trading in Baltasound as Skibhoul Stores (tel: 01957 711304) and selling, well, just about everything.

Whatever, that morning, my ancestors were quiet enough in the space reserved for them in the graveyard at Lund. It is surrounded by a fence and presided over by a red marble memorial to Second Lieutenant Alexander Mundell Sandison, who died of wounds he received during the First World War. Other Sandisons keep him company and it was strange, standing there in the sunlight, contemplating my ultimate destination. Other tombstones reflect the important trading links Unst maintained with Northern Europe: the graves of two merchants from Bremen in Germany, Segedad Detken, who died in 1573, and Henrick Segelcken, who died in 1585. Another grave marks the last resting place of Thomas Mouat (1748–1819), the builder of Belmont House, near to where the ferry arrives and whom we will meet again later in our journey.

About thirty years ago, considerable anger was aroused when the UK government floated the idea of adjusting British Summer Time to bring it into line with European clocks, to make it easier for British companies to communicate by telephone with their counterparts on the continent. The prospect of everyone suffering considerable inconvenience for the benefit of a few created a storm of protest and the proposal was quietly abandoned. Recently, it has re-surfaced in a more user-friendly guise: the government, in their infinite wisdom, want to give us all a "present" of two extra hours of daylight. It is still nonsense, particularly in Unst, where it never really gets dark at all during summer months. For Unst, any alteration would mean almost perpetual daylight during summer and perpetual darkness in winter, and who wants that? Messrs Detken and Segelcken from Bremen seemed to communicate well enough in the sixteenth century without any disruption.

I am an angler and I discovered this truth in June 2009 when Davie McMillan, the president of the Unst Angling Club, asked me to join him and his members and guests at their annual "simmer dim" festival – the longest day, when anglers fish all through the night. It took me about a microsecond to say "yes" because, to me, returning to Unst is like coming home. The club was originally formed back in the 1960s and has always had a thriving membership. Indeed, as far back as 1733, when Thomas Gifford, the Laird of Busta on Mainland Shetland, visited Unst, he found that "the inhabitants are for the most part fishers. They have oxen, cows, some sheep, and plenty of little horses". Today, apart from the oxen, little has changed and fishing is an integral part of most people's activities. We started fishing at around 8pm and finished the following morning at 7am. It was quite wonderful, full of the sound of curlew, whimbrel and oyster-catcher and the happy splash of rising trout. Breakfast with a warming dram was also welcoming.

Unst is the most northern island in the Shetland archipelago and covers an area of some twenty by eight kilometres (117 square kilometres). It lies like a multi-coloured garnet stone, red, orange, violet, green and yellow, encompassed by endless ultramarine waves. Unst is hardly densely populated, being home to fewer than 700 souls, but it has some of the most beautiful and dramatic scenery on Planet Earth: wonderful white sand, near deserted beaches, wild moorlands carpeted with wild flowers, dramatic, seabird-clad cliffs that rise to a height of nearly 210m and the constant music of the sea. There is evidence of human habitation since Neolithic times 5,000 years ago and Unst has a tangled human history embracing many different peoples, from the Iron Age man, Picts and Vikings to the present day.

There are many reasons for spending time in Unst, not the least of which is the fact that it has two of Scotland's most significant National Nature Reserves in the north of the island: Keen of Hamar, near Baltasound on the east coast, and Hermaness, near Burrafirth on the west coast. Both reserves are carefully managed by Scottish Natural Heritage (SNH), the government-appointed body charged with the duty of preserving and protecting Scotland's precious natural environment. SNH describe Keen of Hamar as a lunar landscape, which at first sight seems to be bleak and lifeless, and yet it is home to some of the UK's rarest species of wildflower, including Edmondston's chickweed, slender St John's wort, kidney vetch, hoary whitlow grass and, one of my favourites, mountain everlasting.

The Hermaness reserve is an altogether wilder affair and properly exploring all that it has to offer will involve a vigorous walk; nothing too serious but you will need to be well-shod and clothed, and carry a compass and map and know how to use them. If you walk this way during the breeding season for bonxies, the Shetland name for the great skua, then it is advisable to take along a walking stick to fend off these large, aggressive birds as they crossly defend their nesting sites. But they are magnificent, as are the many thousands of other seabirds to be seen along the way: gannet, guillemot, black guillemot, Arctic skua, razorbill, kittiwake, fulmar, cormorant and puffin.

Start off from the car park at the end of the track that extends north from the B9086 road near Stackhoull, overlooking the battleground of Burra Firth – well, that is the old tale; the firth is enclosed by headlands: to the west, Hermaness (200m), and to the east, Saxa Vord (285m). Tradition has it that two giants lived there, Herman and Saxa, both of whom fell in love with a mermaid named Utsta. The rivals became so jealous of each other that they started chucking huge boulders across the firth, creating such a din that a local witch intervened. She buried Saxa beneath a cover of green grass and turned Herman into a cloud of mist.

Ann and I bumped into Herman during our first visit to the reserve; one moment it was bright and clear, and the next he had enveloped us in his clammy white cloak. With 150-metre cliffs only a step to the left, knifed by isolated stacks and ravine-like geos, we decided it was time for a pause, coffee and some serious compass and map work. Better safe than sorry. When the mist lifted, almost as quickly as it had descended, we found ourselves dangerously close to the cliff edge and sharing the sandy top with a gathering of firework-beaked tammie nories, the Shetland name for puffins.

That day, we also hoped to catch a glimpse of one of the most famous residents of Hermaness, Albert Ross, a black-browed albatross (*Thalassarche melanophrys*) that had strayed from its principal stronghold in the Falkland Islands and for many years visited Hermaness in search of a mate. Albert was first sighted in Scotland in 1967 in the Firth of Forth and for a few years returned regularly to, fruitlessly, court gannets on the Bass Rock. Unrequited in love, Albert then flew north and settled at Hermaness, but we found no sign of Albert. Unrequited again, he must have decided to hunt for love in pastures new.

We did, however, find the spectacular Muckle Flugga Lighthouse on its rocky pinnacle off the north coast of Hermaness between mainland Unst and Out Stack, the most northerly speck of UK territory. Muckle Flugga was begun in 1854 and completed in 1858, at a cost of £32,378 15s 5d (in old, pre-decimal currency). The lighthouse was built by Scottish lighthouse-builders extraordinaire Thomas and David Stevenson, father and uncle of another

Scottish hero of mine, the author Robert Louis Stevenson (RLS). It is claimed that RLS based the island in his book *Treasure Island* on the shape of Unst, a claim made for other islands, but I am sure that Unst has that honour given the remarkable similarity of Unst to the map that appears in the novel.

A sadder story is recounted about Out Stack. Lady Jane Franklin, wife of the Arctic explorer Sir John – who perished in 1845 during a search for the fabled North West Passage – came to Unst seeking help. The incident is recounted in P.N. Guy's excellent book *The Island of Unst* and is based upon information provided by Jessie Saxby: "When Lady Franklin was wandering over Britain in eager quest for men to search for Sir John and his companions, she came to Unst and asked to be taken to the most northerly spot where she could look over the sea and – as she said – "send love on wings of prayer" to the ill-fated adventurer. The weather chanced to be exceptionally fine and my father, with a picked crew, took Lady Franklin to set foot on Ootsta [Out Stack]. Those who were there said she stood for some minutes on the somber rock, quite silent, tears falling slowly, and her hands stretched out towards the north."

Whilst much of the glory of Unst is undoubtedly founded on its landscape and history, the island is also famous for the welcome it gives to visitors amongst the many events, activities and community projects that are organised throughout the year. Indeed, it is probably fair to say that on every day of every month on the island "something" is happening "somewhere". A good start-point is the Uyeasound Up Helly Aa, held in the first week of February. The event celebrates Shetland's links with its Viking ancestors, for until 1468, Shetland was a province of Norway; in that year, King Christian I of Norway pledged the islands to King James III of Scotland as part of the dowry when James married Christian's daughter, Margaret. The money was never paid and, thus, in 1471, Shetland became part of Scotland.

Similar to the festival held in Lerwick, discussed in Chapter 13, throughout the year, a replica of a Viking galley is built and carefully fitted out. It is in itself a work of art but destined to be destroyed by fire during the Uyeasound Up Helly Aa. Teams of local men, Guizers, one hundred-strong, and their leader, the Guizer Jarl, carrying burning torches, march in procession through the town and set the galley ablaze. Be warned, however, that the parties that follow can last for several days. During the months preceding the ceremony, visitors to Unst may visit the shed were the galley is being built and hear about the traditions of the Up Helly Aa, and see the wondrously decorated galley name plates from past occasions.

Further north, in July, is the Baltasound Regatta, the most northerly such regatta in the UK. There are races throughout the day, hotly disputed by crews from other Shetland isles, Yell and Whalsay. Landlubbers are also well-catered for, with activities for children, games and a beer tent for those so disposed, which features the famous Valhalla brew, made at, yes, you've guessed it, the most northerly brewery in UK. The day ends with an evening of entertainment provided by local musicians, fiddlers, accordion players and singers. Nearby, at Saxa Vord, a former Royal Air Force station, visitors can also enjoy superb food at the Saxa Vord Restaurant, based essentially on local produce. The restaurant was a finalist in the 2010 Highlands and Islands "Dining Out Experience" Tourist Awards. And for something simple, but none-the-less excellent, don't miss out on the Chip Suppers which are regularly held in Baltasound Village Hall.

If you have an interest in boats, then head for the Unst Boat Haven, part of the Unst Heritage Trust and dedicated to the maritime history of Shetland boats – all traditionally built for use under sail or oar, double ended and clinker built using a construction method that dates back for more than 1,700 years. They are supremely beautiful. The Haven has seventeen boats, including a nineteenth-century sixareen, rowed by a crew of six, with a square sail for use when the weather was suitable. These boats, which could be nine metres in length, were used for off-shore fishing to a distance of forty miles. The love between a Shetland man and his boat is indivisible. I remember talking to a friend of mine about this "affair". He told me, "Bruce, in Shetland you may do as you please with another man's girlfriend or wife, but you must never, ever, touch his boat."

We now return to Belmont House, near the ferry terminal and built by

Thomas Mouat, son of the Lairg of Garth, whom, you will recall, lies asleep along with my Sandison ancestors in the little graveyard overlooking the sea at Lunda Wick. Before deciding on what Belmont would look like, Thomas visited a number of notable houses near Edinburgh and eventually decided on a Georgian-style dwelling, and in doing so, created an almost perfect example of this design. His family lived there until well into the twentieth century, when the house became derelict. Historic Scotland describes Belmont thus: "As well as being the most ambitious house in the north isles, Belmont is Shetland's least altered classical mansion, its interior being a particularly remarkable survival."

The old house was rescued by the vision and hard work of the Belmont Trust, an independent body with five trustees who purchased the property in 1996 from Edinburgh architect John Hope for just £5. Since then, the trust, with their contractors, The Shetland Amenity Trust, has spent upwards of £1.2 million restoring Belmont to its former glory. The restoration was carried out by unpaid volunteers and specialist contractors were employed when required. I spoke to one of those involved, Wendy Scott, and she confessed that when they began the project, they had no idea exactly how much time and effort would have to be put into the project to bring it to fruition.

Mark Finnie, architect and trustee, has been faithful to the Georgian style of the building: "The drawing room paint is exactly the same as the original colour, wooden floors with oriental rugs and stone flags outside to form paths in the forecourt." The end result is of enormous credit to all involved. Belmont House has taken on a renewed lease of life as a fully-restored Georgian country house sleeping up to twelve people "in a stylish interior for holidays" and will also be used as a venue for weddings, meetings, and art and community events (see http://www.belmontunst.org.uk for details).

For more information on Unst, you could do no better than try to obtain a copy of *Unst, My Island Home and Its Story* by a namesake of mine, Charles Sandison. The author lived at Hammar in Unst and finished the book in January 1966. It is out of print now but Amazon or Abe Books should have copies. The ISBN is 978-0900662003 and the volume was published by

Shetland Times Ltd in 1968. Sandison captured the true worth of Unst in a fine poem, 'The Island's Call':

> To Unst, its high and rock-bound shore,
> And smiling summer bays,
> Its glorious sun and wind and sea,
> And joyous springtime days.
>
> The lapping water between the weed
> When the tide is on the make,
> And the eiderduck with her brood of young
> Scurrying in her wake.
>
> The freedom of bright and long days spent
> In row-boat and in sail,
> The downward swoop of the gannet,
> And the loom of the finner whale.
>
> I will leave the town with its bustling crowds,
> Its one-way streets and all,
> And will hie me away to a northern isles
> For I hear its magic call.

However, perhaps I should leave the last words to another remarkable Scotsman, Sir John Sinclair of Lybster in Caithness, who published his *Statistical Account of Scotland for 1791–1800*. He commented about life in Shetland in the 1790s: "People frank and open in their manners, bold, hardy and humane. Music and dancing are very favoured in winter. Many common people play with skill on the violin." More than two hundred years later, you will find that this is still true. And, I am sure you will also find a goodly number of Sandisons amongst that happy breed.

29.
Cawdor Castle

Every year a Shakespeare play is performed in front of the drawbridge of Cawdor Castle to the east of the City of Inverness. The summer of 2011 featured his wonderful comedy *Twelfth Night*. Cawdor Castle is one of Scotland's oldest and most glorious buildings and has sheltered generations of the same family for more than 600 years. Before the performance, guests picnicked in the Flower Garden and then sat upon the lawn amidst the sweet scent of summer to listen to the tale of mistaken identity and unrequited love. In 1370, more than 200 years before Shakespeare wrote the work, William, 3rd Thane of Cawdor, started work on his new castle and now, people can gather at Cawdor to enjoy both the castle and Shakespeare's plays.

Prior to the building of the present-day castle, the family occupied a smaller castle nearby, probably a defensive fort, about a mile north east of Cawdor and built on an artificial hillock amidst marshy ground. When William made the decision to build the new residence, he decided that the site should be chosen by chance, rather than by design. He is said to have packed gold into a coffer and strapped it to the back of a donkey, then set the animal off to wander where it would. Clearly, the progress of the donkey was closely monitored by William and eventually, at nightfall, the beast settled by a tree on a rocky outcrop where there was a source of water – an excellent building site with a good supply of drinking water and firm foundations for a castle. Thus, William believed, the Cawdor family would be "forever prosperous".

Cawdor Castle is famous for its association with Shakespeare. In his "Scottish play", *Macbeth*, the bard has King Duncan being murdered at Cawdor by Macbeth, then Thane of Cawdor. In fact, Duncan was wounded in a battle at Pitgaveny in 1040 and died at Elgin Castle some miles to the east of Cawdor. Also, given that Cawdor Castle was not built until the late fourteenth century, it is entirely impossible that Duncan could have been murdered there. However, Shakespeare never allowed uncomfortable truths to intrude upon his construction of a good tale, so the myth persists to this day, much to the amusement and pleasure of visitors to the castle.

My own visit to Cawdor occurred in December 2010 on a sparkling morning with Christmas knocking on the door. I was to meet Gräfin Angelika Lažanský von Bukowa, Dowager Countess of Cawdor and widow of Hugh, the 24th Thane. My instructions were precise: "Arrive at 11.30am, enter by the exit, park under the trees and someone will meet you on the drawbridge." I confess that I was intimidated. I was well aware of the link between Cawdor and *Macbeth* and would not have been in the least bit startled to catch a glimpse of three witches brewing up something unwholesome on the bleak moor as I passed by. But what if I arrived late? Would I be bundled unceremoniously into a dungeon to weep and wail, chained to a dank wall? These worries are probably why I got lost, which is hard to do in a tiny place like Cawdor Village.

With time running out, I asked directions from two men in a van. They looked strangely at each other: "Do you see these pillars on the other side of the road?" the driver asked.

"You mean the ones that have a sign on them saying 'EXIT'?"

"Yes," he replied. "Just go through there and follow the road to the castle."

With that, he wound up the window of the van and, still shaking his head in disbelief, drove off. I glanced at my watch, a minute remaining, and shot up the road as fast as I could safely go. Suddenly, there were the trees and the old castle and, thank the lord, the drawbridge, which I was pleased to note was in the lowered position. Grabbing what little was left of my dignity, I hurried to the drawbridge.

Shortly thereafter, I was courteously welcomed by a strikingly handsome woman accompanied by two border terriers. Lady Cawdor settled me in a comfortable chair in her study and took her place behind a large, well-ordered desk. A log fire sparked and crackled in the grate, filling the small room with warmth and the unforgettable scent of wood smoke. I explained again the purpose of my visit and began by asking her about the story of the donkey, the gold and the tree. Was it fact or fiction?

She said, "That is obviously a family legend but my husband, who was someone who liked fact rather than fancy, complained that he couldn't possibly tell the tale to unsuspecting visitors without some evidential proof. On the ground floor of the castle there are the remains of a fossilized tree – I will show you in a moment. He chopped off a bit of wood from the tree and had it analyzed by carbon dating. The answer came back that the tree was alive in 1372, plus or minus forty-five years. Now, this tree is exactly in the middle of the central structure of the castle, exactly opposite the drawbridge and there is no doubt that the original tower was built over the tree."

For years, the family thought that the tree was a hawthorn, which is not surprising; Hugh Fife, in his wonderful book about native Highland trees, *Warriors and Guardians*, notes that "the belief that this tree [hawthorn] has a strong affinity of things beyond the obvious world has persisted for thousands of years. There also appears to be some special link between the tree and hereditary chiefs." Fife also incorrectly identified the Cawdor tree as being a hawthorn: "At another location in the North East Highlands," he said, "a very famous castle was built over a hawthorn tree and some centuries later, the tree was still alive in the building's cellar."

The inquiring mind of the 24th Thane and modern technology resolved the issue of the true identity of the tree: it was not hawthorn but holly. This discovery gave considerably more credence to the story about William, the gold and the donkey, in as much as holly, in Gaelic culture, was considered to be a "protective" tree and, like other evergreens, had the power to ward off evil spirits. Yes, indeed, just the right place to build the castle to ensure that he and his descendants would be "forever prosperous".

Nevertheless, the word "prosperous" can have different meanings to different people: to turn out well, success, good fortune, health, wealth, happiness, thriving. So I asked Lady Cawdor what she thought the previous

Thanes, looking at the castle today, would think about Cawdor and if they would agree that the family had been "forever prosperous". She thought about this for a moment, looking down for guidance at the younger of the two border terriers, which was comfortably ensconced on her lap.

"I think that I would take that as meaning that the family, in a long line, continued here. The statement, in that sense, to prosper, seems to me to mean to continue, rather than in any monetary terms. And, considering the history of Scotland during that period, the early and middle-ages, it was indeed good fortune that the family did survive, in a direct line, during these often bloody times," she answered.

Few would doubt the veracity of Lady Cawdor's statement. The family lived through some of the most turbulent events in our history: the Scottish Wars of Independence, Henry VIII's "Rough Wooing" of our realm and the turmoil of the Reformation; the bloodshed and mayhem of religious wars; the death of Mary of Guise (1560), mother of Mary, Queen of Scots, which left Scotland in a state of civil war; Oliver Cromwell's tenure, when Cawdor was one of the few Scottish castles that he did not "knock about a bit"; the Jacobite Rebellions of 1689, 1715 and 1745.

However, towards the end of the seventeenth century and in spite of the uncertainty of these times, Hugh, the 14th Thane, embarked upon an ambitious programme designed to alter the character of Cawdor from fortress to family home; a good idea given that he had nine children aged from four to twenty-one and a numerous household, including the chaplain, the gentleman, the butler, the cook, the cook's man, the porter, the coachman, two footmen, two gentlewomen, the chamber maid, three byrewomen and a dairy maid – twenty-seven people in all. The work was completed to Hugh's satisfaction in 1702 and Cawdor, as it is today, is very much his legacy to the family home.

When Hugh died in 1716, his successor, his grandson John, moved the family south to live in London and on the family estates in Wales; a custom subsequently adopted by many of his peers, when, after centuries, the Lairds essentially abandoned their Highland clans; thus paving the way for the savage clearances of the nineteenth century when the descendants of these Lairds chose to populate their Scottish estates with sheep, rather than with people. Cawdor Castle was left, unchanged, and cared for by a succession of factors, employed to do so by Cawdor Estates.

Lady Cawdor cares for the castle today, with support and help from a small staff of key helpers: Martin Nelson, Lady Cawdor's chef, who has been with her for twenty-seven years; Alison Clark, her assistant in the tourism office, who has worked there for twenty-eight years; Derek Hosie, the head gardener, who has nurtured the famous Cawdor Gardens for nearly thirty years. In all, there are fourteen full-time members on Lady Cawdor's management team, along with seasonal staff numbering fifty-four, mostly from Cawdor and the surrounding area. The castle is open seven days a week from 1 May until the first Sunday in October and attracts upwards of 80,000 visitors each year.

Gardening has always been a passion with Lady Cawdor, clearly reflected in the three principal gardens adjacent to the castle: the Flower Garden, Old Walled Garden and the Wild Garden. I asked about her special interest in the gardens and she told me: "I love gardens. And the great fortune is that I have this excellent head gardener who has been here, as I say, twenty-nine years. We have done a lot of work in the gardens. The most recent is that we have created a slate garden, with some of the old slates when we replaced slates on the roof of the castle. We redid a small area of the flower garden, with a beautiful fountain made out of slate in the middle, a lovely grey colour. The slates came from a quarry near Elgin 250 years ago, the last time the castle was reroofed.

"We are completely organic here. My vegetable gardens, my summer and winter vegetable gardens, have been organic for thirty-one years. That is my major passion, well, one of them. We grow all our own vegetables. In the summer, a lot of those go to our restaurant for the benefit of the visitors. We are self-sufficient, except for milk and butter, and olive oil, of course. But basically, self-sufficient; we have salmon in the river, partridge, grouse, pheasant, hare and roe deer – you can't really ask for more."

Lady Cawdor fiercely guards the integrity of organic farming in the area and, in 2002, played a leading role in opposing the trial-plantings of genetically modified crops near the castle because of uncertainty about the impact these crops might have on crops produced by organic farmers. She managed to have two of the trials stopped but a third trial, on Roskill Farm near Munlochy, across the Moray Firth on the Black Isle, went ahead. The public debate she organised was attended by 350 people, with many more being turned away because of lack of space.

Since then, she has continued her support for organic farming and told me, "For five or six years now we have held a 'Living Food' day on the last Saturday in September. We invite all the good organic producers in the Highlands to join us and there are usually about forty to fifty different stalls. Last year, we had over 2,000 visitors during the day. It is an excellent showcase for the wonderful produce of the Highlands. I really do think, as far as food is concerned, that we produce some of the best raw materials in the world."

With that, Lady Cawdor conducted me on a tour of the principal rooms in the Castle: the drawing room with its wonderful paintings, including works by Sir Joshua Reynolds, Sawrey Gilpin, Thomas Lawrence and Frederick Say; the Tapestry Bedroom with its magnificent Venetian headboard on the four-poster marriage-bed of Sir Hugh Campbell, the 14th Thane of Cawdor and Lady Henrietta Stuart, wed in 1662, and the lovely Flemish tapestries purchased in 1682 at a total cost of £483, including £3 customs duty; the Woodcock Room, Pink Bedroom, Pink Dressing Room, Tower Room and, finally, the Thorn Tree Room with the famous fossilized holly, over which the castle was built.

Hugh, the 24th Thane and 6th Earl Cawdor, who died in 1993, left a splendid and detailed account of all the furnishings, ornaments and artifacts in the castle. You will find this at the back of the guide book to Cawdor, which was also written by Hugh. Both are highly entertaining and absolutely essential if you are to get the most out of your visit to the castle. I have visited quite a few castles in my time, carefully reading the attendant literature. Invariably, it is, more often than not, as dry as dust. Hugh's writing is a perfect example of how such subjects should be tackled: fact-packed but with a liberal sprinkling of fun and good humour.

I had asked Lady Cawdor what the previous Thanes would have thought about the present status of the castle and I wondered how she felt about the future – would the family continue to prosper? "Cawdor Estate is a very large entity. The Castle and the land that belongs with the castle is very much part of that. The Castle and the Estate are run in two different ways. The whole thing is 58,000 acres. My stepson, Colin Cawdor, [the 25th Thane and 7th Earl of Cawdor] runs a very good shoot and we have a beautiful grouse moor. We have an excellent partridge shoot, pheasant shoot and, of course, salmon fishing on the River Findhorn. The Estate has a formal factor; I have a general manager. As to the future, well, the next generation is very much alive and well, which is my stepson and he also has a son, so as far as I can look down the line, I think that everything will be all right."

But before I left, I had one final question to ask Lady Cawdor: what did the castle mean to her? "What it means to me is that I am the current guardian thereof and that is what my husband wanted me to do, which is why he left it to me. I am just a link in a very long chain and although it belongs to me, it is really the other way round – I belong to it. I do my very best to look after it, like an old relation really. An old house is very much a being in its own right. I just see myself as the guardian now," was her reply.

As I drove home, I thought to myself, "Well, an old house it may be but it could not have a more caring and committed guardian," whilst making a careful note of the date 23 July, Cawdor Castle, *Twelfth Night*, and keeping a weather eye open for witches along the way.

For full details about the castle and annual events, contact: Cawdor Castle Ltd, Cawdor Castle, Nairn, Scotland IV12 5RD; Tel: 01667 404401; Fax: 01667 404674; Website: http://www.cawdorcastle.com; Email: info@cawdorcastle.com

30.
Alladale Wilderness Lodge and Reserve

Little of lasting worth in this world has ever been achieved without passion and commitment. Governments – well, some governments – in their various ways, seek to do so but all of the available evidence seems to indicate that, for much of the time, they labour in vain. Nowhere is this more self-evident than in the field of conservation: our environment is continually under pressure from commercial interests, the rape of our seas, the destruction of native forests, industrial pollution, profit before probity. A Cree Indian prophecy encapsulates this belief: "Only after the last tree has been cut down / Only after the last river has been poisoned / Only after the last fish has been caught / Only then will you find that money cannot be eaten."

Happily, there are people, individuals, who are prepared to accept these challenges and to confront these issues. Mostly, they are personally wealthy and prepared to give of their time and money to try to restore degraded parts of Planet Earth to their natural state. And, of course, there are many others, less enriched, who toil in the same way as best as they can. But they all have one thing in common: an enhanced desire to leave nothing behind for future generations other than the friendly imprint of their care for the land that gives us all life. This is the story of one such project in the Highlands of Scotland, a story that is just beginning.

The announcement a few years ago that the Alladale Wildlife Reserve proposed to reintroduce wolves, lynx, bison, brown bear and elk to the Highlands was met with mixed feelings. The Scottish Mountaineering Council, Ramblers Association and the Mountain Bothy Association all launched fierce attacks on the proposals because, they insist, the building of fences will restrict access to the hills. The Highland Council, Scottish Government, Scottish Natural Heritage, *et al* also expressed concern. Neighbouring estates have expressed alarm about the reduction of the Alladale red deer population and how such a reduction will impact upon their deer.

As such, this response was similar to the public response that has greeted other schemes; most recently, the reintroduction of white-tailed eagles, commonly known as sea eagles – great raptors that were driven to extinction in Scotland in the early years of the twentieth century – and the reintroduction of European beavers, a species that has been absent from Scotland since the seventeenth century.

In spite of predictions that life in Caledonia as we know it would come to an immediate end if the sea eagles and beavers arrived, they are here; sea eagles in Mull and Sutherland and other areas of the north, and beavers in the Knapdale Forest in Argyll. The sea eagles are doing well, thriving mightily, and they delight thousands of visitors and local people every year. The beavers have settled in comfortably, thank you, and are busy building their lodges and getting on with what nature intended for them, propagating their kind.

As far as I can judge, the prophets of doom have been confounded. The sun still rises from the east each morning and still sets in the west at the end of each day. But the doubters persist in their complaints: allegedly, sea eagles kill and eat hundreds of lambs and sheep each year and the beavers severely disrupt riverine habitats and wild fish stocks with their tree-felling and dam-building proclivities. There is only anecdotal evidence to support such claims but they continue to exercise the minds of many of those opposed to any form of radical change.

Such complaints are nothing new amidst Scotland's wild lands. Any creature that is perceived to be a threat to the inalienable right of humans to make a profit, regardless of collateral damage, goes on to many land-owner's and land-worker's hit lists: sea eagle, golden eagle, buzzard, hen harrier, cormorant, goosander, merganser, heron, otter, seals, and, at least until the Land Reform (Scotland) Act was passed in 2003, in extreme cases, climbers, hill walkers, ramblers, bird watchers *et al.*

This is the historical background against which the reintroduction of wolves, lynx, bison, brown bear and elk has to be viewed. Those who express concern about these matters have the right to be fairly heard. Scotland's legal freedom-to-roam legislation has been hard won and has to be vigorously protected. Those who propose these reintroductions will always fail in their aim to do so unless they obtain the support of our political masters, the general public and the majority of the local communities upon which the proposals will impact. It is right and proper that this is the case; after all, we live in a democracy.

Mr Paul Lister, co-founder of the MFI furniture chain, is the owner and leading visionary of the 23,000-acre Alladale Wildlife Reserve, about forty miles north from Inverness, the capital city of the Highlands. He is a passionate conservationist and the driving force behind the proposed reintroductions described above. Paul Lister is also the founder of The European Nature Trust (TENT), an organisation committed to the protection and restoration of threatened wilderness areas, wild habitats and the wildlife living within them.

Hugh Fullerton-Smith, for five years general manager at Alladale, is every bit as passionate and committed to the concept of conservation as is Paul Lister and he has recently been appointed as director of TENT. Fullerton-Smith has extensive experience of conservation issues throughout the world: in the UK, USA, Mongolia and in the Carpathian Mountains, across Romania, Ukraine, Poland, Slovakia, the Czech Republic and Hungry where TENT is seeking philanthropic and institutional funding to safeguard large tracts of forest and other wild areas.

I set off early one morning in August to find out exactly what was going on at Alladale and why it had raised the hackles of so many of our fellow Scots. Alladale lies at the heart of Clan Ross country and bestrides the boundary between Sutherland and Ross-shire. It has a considerable history of angst, most known for the little church at Croick, a few miles to the west of Ardgay at the head of the Dornoch Firth. This provided shelter for the people of Glencalvie, part of the Alladale lands, when they were evicted from their homes in 1845 to make way for sheep. About ninety souls, destitute men, women and children, huddled in the churchyard under plaids and blankets.

They engraved sad messages on the windows of the church: "Glencalvie people was in the churchyard here on 24 May 1845." "Glencalvie tenants residing here." "Glencalvie people, the wicked generation." Many of those evicted had been told by their ministers, appointed by the Lairds conducting the clearances, that they were being evicted because of their sins before God, although those so-called sins were never detailed. All that was required of those whose ancestors had lived and toiled the land for generations was to immediately pack whatever they could carry and go.

Today, this area is very much the sporting and recreational paradise of southern owners and their guests. My friend Mike and I drove past their lodges, Gruinards, Amat and Glencalvie, and then followed the blue ribbon of the River Carron through magnificent forests of ancient Scots Pine up a small hill to Alladale Lodge. The great house is splendidly set amidst well-tended lawns and fine gardens. Having announced our arrival, we were welcomed by the reserve manager, Innes MacNeill, a sparse, strikingly fit young man with a natural air of command and common sense. His experience spans almost twenty years of habitat management, flora and fauna on the reserve. We sat round the dining room table over coffee and home-made shortbread whilst Innes outlined his plan for our day on the reserve.

The key question in my mind was to determine the position in regard to the reintroduction of the major predators: wolves and brown bears. Personally, I harbour doubts about doing so. Not because I think that it is in any way wrong, but rather my concern that these animals would be persecuted today as much as they were persecuted when they naturally roamed these lands. It became clear that Paul Lister and his team could not proceed with the reintroductions until such time as they were certain that the habitat provided was sufficiently large to safely sustain them.

Alladale extends to 23,000 acres but to establish an area large enough to safely accommodate two small packs of wolves requires a minimum 50,000 acres. This means that either Alladale's neighbours have to be persuaded to sign up to the proposal or that Alladale will have to try to buy adjacent land on the open market if and when it becomes available. Until these conditions are met, the reintroduction remains uncertain.

With Innes at the wheel of a Reserve Land Rover, we set off along the bumpy road leading up Gleann Mór into the Glencalvie Forest, centred by a white, rocky, tumbling stream, the Abhainn á Ghlinne Mhóir. Although there are no Munros on the Reserve, the hills are considerable and majestic: to the south, the long ridge of Dunach Liath (554m), Dunna Liath (690m) and Carn Feur-lochain (694m), to the north Sron Gun Aran (622m) and An Socach (745m). These hills are scattered with wild brown trout lochs that delight anglers: Crom, Sgeireach, little Lochan nam Breac Buidh, Pollaig, Lochan nan Leac and na Gabhalach Nodha, full of hard-fighting fish.

Innes commented, "Man has destroyed the glens, not the deer or the sheep, but man. He cut down the trees and burned the ground. Any young saplings that have tried to come through during the past 200 years, the sheep and deer have had them. Putting it back is a tall order for us and we are trying to replant areas. It is great to think that the trees will self regenerate, but they will not, because of sheep and deer, this why we have to move in and help."

The hills host a wide range of wildlife, including purple swaths of bell heather, stands of Scots pine, amidst newly planted trees of the same species, cautious ptarmigan on the high tops, red grouse, the great raptors, golden eagle, buzzard, peregrine, kestrel, delicate merlin and vast, coal-black raven. By the river and on the lower slopes, you will find otter, fox, pine marten and badger. Throughout the reserve, red deer abound. This is the largest mammal in Britain and it has survived in some form or other since time immemorial. Currently, there is a population of some 1,000 red deer on the reserve, although numbers have been reduced to allow the natural regeneration on both old and newly planted forests.

The reserve's commitment to the re-establishment of the old forest is total. I asked Innes how many trees had been planted in recent years and he told me, "From 1992 until 2011, upwards of 500,000 native trees will have been planted. Rowan and birch are quickly established, the Scots pine are much slower. We have designed open plan thickets and natural scatterings. The hill crests are planted with pine and we think, and hope, that it looks like how it possibly did look in the past. After fifteen years, it is safe to take down the fence that has protected them from predation by deer – there are no longer sheep on the reserve. All the species we plant here are native to this region. We are just about to start planting 67,000 trees in this area; mainly pine but birch, rowan, holly, willow, juniper, alder and aspen as well. This is long-term work. We won't see the result but future generations will, and they will benefit from doing so. It's a 100-year restoration project."

Half way up the glen, we stopped to say good morning to the reserve's five Highland ponies, two of which are used to bring in stalked deer, the others taking visitors on adventure treks through the hills. That morning, two of the beautiful beasts were being saddled by John Calder, who looks after them for the reserve, and a lady guest accompanied by her boisterous, talkative dog, Reah. We next stopped at a wonderful badger hide, carefully disguised into the side of a small hillock overlooking the stream. Innes pointed out the set, on the far bank, where the badgers had been busy, house-keeping, clearing out unwanted earth from their home. We were also introduced to the reserve's wild boar colony, curious animals that ran down the hill to greet us. We were similarly introduced to Hercules and Hulda, elk brought onto the reserve recently. They are designated as being dangerous wild animals and are safely contained within a considerable area of ground, but they were friendly enough when we said hello.

The reserve also provides, in conjunction with the Challenger Trust programme, wonderful opportunities for young people to become involved in the work of the reserve. The Challenger Trust is a registered charity and Alladale runs a "challenge", funded by the Young People's Fund for Scotland and the Lister Charitable Trust. It provides facilities for twenty-four young people to take part in development adventure activities whilst working with rangers on conservation projects and helping with running the reserve, building self-confidence and learning new skills.

The Alladale Challenge starts on Monday mornings and finishes the following Friday evening, during April, May and June. Innes explained some of the tasks the boys and girls are set: "They recently helped plant about 2,000 trees in the boar's compound. The children and their teachers camp out and love it. They come from a catchment area of within forty miles of Alladale and, currently, six high schools are involved: they undertake tree planting, tree surveys, pulling down fences, guided wildlife walks and talks, fly fishing on the river, abseiling, team leadership skills and route finding."

The Alladale Reserve also supports twenty full- and part-time jobs in an area where employment opportunities are limited. The reserve has its own saw mill and much of the furniture that adorns the reserve properties is made from their own wood, in their own workshop; designed and built by the reserve handyman, Blair Barnet. Alladale generates much of its own electricity from water power and up to 70% comes from this source, depending upon water levels in the rivers.

Clearly, the capital investment in setting up and developing the Alladale Wilderness Lodge and Reserve has been considerable and, as such, it also has to generate income to sustain that development. Alladale Lodge and the reserve properties provide that source of income. The Lodge and the luxurious self-catering "bothies" are available to rent and are increasingly well patronised. Those with the means to do so enjoy a standard of accommodation and service that is beyond excellent and many have become regular Alladale guests, experiencing all that is finest in Scottish scenery and hospitality.

They are also exposed to the passion and commitment to the environment that Paul Lister and his team have brought to their dream of returning a degraded part of the Highland landscape to its rightful former glory. I, for one, welcome this commitment. As to reintroducing wolves, brown bear and lynx, I also hope that this dream becomes a reality. Only time and the continued passion of people like Paul Lister can make it happen.

For further information, contact: Alladale Wilderness Lodge & Reserve, Ardgay, Sutherland, Scotland IV24 3BS; Tel: 01863 755338; Fax: 01863 755352; Email: reservations@alladale.com; Website: www.alladale.com

31.
Ardtornish, a Dream in the West

Morvern and Ardtornish in the West Highlands of Scotland is one of the least visited and yet most beautiful areas of the land I love. It retains a sense of peace often lacking amidst Caledonia's more popular airts. Even today there is no easy way into this magnificent wilderness. The best route is by the short ferry crossing over Loch Linnhe at the Corran Narrows, eight miles south from Fort William. But you will still be gripped in the embrace of a tortuous, single-track road for the last part of your journey, climbing from shores of Loch Sunart between Beinn nam Beathrach (582m) and Taobh Dubh (352m) before descending to the sea through the glory of Gleann Geal, the White Glen of Morvern.

I became interested in the area after reading Philip Gaskell's book, *Morvern Transformed: A Highland Parish in the Nineteenth Century*, and, particularly, coming from North Sutherland, by the infamous Patrick Sellar's association with Ardtornish. In 1838, Sellar – who had been an agent of the Duke of Sutherland and personally oversaw the brutal Strathnaver Clearances between 1813 and 1819 – acquired 6,810 acres of land around Loch Arienas and brought sheep down from his Sutherland estates. Clearances soon followed. Forty-four families amounting to 230 people were immediately evicted.

Eventually, Sellar had control of upwards of 30,000 Morvern acres and he settled himself in the original Ardtornish House, once the home of the Duke of Argyll's factor. This grand building stood on a high promontory jutting out into the Sound of Mull, close to the ruins of Ardtornish Castle; a tumble of broken walls with a stubby tower clinging to the edge of gull-cry-filled cliffs that look west over the sea to the Island of Mull.

I walked out to the castle with young Russell MacIntyre, the Ardtornish Estate acting visitor manager, and we talked about those who had lived there down the ages – from the earliest Mesolithic people, Neolithic man, Celts, Picts, Vikings and Highlanders – and the struggles they must have endured to survive in such an inhospitable environment. Sellar's home, like the castle, is now in ruins. The few remaining walls and arches are moss-covered and almost invisible amidst the tangle of branches and bushes that have invaded the remains of the great man's residence.

John Macdonald was one of the casualties of the clearances and, as an old man, he was appointed spokesman for the community when, in 1883, the Napier Commission came north to take evidence about these sad events. At a meeting in the Free Church Hall at Lochaline, he was asked by the Commission what he wanted and he replied: "I would like it to be the way it was before, if it were possible, that is. I should like to have a croft and my cows back again, as before."

After the clearances, two men owned most of the land in Morvern: Patrick Sellar, who had Ardtronish Estate, and his neighbour, Octavius Smith, who had made his fortune distilling and selling gin in Victorian London and owned Achranich Estate. Smith's family built the present day Ardtornish House, a vast, imposing Victorian mansion.

But the Achranich Estate lay between Sellar's land and the men were soon at loggerheads. The dispute centered on salmon fishing rights in the River Aline. Although Smith owned one bank of the stream, Sellar had the sole rights to fishing. As relations deteriorated, Sellar refused Smith permission to fish and Smith responded by denying Sellar access across his land to tend to his business at Loch Arienas.

The matter was placed in the hands of their respective lawyers and the young families of the stubborn adults were ordered, on pain of severe retribution, to ignore each other. Happily, however, before the dispute came to court, it was resolved; Sellar agreed to sell half of his fishing rights to Smith, whilst Smith agreed to give Sellar a right of way across his land. Thus, Victorian propriety and honour was satisfied and thereafter the two families lived amicably together. Eleanor Sellar later recalled, "I remember Gertrude, Mr Smith's youngest daughter, telling me how the new peace was inaugurated by her mother and herself, then a child of eight, lunching at Ardtornish. Mr Sellar set her beside himself and called her his little lady. The goings to and from between the two places was as perpetual as they had been strictly forbidden the year before."

In time, the families were united by marriage and the estates merged into what is now Ardtornish Estate and, because of Queen Victoria's love of all things Scottish, the great and good flocked to the Highlands, to walk, fish, hunt stags and generally disport themselves far from the madding crowd. Ardtornish welcomed many famous visitors, including, in 1853, Alfred Lord Tennyson, poet laureate, accompanied by his friend and fellow poet, Francis Turner Palgrave of *Golden Treasury* fame. Their host was Patrick Sellar's son and heir, William, Professor of Humanities at Edinburgh University. Although Tennyson and Palgrave had intended to visit Loch Coruisk in Skye, they were so captivated by Ardtornish that they decided to stay there. Tennyson later wrote, "For though he missed a day in Skye / He spent a day in heaven."

John Buchan, statesman, soldier, author, poet and angler, met Gerard Craig Sellar, Patrick's grandson, in South Africa in 1902 and he and his wife regularly visited Ardtornish. Indeed, Buchan probably conceived the idea for his marvelous book *John Macnab* from the earlier dispute between Smith and Sellar. The story is based upon a public challenge to poach a deer and a salmon from a neighbour's land, on a given day, without the participants being caught. Buchan dedicated his book to Rosalind Maitland, Craig Sellar's sister.

When I last visited Ardtornish in March 2010 the estate provided me with comfortable accommodation in a cottage by the river. The estate has a number of excellent self-catering properties where guests can enjoy a fulfilling holiday amongst wonderful scenery. Not the least of which is the magnificent Ardtornish gardens, approximately thirty acres of splendid parkland: shrubs and trees, native birch, larch, firs and pines, dark green against the pink sandstone façade of the great house. Owen and Emmeline Hugh Smith bought the Ardtornish estate in 1930 and each year they received gifts of named and un-named hybrid rhododendrons from Sir John Stirling Maxwell, of Pollock House in Glasgow. Consequently, the Ardtornish plants are famous throughout Scotland for their diversity and vibrant colours.

The gardens at Ardtornish have been developed over a period of 150 years and today they enfold an amazing sense of calm. Well-defined walks lead through this wonderland following the Keeper's Path to a graceful Alpine meadow, Amphitheatre and Eucryphia garden, with a number of "diversions" leading off to further delights. The present incumbents of the estate, the Raven Family, along with local people, have continued to care for the gardens, primarily Faith Raven, who recently published a comprehensive history of the gardens, *The Ardtornish Garden – A Highland Garden in Morvern, Lochaber: History, Gardeners, Seasons and a Tour*. The book is available from the estate office.

Ian Lamb is the present Ardtornish Estate gardener. For twenty-seven years, Ian and his wife, Helen, ran the estate kitchen garden as an independent nursery selling a wide range of both indoor and outdoor plants until, in 2007, they took on the task of helping to care for the main garden. I met Ian on a brisk morning when he was busy pruning the roses that adorn the front of the house. This is no mean task and requires the use of a hydraulic lift to reach the upper areas of the display. Ian lowered his working platform to ground level and came over to speak to me. He is a well-built, bearded man with a ready smile, and the character and stature of one who obviously loves his work. He knows, intimately, every inch of his domain and listening to him talk about the plants and animals that he encounters during his daily tasks was entirely fascinating and inspiring.

Just as fascinating was the time I spent with Simon Boult, the estate head stalker. Simon guides guests on both hill and river and I chatted to him by the old bridge where the River Aline greets the sea in sheltered Loch Aline. Simon had brought along a fishing rod, more in hope than earnest endeavour because the river was running very high. It quickly became apparent to me that he was well versed in its use, casting neatly over the stream whilst avoiding the trees and undergrowth that lined the bank behind him. Simon originally hails from Somerset, in England, but has worked in Scotland for the last twenty-one years, gaining experience in his craft in the Outer Hebrides, Islay, Perthshire, Kintyre and Speyside. As with Ian Lamb, Simon mightily impressed me both with his knowledge and his enthusiasm.

Back at Ardtornish House, Isobel Carmichael, the housekeeper, gave me a guided tour of the building. Isobel, who was born at Ardtornish, has a ready laugh and a wicked sense of humour. The house is huge and if Isobel hadn't been leading the way, I would have very quickly become lost. "Below stairs", where the staff lived, still retains some of the features that must have been in daily use when John Buchan was a guest: a long row of numbered bells, connected to the principal rooms upstairs, set high on the wall and readily visible to the alert eyes and ears of the house staff and butler. What a flurry there must have been when the bells clanged their summons, men and women dashing in all directions to attend to the orders of family and guests.

The entrance hall is magnificent; portraits of family members and Highland scenes adorn the walls and a graceful flight of wide stairs, with a delicately sculptured, shining white banister leading up to the first floor. The great house has been divided into five, private and individual guest suites but Ardtornish still retains a remarkable sense of "wholeness". Magnificent carpets, which have been in place for many years, are preciously guarded and carefully maintained. Each of the suites has similar characteristics: the comfortable sense of a time and way of life that is passing yet, at Ardtornish, is still accessible, fortified with the accoutrements of present-day living.

I asked Isobel what she felt about Ardtornish and she replied instantly, "It is a very special place because it is my home and it is beautiful and I love it." Isobel's father was the estate Foreman and her mother cooked for the Raven Family. I left Isobel with her cheerful team of girls, all busy hoovering, dusting and polishing, preparing the house to receive a flood of eager guests who were to attend a weekend wedding reception at Ardtornish House.

In times past, the estate provided employment for nearly 100 local people. This tradition continues today when fifty to sixty people are recognised as gaining employment from the assets and activities of the estate. The estate was eventually inherited by the Raven Family and it extends to 35,000 acres, occupying the southeast corner of the Morvern peninsula, and, in 1967, the title was transferred into the name of Ardtornish Estate Company Limited. The stated objectives of the company are: To manage the estate, to support the strength and prosperity of the community, to maintain and enhance the natural and cultural heritage, and to develop in a sustainable way the value of the estate for the benefit of both the owners and the community.

This bald statement belies the reality that is Ardtornish. Has the estate succeeded in its aim? The truth is that I don't really know. What I do know, however, is that when I leave the main road and drive down the hill into Ardtornish, it is as though I have passed through an invisible curtain into a different world. A magical land full of "noises and sweet airs that give delight and hurt not". A place where all things are possible and where there is a sense of sublime peace. Go there and discover for yourself the joy that is Ardtornish.

For further details about Ardtornish Estate, accommodation, visitor centre and holiday services, activities, Ardtornish gardens, stalking, shooting and fishing, booking and other information, visit the Ardtornish Estate website at: http://www.ardtornish.co.uk/; Email: stay@ardtornish.co.uk or contact: Ardtornish Estate Office, Morvern, by Oban, Argyll, Scotland PA80 5UZ; Tel: 01967 421288; Fax: 01967 421221.

32.
Glenelg

~~~~~~~~

If I believed in reincarnation, I would choose, if I could, to come back as an otter. Of all the creatures that grace this magical land I love, *Lutra lutra*, the European otter, is supreme: an outdoor existence, swimming on demand, a highly developed sense of fun and unlimited fishing; all of the things that give me purpose and pleasure in life.

I thought of this as I looked down on Sandaig, a few tortuous, single-track-road miles south from Glenelg in Inverness-shire, with its scattered islands and deserted, shell sand beaches guarding the southern approach to the fierce waters of the Kylerhea narrows. Another otter-lover, Gavin Maxwell, author of *Ring of Bright Water*, lived there in a cottage by the lighthouse on Eilean Mor. His book tells of the otters he befriended at "Camusfearna", the name he gave to Sandaig in his stories.

Visitors make the pilgrimage to "Camusfearna" to pay their respects to Maxwell. He is buried there alongside Edal, his most famous otter, and a huge stone marks the place where his cottage stood. A fire destroyed the cottage in 1968, after which he moved to a cottage by the lighthouse on Eilean Ban – "The White Island" – which now supports one of the piers of the Skye Bridge, built in the 1990s.

Getting to Glenelg, "The Glens of Hunting", is not for the faint-hearted. Loch Alsh and Loch Duich, along the Road to the Isles by gaunt Eilean Donan Castle, bound it to the north. To the south, the dark, cold waters of Loch Hourn separate the Glenelg peninsula from the rough bounds of Knoydart. Westward across the Sound of Sleat is the misty island of Skye and its blue-grey Cuillin hills.

Glenelg, population in the order of 200 souls, is the principal community in this wilderness land, a land dominated by fractured mountains knifed by steep, tortuous passes; Beinn nan Caorach (773m) "Hill of the Rowan Berries", Beinn na h-Eaglaise (804m) "Hill of the Church", Sgurr Mhic Bharraich (781m) "Peak of the Son of Maurice", Beinn Sgritheall (974m) "The Scree Hill". The only other substantial village here is Arnisdale, where the road ends, past Sandaig, a dozen or so miles south along the shores of Loch Hourn.

This road is the only way into this remote peninsula and it follows the line of General Wade's military road built in 1770. Join it at Shiel Bridge at the head of Loch Duich on the A87 road from Invermoriston to Kyle of Lochalsh. The route was constructed in the aftermath of the Jacobite Rebellions and links Fort Augustus at the head of Loch Ness to Bernera Barracks at Glenelg, then the main point of access to the Kylerhea ferry over the sea to Skye.

The road climbs spectacularly from Shiel Bridge across the Bealach Ratagan, giving unforgettable views north to the magnificent peaks of the Five Sisters of Kintail and into the hills and mountains of the Inverinate Forest. Three years after it was completed, two illustrious travellers, Johnson and Boswell, passed this way, as recorded in Boswell's book, *The Journal of a Tour to the Hebrides with Samuel Johnson, LL.D.*

Of the road over the bealach, Dr Johnson commented: "We left Auknasheals and the Macraes in the afternoon and in the evening came to Ratiken, a high hill upon which a road is cut, but so steep and narrow that it is very difficult. Upon one of the precipices, my horse, weary with the steepness of the rise, staggered a little, and I called in haste to the Highlander to hold him. This was the only moment of my journey in which I thought myself endangered."

Even today, drivers treat this road with respect but once the bealach is surmounted, the vista that unfolds is remarkable. It is as though the traveller has discovered an entirely unexpected, secret world: a sudden, fertile strath, graced by a tumbling stream, busy with fine black-faced sheep, cattle and croft cottages; bounded on either side by majestic peaks and, ahead, the splendid mountains of Skye. The road twists and turns down to Glenelg village, clustered comfortably about a sheltered bay facing the blue waters of the Sound of Sleat.

Johnson and Boswell stopped at the old Ferry Inn, by the Kylerhea narrows, and the following morning crossed over to Skye where they met Flora MacDonald and her husband at Kingsburgh. Johnson famously said of the lady, "Her name will be mentioned in history and if courage and fidelity be virtues, mentioned with honour."

After the 1715 Jacobite uprising, the sea-crossing was deemed to be so important to the security of the country that government ordered the building of the military barracks at Bernera to protect it. A ferry, the *Glenachulish*, the last working example of a turntable-ferry in Scotland, still plies the Kylerhea narrows during the summer months and is owned and run by the Isle of Skye Ferry Community Interest Company.

Two less-illustrious travellers, your correspondent and a friend, made the journey last November. We caught the last rays of the winter sun as we arrived at the top of Bealach Ratagan and were, like so many others, captivated by the majesty of the view that lay before us. However, by the time we arrived in Glenelg, darkness enfolded us, but the light was on in our cottage and our host was there to greet us.

Sunset in these airts during winter months comes at about 3.30pm, so, after unpacking, we went up to the village where we found the community hall busy with residents enjoying afternoon tea and home-made scones to die for. Within moments, we were chatting happily to local people, sharing our thoughts on Glenelg and learning a little of what makes it such a friendly and welcoming place. A gaggle of laughing boys and girls joined us, freed from school, soon to be hurried off homewards to waiting parents.

As is often the case in Highland communities, the population is astonishingly cosmopolitan – a mix of people who were born and bred in Glenelg and had lived there all their lives, and others who had left to find employment in the south and then returned to the place they so clearly loved; and, of course, refugees from the mad, satanic mills of Glasgow and

Edinburgh and the Central Belt, and even from further afield. Indeed, the woman serving tea, a happy, bright, smiling, vibrant presence, was from São Paulo in Brazil.

I fell into conversation with one such refugee, Edwin Stiven, playwright, scriptwriter, tutor and occasional actor. Eddie originally hails from Ayrshire and is gloriously bearded and articulate. I asked what had brought him to Glenelg and he told me, "It is just a wonderful and inspiring place for a writer, peaceful and quiet." Eddie is a member of the Scottish Society of Playwrights and of the actors union, Equity. His work has appeared at the Edinburgh Festival Fringe and the Traverse Theatre and at the Tron Theatre in Glasgow. When I spoke with him in 2010, he was working on a commission for BBC Radio Scotland for his play *Wings of the Morning* (see: www.eddiestiven.co.uk).

The following morning, I headed for the village shop, indeed just about the only shop in Glenelg, for bread and a newspaper. There we met the owners, two more refugees from the suburbs of Glasgow, Jane and Craig Scobie. I asked Jane if she missed the bustle and hustle of the "Dear Green Place". Without hesitation, she replied, "We have been here for four years now and would never go back. Living here is like the difference between living in heaven and hell." The shop was full of laughter, reflecting the character of the proprietors.

I met another group of characters in the afternoon, the members of the Glenelg fire service. They had agreed to be photographed during a practice meeting and gathered, laughing and joking, round their fire engine for the event. They were a supremely happy team but it was immediately obvious that they were also highly disciplined and capable in their role. The vast area they have to cover and the difficult roads they have to traverse in order to reach outlying communities is awesome, but they carry out their vital work with the utmost professionalism.

One of the most surprising sights in Glenelg is the War Memorial. It stands in a clear space by the shores of the Sound of Sleat and is magnificent: a startling group of bronze figures set on a tall plinth. It was created by the sculptor and artist Louis Reid Deuchars (1870–1927), and planned over two years in collaboration with the famous Scottish architect Sir Robert Lorimer (1864–1929). The statue shows an angel holding aloft a laurel wreath, reaching down to help a kneeling woman. They are flanked on the left by the figure of a soldier, a Cameron Highlander, standing at ease with his rifle and steel helmet.

The memorial was commissioned by Lady Scott of Eilanreach to commemorate her son, George, and her son-in-law, Roland Hebeler, and the twenty others from the community who were killed during the First World War. The first name on the memorial is Major Valentine Fleming DSO, the father of Ian Fleming, the writer and creator of "James Bond". The family owned the Arnisdale Estate. Winston Churchill wrote an obituary for Major Valentine that Ian Fleming framed and kept by him all his life.

There are memorials to an older people who lived and worked here more than 2,000 years ago: the dramatic remains of their brochs in Glen Beag, to the south of Glenelg. The brochs were circular, dry-stone-built towers, enclosing a space of 40yds and approximately 12m in height. Dun Telve Broch is one of the best preserved of these structures in Europe. Nearby, on the side of the hill to the left of the road, are the remains of another broch, Dun Troddan, which, if anything, is perhaps more dramatic than Telve. I climbed the hill and mounted the wall enclosing the inner courtyard. From this vantage point, I looked out over the same landscape that these ancient people must have surveyed and felt their presence by me.

The presence of Alice Macalonan was just as impressive. Alice was born and brought up in Glenelg and had agreed to meet me. She is a charming lady, with kindly eyes and a smile that mightily brightened the grey, winter's day when we sat chatting before the fire in her comfortable living room. Like many of her peers, Alice had to leave Glenelg to find employment and worked for many years with children at Yorkhill hospital in Glasgow.

Her parents had the village post office and shop, and during the Second World War, they managed the local telephone exchange. Her mother used to get up at 4am and, after milking the cows, would "man" the phone so that her husband could have a rest. Life was simple when Alice was a girl, entertainment homemade, playing chess, draughts, whist and a lot of knitting. Electricity didn't arrive in Glenelg until 1950 and coal was brought in by sea.

Her mother used to say that the best part of her days was the early morning, in the spring of the year, in the fields, listening to the cry of green plover, the constant tide washing the shore, the silence and the smell of peat smoke and of the sea. "I just love Glenelg," Alice told me. "Its roots are so deep in me that I know that I could not be happy anywhere else."

When I left Glenelg, I paused on Bealach Ratagan and looked back. The village by the shore glinted silver and gold in winter sunlight. Smoke drifted lazily from the croft cottages that lay scattered up and down the glen. A dog barked somewhere and a hunting buzzard circled above the white thread of a tumbling stream where otters still play. It was hard to leave such peace and certainty, hard to turn our backs on such magical beauty.

33.
John O'Groats to Durness Drive
Part One:
John O'Groats to Forss House Hotel

Come with me this morning on a magical journey through time and history, along the furthermost reaches of mainland Scotland's north coast; by croft and castle and red-scarred cliffs loud with the cry of wheeling gulls, where white-fingered green waves endlessly caress near-deserted yellow sand beaches, distant blue mountains beckon and golden eagles soar.

To get the best out of this drive, you need three UK maps: Ordnance Survey Map 12, Thurso, Wick and surrounding area; Map 10, Strathnaver; and Map 9, Cape Wrath – all in the Landranger series, Scale 1:50,000. View these maps at http://getamap.ordnancesurvey.co.uk or buy paper copies direct from the Ordnance Shop on the same site. Be well prepared.

We begin in the east, at Duncansby Head, near John O'Groats, and travel west from there along the A836 through Thurso to Tongue, and thence follow the A838 round sea loch Eriboll to journey's end in the tiny village of Durness, a total distance of 100 miles. Along the way, we will pass through the ancient heartlands of clans Sinclair, Gunn, Sutherland and Mackay, who for centuries filled the straths with the bellowing belligerence of their constant feuds.

How long the journey takes is entirely up to you but you should plan for at least one overnight stop. A week is much better, because there is so much to see and do and explore amidst this amazing landscape. You may be as active or as passive as you wish, but my advice would be to pack at least stout walking boots and wet weather gear; in Caithness, the walking is easy, however, out in the wilds of Sutherland, leaving the car and striking off into the wilderness can be much more vigorous entertainment.

Ann and I have lived in these airts for nearly forty years, firstly in Caithness and, for the past twenty years, in a cottage overlooking the Kyle of Tongue, out beyond the "split stane", the old boundary stone dividing Caithness from Sutherland. We know and love the area dearly, and have tramped and hiked over most of it, under the cathedral-like skies of the wonderful Flow Country moorlands of Caithness to the jagged peaks of Ben Loyal, the Queen of Scottish mountains. We find comfort and pleasure in every season the Good Lord sends us and there is no other place on Planet Earth where we would rather live.

In truth, John O'Groats can be a disappointment, although there are plans to brush up its image. It is, nevertheless, a landmark Scottish destination and, as such, it is a must-see port-of-call for most visitors. However, if you follow the little road east from John O'Groats to Duncansby Head and park by the white-painted lighthouse, you will begin to appreciate the real worth of Caithness. The view from the lighthouse is reason enough for making this detour: a distant prospect over the deserted island of Stroma to the Orkney Isles and, even nicer, if you walk south along the cliff path, the jagged Stacks of Duncansby; sea-girt sandstone pillars, the tallest of which, the Great Stack, is 61m in height. During the nesting season, the cliffs are crowded with squabbling birds, including stiff-winged fulmar, guillemot, black wing-tipped kittiwake and firework-beaked puffins.

Driving west from John O'Groats, the island of Stroma dominates the northern view. Stroma was inhabited for hundreds of years and the population was essentially self-sufficient, growing most of their own food. In the first *Scottish Statistical Account*, published in 1793, the minister of Canisbay Church, the Rev. John Morrison, describes the people of Stroma thus: "From their political situation, and the simplicity, sobriety and industry, natural to them, there are perhaps few islanders on earth happier than those of Stroma." Stroma was once home to nearly 400 people but by 1962, the island was deserted as the population left to seek greater opportunities on the mainland. You may visit Stroma by charter boat from John O'Groats.

At Kirkstyle, two miles west from John O'Groats, call and make your peace with your maker at lovely Canisbay Church. The late Queen Mother often worshiped there when staying in her northern home at the Castle of Mey. The original structure probably dates back to the fifteenth century, although there is mention of a church here in 1222. The pre-reformation tower in the centre of the west front is an echo of the enormous changes that were reshaping religious attitudes throughout Europe at that time. By 1581, Caithness had been divided into presbyteries, however, after the restoration of King Charles II in 1660, the old Episcopalian faith flourished again in the county.

Throughout our journey, the sea will be our constant companion, from the ever-turbulent waters of the uproarious Pentland Firth, to the wide reaches of the Atlantic Ocean. Bewhiskered seals abound, curiously marking your passage. Porpoise, dolphin and orcas are often seen, particularly in the Pentland Firth, and sightings of great minkie whales are not uncommon. At Gills Bay, where the ultra-modern catamaran *Pentalina* operates a car and passenger service to St Margaret's Hope in Orkney, the road runs close to the shore. I have never passed this way without seeing seals resting and preening themselves on the rocks below the road. Stop and make their acquaintance.

An excellent place for lunch is in the new restaurant adjacent to the Castle of Mey. The castle and gardens are open to visitors from April through to September and offer the opportunity to explore the late Queen Mother's home, which she bought following the death of her husband in 1952. It is very much as she left it, with her favourite personal belongings on display – books, pictures and memorabilia of her lasting fondness of Caithness and the surrounding lands.

A few minutes further west brings you to Loch St John's, one of Scotland's most famous wild brown trout lochs where, if you are so inclined, fishing is readily available to visiting anglers. St John's is also famous for its ability to cure physical and mental ailments. Those who suffered would walk or be carried round the shores of the loch, bathe in its waters, throw a silver coin into the loch and depart without looking back. In Dunnet village, look forward to a visit to Mary-Ann Calder's croft house, built more than 150 years ago and in which Mary-Ann lived for nearly ninety years. The cottage is now owned by the Caithness Heritage Trust and remarkably reflects the way in which crofters lived and worked during the nineteenth century and early years of the twentieth century.

A minor road points north from Dunnet, leading you through the scattered township of Brough to the lighthouse on the cliffs at Dunnet Head, the most northerly point on mainland Scotland. The lighthouse stands 91m above the silver-leaden sea and the structure is 20m in height. Robert Stevenson, grandfather of the wonderful Scottish author and poet Robert Louis Stevenson, built it in 1831. Dunnet Head marks the westerly entrance to the tortuous waters of the Pentland Firth – the eastern limit is Duncansby Head. In the days of sail, pilots were ferried out to waiting ships to safely conduct them through these dangerous seas.

There are a series of little lochs on Dunnet Head, the largest being the Long Loch, which was traditionally used for racing model yachts. Another of the Dunnet Head lochs, Loch of Bushta, in the southwest quarter of the peninsula was, when we lived in Caithness, my private swimming pool. On hot summer days, I would walk out past the tiny beach below the statuesque House of the Northern Gate, and along the edge of the jagged cliffs over Dwarick Head to reach the loch. The water is crystal clear and the south end has a soft, sandy bottom, making it ideal for an invigorating splash. When I arrived at the loch, I was invariably greeted by a curious red-throated diver who would flap off crossly the moment I invaded his privacy. Dunnet Head really requires a whole day to properly appreciate all that it has to offer. It is, in its own right, a wildlife paradise, rich in flora and fauna, and a circuit of the whole headland is one of the great walks of Caithness.

Nearby Dunnet Bay has one of Scotland's most stunning beaches, two miles of spotless, golden sands. The beach is considered to be "crowded" if you can see a few other people in the distance. This was one of our favourite family walks at Christmas and New Year, the whole of Clan Sandison, complete with friends and relations and dogs various, marching together companionably along the shore. Visiting snow buntings, flocks of fluttering flakes, whisked by. Seals sometimes followed our progress with sad-eyed caution and, on one occasion, we were blessed with the company of a great northern diver, majestically afloat beyond the surf.

Castletown, our next stop, has many claims to fame, not the least of which is being the birthplace of the ancestors of one of America's most iconic heroes, General George Armstrong Custer, he of Little Bighorn fame. But Castletown is best known as being the birthplace of the Caithness Flagstone industry, which blossomed under the tutelage of James Traill of Rattar (1758–1843), Sheriff of Caithness. Nearly 400 million years ago, the whole of the north of Scotland, well out into what is now the North Sea, was covered by what is known as the Sea of Orcadies. As the sea dried, successive layers of sediment were laid down and this was the source of the flagstone for which Caithness became renowned during the nineteenth century and for which it is still renowned to this day; the beauty of the flagstone lies in the simplicity with which it can be split and dressed, often by hand, without the need for mechanical intervention. The stone has been used for hundreds of years by Caithness people, as fencing in a largely treeless landscape and for house building, roofing tiles and walls.

The industry thrived in an age when railways were being developed throughout Britain. Many of the platforms required to service the puffing steam-driven monsters were paved with Caithness flagstone. The Strand in London was paved with the material, as was the concourse of Euston Station and Waverley Station in Edinburgh. At its height in 1902, the industry produced 35,363 tonnes of flagstone valued £23,239 and Caithness flagstone was being sent all over the world, including to Australia and South America. Much of the stone was exported from Castletown Harbour and the harbour has been finely renovated using this most enduring of all building stones. Find out more about the industry by following the Castlehill Flagstone Trail in Castletown, a substantial community initiative that will lead you through the story of the stone with past sculptures formed from it by local artists.

Fifteen minutes further west brings us to the Royal Burgh of Thurso, clustered around a bay at the mouth of the Thurso River, one of Scotland's most notable salmon streams, where anglers catch upwards of 900 wild salmon each year. Thurso is a welcoming place that has expanded mightily since the building of the UK's first nuclear power station at Dounreay, a few miles to the west of the town, in the 1950s. However, Thurso has a long history of occupation, through Neolithic times and the days of Viking domination of the far north, to the battles and struggles of the Middle Ages when the Kingdom of Scotland was being forged. Members of the Sinclair family are the pre-eminent Lairds here and their leaders have always played an important role in the great affairs of state throughout the ages.

Sir John Sinclair (1754–1835), born in Thurso Castle, is perhaps most famously remembered for introducing cheviot sheep to Caithness and Sutherland, an introduction that subsequently led to the tragedy of the great clearances of the nineteenth century. Sir John was President of the Board of Agriculture and he was responsible for the publication of the remarkable first *Statistical Account of Scotland (1791–1799)*, a detailed description of every parish in Scotland written primarily by their local ministers. The present Laird, John Sinclair, Lord Thurso, represents the county in the UK's Westminster Parliament.

Thurso is our principal shopping centre, an hour's drive from where we live in Tongue, and we visit it generally twice a month to restock the Sandison larder. The journey is never irksome, always exciting and full of interest along the way. However, my favourite part of Thurso is somewhat less modern than the local supermarkets. It is the ruins of St Peter's Church, near to the harbour and in the oldest part of the town. There has probably been a church on this site since the thirteenth century, although the present structure dates primarily from the sixteenth and seventeenth centuries. There is a beautiful stone-latticed window and St Peter's has, to me, an air of serenity that is almost touchable, a corner of calm amidst the storm of living.

Another corner of serenity, for an entirely different reason, may be found at Scrabster Harbour: the Captain's Galley (Tel: 01847 894999), adjudged in 2009 to be the UK's "Best Seafood Restaurant". After such a busy day, you deserve nothing but the best. And for complete rest and relaxation, drive west from Thurso for ten minutes to spend the night at Forss House Hotel (Tel: 01847 861201), a gracious building on the banks of a small river set amidst ancient woodlands, close to Crosskirk Bay and the endless chorus of the sea.

34.
John O'Groats to Durness Drive
Part Two:
Forss House Hotel to Durness

Forss House Hotel stands on a green space overlooking a gracious salmon stream. To the left of the house, by the side of the lawn, a path leads to a promontory overlooking a dramatic waterfall, ever more dramatic after heavy rain. A thoughtfully placed seat overlooks the falls and the dark pool below. Early one morning, as I sat there, I watched an otter slide confidently into the pool. His whiskers twitched as he scented the air for the hint of any unwanted presence. I watched him pursue, capture and bustle ashore a large salmon, rushing the doomed fish into the undergrowth, anxious for breakfast.

A track at the back of the house, through an iron gate, takes you along pine-wooded hills above the river, where, below, the Forss glides gently seawards through green meadowlands adorned with spotted orchid, marsh marigold, buttercup, violet, forget-me-not, comfrey and speedwell, milkwort and primrose. In warm corners *Primula scotica*, one of the rarest and most unique of all Scottish plants, blushes purple-pink in spring sunlight. Black and white wagtails dip and bob by the stream as it hurries under a footbridge to greet the cold Atlantic in Crosskirk Bay. On the cliffs above the west shore, visit the ruins of one of the oldest places of worship in the north, the twelfth century St Mary's Chapel. Tread softly amongst the grey stones and listen to the whisper of the passing winds of time.

Reluctantly leaving Forss House, we now head west and continue our journey into the depths of Sutherland and the Land of Clan Mackay, past the ominous form of Dounreay Atomic Power Station, now being decommissioned, and the ever-expanding village of Reay. Those inflicted with the pain of golf should consider a round at Reay, a traditional and very attractive 18-hole links course established in 1893. No need to book a tee time, £25 per round, excellent value for money and famous for the friendly welcome visitors receive. A few miles further west from Reay, on the right-hand side of the road, stands the "Split Stane"; a huge boulder that, according to legend, the Devil, angry with delays on his journey west, cleaved with a mighty blow of his tail.

The "Split Stane" also marks the traditional boundary between Caithness and Sutherland. It was here, during the terrible years of the nineteenth-century Sutherland Clearances, that the people of Caithness gathered to greet these destitute families and offer them comfort and assistance. It was not always thus, for Clan Mackay were once one of the most powerful clans in the north, famous for their constant feuding, both with their neighbours and amongst themselves. Their most persistent foes were Clan Sutherland, with whom they were forever at odds. However, that which the Sutherlands could not obtain by force of arms, they eventually achieved, in 1829, through purchase. In that year, the last of the Clan Mackay lands were acquired by the Earl of Sutherland from his financially distraught neighbour. The "Bratach Bhan", the white banner of the ancient clan, fluttered no more.

A series of long, lonely river straths, running north to south, divides these northlands. The first, Strath Halladale, where the River Halladale empties into the sea through the golden sands fringing Melvich Bay, gives visitors their initial glimpse of the remarkable beaches and bays that lie ahead, each one demanding further inspection. Strath Halladale itself offers much to delight both eye and mind, not the least of which is the Royal Society for the Protection of Birds (RSPB) Flow Country nature reserve. The Flow Country of Caithness and Sutherland is one of the last remaining and most important examples of blanket bog peatlands on Planet Earth. My family and I have spent many, many happy days walking in the Flow country; fishing its sparkling silver and blue lochs for wild brown trout; meeting fearsome, scowling wild cats, playful families of otters, statuesque red deer, soaring golden eagle and hunting hen harriers. Visit the RSPB centre at Forsinard and join one of their guided walks to discover the full glory of this entirely magical wonderland.

A fine new road hurries the traveller west now, across the moor to the tiny township of Strathy, which has its own, yellow gem of a beach. Turn right in Strathy and follow the narrow, twisting road out to Totegan to visit Strathy Point, where a lighthouse casts its welcoming beam to mariners for a distance of up to twenty-six miles. Strathy is also remarkable for the fact that it has no less than four churches, built between 1829 and 1910. The first of the churches was designed and built by Thomas Telford (1757–1834), a towering genius who made an enormous impact on the far north: piers, harbours, canals, towns – such as Ullapool in Wester Ross and Pulteneytown in Wick, Caithness. His Strathy church was funded by the government, in one of the first acts of "public relations", to try to persuade highlanders that those in far off London really cared for both their physical and moral welfare. When the church was completed, the government also paid the minister's stipend, the princely sum of £120 per annum.

At the start of our journey to Durness and Cape Wrath, back in Caithness at John O'Groats, I suggested that those following this trail should consider taking at least a week to complete the route. Perhaps now is a good time to remind you of this suggestion. There really is so much to see and do, so many places to visit and explore, that it would be sad to miss them. As such, as we come to the heart of the Mackay Country, around the small communities of Bettyhill and Tongue, it is useful to note that there is a wide range of accommodation here to suit everyone: excellent hotels, guest houses, B&B establishments and camping sites. Find out which is for you by visiting www.scotland-inverness.co.uk/caithness.htm. Spend a few days exploring the surrounding countryside, enjoying the beaches, hills and mountains that make this area one of the jewels in Scotland's crown.

Bettyhill, which we reach after a half hour's drive from Strathy, is forever linked to the infamous Sutherland Clearances. Many think that the name, "Bettyhill" is inherited from Elizabeth, Countess Duchess of Sutherland, whose husband, George Leveson-Gower, 1st Duke of Sutherland, was a prime architect of this atrocious act. But there are indications that the little township clinging to broken cliffs at the mouth of the River Naver had been known as Bettyhill for many years prior to the clearances: an old woman called Betty lived in a house on a hill there and gave her name to the community.

Whatever the truth of the origin of the name, it is forever emotive of all the hardship the Sutherland family visited upon their defenceless dependents. The full story is told in the old church by Farr Beach, now the Strathnaver Museum, on your right just before you enter the village. In 1819, the Rev. David Mackenzie read the eviction notices from the pulpit. Not so very long ago, I stood in that same pulpit, recording a programme for BBC Radio Scotland, and read out paragraphs of what the minister had said. It brought tears to my eyes then and still does to this day when I think about how helpless and hopeless those who heard the words must have felt.

For me, the River Naver, which flows down from the heights of Ben Klibreck and Ben Hee, will always be the "river of a thousand tears". But it is hard to be sad for long in Bettyhill today. This is a thriving, bustling community with a vibrant secondary school that offers local children all that is best in education; and I speak from personal experience, given that three of my grandchildren are pupils there. And the history of Strathnaver records remarkable evidence of human habitation reaching back to Mesolithic times, 10,000 years ago, when the first hunter gatherers settled on the shores of Torrisdale Bay, where the river tumbles into the sea.

On the raised beach on the west bank of the Naver, buried under centuries of sand, are the remains of more than a dozen hut circles built and inhabited 5,000 years ago during the Neolithic period. Ruined brochs, circular stone-built towers of up to 12m in height, zig-zag south on either side of the river for a distance of nearly twenty miles, built during the period 200 BC to AD 200. There are relics from the days of Viking dominance, from the ninth century, and the outlines of traditional turf-roofed long-houses from the Middle Ages; and there are scattered boulders of the homes of those who were evicted. For full details on all the above and details of the Strathnaver Trail, which takes you to these sites, see: www.strathnavermuseum. org.uk.

I have to confess a vested interest in the village of Tongue, our next stopping place on the way west: I have lived there for almost twenty years and many members of my family have also made their homes in the vicinity. We live in a small croft cottage looking directly onto the jagged ridge of Ben Loyal, the Queen of Scottish mountains. To the west towers Ben Hope, Scotland's most northerly Munro, whilst from our back door we survey the wide, shallow Kyle of Tongue, dominated on a hill overlooking the village by the ruins of Castle Varrich, a fifteenth-century Clan Mackay fortress, which probably also served as a Viking stronghold in earlier times. On warm summer evenings, the scent of peat smoke spreads from the chimneys of village houses and, in winter, the black night sky twinkles with myriad stars and, often, the breathtaking sparkle of the Northern Lights.

As is the case with most of these far-flung lands, signs of man's activity abound. Close to the east shore of Loch Hakel, a few minutes' drive from the centre of the village, there is a vast boulder on the surface of which are inscribed the most significant assembly of cup-and-ring markings to be found anywhere in Europe, cut there some 5,000 years ago by people who lived by the loch. There are the remains of a ruined Pictish fort on a tiny island nearby and, on a ridge to the south east of the loch, at Drum nan Coup, the site of the last battle fought in Sutherland between Clan Sutherland and Clan Mackay; reported to have been a bloody, broadsword and battleaxe affair that the Mackays famously won. Loch Hakel is also reputed to be where, in 1746, survivors of the French vessel *Hazzard*, pursued and attacked by British warships in the Kyle of Tongue, flung into the loch handfuls of gold coins destined for the embattled Highland army of Bonnie Prince Charlie at Culloden.

There are wonderful walks along the wide, near-deserted sands at Torrisdale, by the scattered township of Skerray, and the chance, on calm days, of sailing to deserted Island Roan, "The Island of Seals", a mile off-shore from Skerray Harbour. The island was once the home to a self-sufficient community of nearly 100 people. Enjoy lazy, sunny picnics on warm beaches at the Rabbit Islands, guarding the mouth of Kyle. The Kyle itself is popular with windsurfers and small-boat sailors, as it is with anglers fishing for the sea-bass and sea-trout that enter on successive tides. From our cottage windows, we often see golden eagle, buzzard, raven and peregrine falcons going about their daily affairs, and on one memorable occasion, sea eagles, attacking sea gulls, sheltering in our glen from the full force of a mighty storm. You will always find a warm welcome in Tongue and friendly people always willing to help.

We are now nearing the end of our journey, crossing the narrow ribbon of the causeway that bridges the Kyle of Tongue, speeding over the desolate moorlands of the Moine Peninsula towards the River Hope and Loch Hope. The horizon is lined by majestic mountains: Ben Hope itself in the foreground, backed by the Reay Forest peaks of Arkle, Foinaven, Cranstackie and Beinn Spionnaidh, and in the far distance, the hills of Cape Wrath.

Our way winds round Loch Eriboll, the deepest sea-loch in the north of Scotland, from where *HMS Hood* sailed into the Atlantic to confront and face disaster from the guns of the German battleship *Bismarck*. On a hill to the west, overlooking the loch, stones, painted white and formed into the names of the ships that anchored there, are set out near the summit.

A remarkable change in the landscape occurs as you leave Loch Eriboll and turn west on the final run to the village of Durness. Where, before, wild heather and sphagnum-clad moors crowded the way, the land changes to verdant, green pastures. This change has been caused by a limestone outcrop, born many miles to the south in the islands of the Inner Hebrides, which surfaces again before dipping once more below the cold waters of the Atlantic Ocean.

This gives Durness and the surrounding area a special character and provides a wonderful habitat for a wide variety of flora and fauna. The crystal-clear lochs here offer some of the finest trout fishing in the world. During the early months of the year, the sea-girt cliffs are home to thousands of nesting birds. Shore-side, cathedral-like caves invite easy exploration. Stay in Durness for a few days and enjoy the peace and content that it enfolds.

Whilst doing so, prepare for one final, exciting expedition by sea, mini-bus and foot to the lighthouse on the north-west tip of the Cape Wrath peninsula, to marvel at the stark, vast, 160-metre-high cliffs, constantly washed by 3,000-mile-old, green Atlantic waves, and, surprisingly, for a coffee in the most remote café in Scotland. John Ure and his wife Kay bought and renovated one of the disused lighthouse keeper's cottages and opened it as a café. Have a look at www.durness.org for all the details of visits to Cape Wrath and for full information on all that Durness has to offer.

Thank you for joining me on this journey. We have travelled a long way together and, yet, I feel that there is so much that I have left unsaid, and so much more to what I have said. However, I hope that you have enjoyed the trip, and that you might be tempted to head north and discover it in reality. When you do, you will not be disappointed.

35.
The Royal and Ancient Burgh of Wick

Hidden within our souls is a deep-rooted love of the land that gave us birth. Those of us who were born in Scotland and those who have Scottish ancestors celebrated this truth during 2009, the Year of the Scottish Homecoming. I began my journey home in 1976, after many years living in the north east of England. Circumstances meant that we could choose any place on Planet Earth in which to live. My wife, Ann, and I talked it over with our four children; well, to be precise, three of them – the fourth, little Jean, was only six months old then. We agreed that we should move to Caithness, where my paternal grandfather had been born in the tiny fishing village of Staxigoe, close to the Royal Burgh of Wick.

My father spent many of his childhood holidays staying with an uncle, George Rae, who farmed near Wick. He told me that when Granddad was a young man, he and a group of friends were walking across the old bridge that arches the River Wick in the centre of town. On the opposite side of the bridge, a group of pretty girls were hurrying by, talking and laughing as only a group of pretty girls can do. Granddad and his friends were watching them, as young men do, and one said to him, "You see that girl over there, the brown-haired lassie in the middle? I bet you wouldn't dare go across and kiss her." My granddad didn't hesitate. He crossed the road and kissed her, and two years later they were married.

I have a formal picture of them on the wall above my desk, monochrome and fading, taken in later life. They are in their Sunday best, sitting at a table graced by a vase of spring flowers. They are smiling, grandmother in a simple dark dress with a single strand of pearls at her throat, grandfather sporting a neatly trimmed moustache, in a suit, wing-collared shirt and tie, with the chain of a pocket watch glimpsed across his waistcoat. Grandma was a Macgregor from Amulree in Perthshire and she and her family were travelling people, coming north each summer to Caithness to sell the goods that they had made during the winter months.

Wick is still a busy, bustling town and offers a wide range of activities throughout the year that are guaranteed to keep everybody happy and occupied, local and visitor alike: a vibrant Gala Week with fun events every day and concluding with a splendid bonfire and fireworks display by the banks of the Wick River; a Continental Market in the town square featuring food and flowers and other produce from a dozen countries; the annual Music Festival, in the town's Assembly rooms, with performers of all ages from all aspects of Wick society; theatre and dance, art exhibitions in the library's St Fergus Gallery, ceilidhs and concerts, lectures and slideshows.

Wick is the administrative centre and the county town of Caithness, often known as the "Lowlands beyond the Highlands" because, unlike neighbouring Sutherland, Caithness is low lying with only a few mountains in the south. The town is backed by fertile farmlands and clusters round the shallow, rock-strewn waters of Wick Bay, which has been an important harbour and trading port almost since history began. The name Wick is derived from the Norse word "Vik" meaning "bay" and for many years Caithnesians lived under Viking rule. That rule ended in September 1263, when the young King Alexander III of Scotland defeated the forces of King Hakon IV of Norway in the Battle of Largs.

The man who led the king's soldiers into that battle was Sir William Sinclair and as a reward, he was granted the lands of Rosslyn near Edinburgh and most of what is present-day Caithness. In spite of being so distant from the centre of power, Clan Sinclair has always played an important part in the events that shaped Scotland. From their arrival from France with William the Conqueror, the Sinclairs served Scotland: they fought with William Wallace at the Battle of Stirling Bridge in 1297, with Robert the Bruce at Bannockburn in 1314, and died with King James IV on Flodden Field in 1513.

Caithness is a land of cliffs and castles, twenty-five in all, and one of the best preserved of these lies close to Wick: Sinclair and Girnigoe Castles, one of the most dramatic ruins in the north of Scotland and built towards the end of the fifteenth century by William, the 2nd Earl of Caithness. The twin castles crown the crest of a narrow, finger-like promontory four miles to the north of town, near Noss Head Lighthouse. They are easily accessible and have recently undergone substantial repairs to preserve them and make them as safe as possible for visitors. Just as dramatic is the Castle of Old Wick, on the southern skirts of the town. It probably dates back to Viking times and was certainly an important castle when Robert the Bruce restored Scottish independence. It is now a roofless tower but still three stories in height with two-metre-thick walls, overlooking the sea and guarded on two sides by twenty-four-metre-high, sheer cliffs.

The old, grey town of Wick, with its narrow streets and sombre buildings, seems to ring with echoes of its turbulent past. The principal street – indeed, the only street for quite a few centuries – is High Street, running from the Parish Church in the west, down to the harbour in the east; still known to this day as "the camps" because Oliver Cromwell's soldiers were billeted there during the seventeenth century when they visited Wick to suppress any unseemly mirth and jollity in the Lord Protector's austere Commonwealth. The officers in Cromwell's army were more appropriately accommodated in Ackergill Tower, a fifteenth-century tower, restored and renovated in the 1980s, complete with the UK's most northerly opera house, and now run as an internationally renowned corporate business venue.

Wick was granted the status of Royal Burgh in 1589 by King James VI, giving the elected councillors powers to hold markets, deal in all manner of goods and other transactions and to levy taxes to be used in the furtherance of the common good of all the people of the Burgh. They did so to excellent effect, particularly in the nineteenth century, during the silver years of the great herring fishings. During the short summer fishing season, more than 1,000 boats crowded the harbour and upwards of 5,000 Gaelic-speaking people from throughout the Highlands flocked to Wick to crew the boats and to clean, pack and sell the fish caught. However, Wick, like Kirkwall in Orkney and Lerwick in Shetland, has always been more Norse than Gaelic and the Gaelic language was rarely heard outwith the fishing season.

The sea is a constant facet of life in Wick, ever present and ever changing, from the mirror stillness of the bay on a warm summer day to the outrageous temper of huge winter storms. Evidence of these days is wonderfully displayed at the Wick Heritage Centre, an award-winning museum near the harbour in Bank Row that was born out of the dedicated efforts of a few local people determined to honour and preserve the history of their community. One of the exhibits is the original light from Noss Head Lighthouse. Like the word "wick", the word "noss" is also derived from Old Norse and means "nose". The lighthouse was designed by Alan Stevenson, one of the members of the famous family of engineers who built so many lighthouses round the coast of Scotland, and it was completed in 1849.

One of the oldest traditions associated with Wick and the herring fishings was the annual appointment of the Wick herring queen. The herring queen reigned for three days and opened her reign by sailing into Wick harbour on the bow of a finely decked-out fishing boat at the head of a flotilla of other fishing boats. The ceremony was last performed more than fifty years ago and has been revived to coincide with the Wick Harbourfest, a special homecoming event that has attracted not only regional, but also national and international recognition. After being crowned, the queen and her court travels in procession around the Pulteneytown area of Wick, built in the nineteenth century to accommodate the expansion of the herring fishing industry. On the Sunday, the herring queen conducts a farewell ceremony before the flotilla sails away and a "Hymns of the Sea" church service is held in the evening.

Often, on visits south, when I had to attend to business in London, Edinburgh or Glasgow, the people I met asked where I lived: "Wick" I would reply. "Really?" would come the astonished response. It was difficult for them to appreciate everything that remote communities such as Wick have to offer: a close-knit society where children can play safely and where serious crime is essentially absent; schools that are amongst the finest in the kingdom. Our children thrived mightily and we never regretted our decision to come home to Wick.

It is only fair to confess, however, that Ann and I did have a vested interest in making that decision: we both love the great outdoors. In that regard, Wick not only provided a comprehensive array of urban facilities, but also wonderful access to the wilds: the amazing beauty of the Caithness moorlands and its unique flora and fauna; superb salmon, sea-trout and wild brown trout fishing; stunning golf courses; glorious, near-empty beaches; cathedral-like skies and the endless peace of the long, endless summer days of the "simmer dim".

One of our first outings after we settled in Wick was a visit to Staxigoe to see where Grandfather had been born. We found a sheltered, boat-bobbing harbour, guarded by a pillar of rock, backed by a few houses and the ruined outlines of the fishermen's cottages where he and his parents once lived. We had taken along a picnic and a bottle of champagne. On the quayside in afternoon sunlight, amidst the music of white-tipped waves gently rocking the little pebbles on the shore, I proposed that famous old Scottish toast, "to absent friends".

36.
Her Majesty The Queen Mother
and the Castle of Mey

On a warm autumn afternoon last year, I stood in the sunlit library of the Castle of Mey, the Caithness home of Her Majesty The Queen Mother. In her later years, the Queen Mother used the library as her private sitting room. It remains today much as it must have been when she was there, surrounded by her most favourite books, alongside treasured personal gifts and precious family photographs.

I was not surprised to see volumes on the shelves about Aberdeen Angus cattle and North Country Cheviot sheep, native breeds that the Queen Mother introduced to her nearby farm at Longoe, as well as books on the country sports that she enjoyed all her life. For many years, the Queen Mother's holiday reading list was published in the national press and one of my proudest moments came when I found that one of my books, *The Sporting Gentleman's Gentleman*, appeared on that list.

When the Queen Mother died in 2002, shortly before her 102nd birthday, and because I am an angler, I was asked to write a few notes about her love of fly-fishing. Fly-fishing is a universal pleasure that transcends the boundaries of age, race, class or creed. It brings together people from all walks of life who share common interests: a deep love of the countryside, respect for their quarry and consideration for the aspirations of others.

Few anglers expressed these sentiments more graciously than the Queen Mother, who was one of the world's best known and best loved fly-fishers. However, the Queen Mother was not only a keen angler, but also active in promoting the best interests of the sport. For many years, she was the Patron of the Salmon & Trout Association, a position that is now filled by His Royal Highness Prince Charles, who, as a youth, was much influenced by his grandmother's love of fishing.

When the Queen Mother purchased Barrogill Castle in 1952, she restored the castle's name to its ancient title, Castle of Mey. The castle had been built in the later years of the sixteenth century by George Sinclair, 4th Earl of Caithness, and remained in the hands of the Sinclair family until 1889. The Queen Mother discovered Barrogill Castle on a visit to her friends, Commander Clair Vyner and his wife, Lady Doris, who lived at the House of the Northern Gate on the cliffs of Dunnet Head, the most northerly point on Mainland Scotland.

Looking east from one of the upper floor windows of the house one day, the Queen Mother noticed the tower of the castle. It had recently been put on the market by the then owner, Captain Imbert-Terry, of the York family who produce the famous chocolates that still bear his name. After visiting Barrogill, the Queen Mother bought it and set about the considerable task of modernising the property.

The Queen Mother spent many happy months in Caithness over nearly fifty years. She loved the remote lochs of the Caithness Flow Country where she used to fish for wild brown trout on Loch Caluim on the Dorrery Estate. She also came to know and love the Thurso River and was a frequent guest there, often accompanied by her favourite corgis, Billy and Bee. David Sutherland, the River Superintendent, remembered being with the Queen Mother one day in 1953 when she was fishing with Commander Vyner and Sir Arthur Penn, her then Private Secretary.

He recalled, "The day was calm and thundery and although we saw plenty of fish on the move, none were taking. But this did not deter the Queen Mother. She threw a beautiful line and fished continuously for four hours and enjoyed every minute." The Queen Mother always had a kind word for fellow anglers, sharing stories of ones that got away and the few that didn't. But perhaps the most famous story recounts how a lady angler, fishing the Royal Dee, suddenly discovered that she was sharing a Beat with the

Queen Mother and instinctively curtsied, receiving two bootfuls of icy water in the process.

It was always the Queen Mother's wish that, when she died, her Caithness home should be continued in the way that she had established and nurtured it for nearly half a century. Above all, she was proud of her pedigree herds of Aberdeen Angus cattle and North Country Cheviot sheep. To achieve this, in June 1996, she set up the Queen Elizabeth Castle of Mey Trust and, to secure its future, endowed it with the castle, farm and estate. When the castle was opened to the public in August 2002, more than 900 visitors were welcomed on the first day. Today, the castle receives upwards of 25,000 visitors each year and employs fifty people during the season.

Along with King George VI, the Queen Mother had been patron of the Aberdeen Angus Cattle Society since 1937 and, after her husband's death, she remained patron for the rest of her life. The Castle of Mey Aberdeen Angus Herd was established in 1964 and soon began to produce a long succession of magnificent animals and show-winners, including, and perhaps the most outstanding, Castle of Mey Elscot, which sold at the Perth Bull sales in 1996 for the then record price of 8,000gns.

The Queen Mother was also patron of the North Country Cheviot Sheep Society and the Longoe Flock was established in 1960. Sheep from her flock have won Breed Champion awards nine times at the prestigious Royal Highland Show at Ingliston near Edinburgh. The most famous wins, however, came in 1991 and 1996. In 1991, the shearling ewe, Longoe H3, not only won the breed champion award, but also went on to win the Supreme Interbreed Sheep champion award out of 2,500 entries, as well as the coveted Queen's Cup – thus, her daughter's trophy was presented to the Queen Mother by her granddaughter, Her Royal Highness Princess Anne. In 1996, at the fiftieth anniversary show of the North Country Sheep Society, the shearling ram, Longoe Majestic, took top place out of 254 entries.

I came to know the Castle of Mey in the 1970s, when I was manager of an agricultural land drainage company. The Queen Mother's factor, Martin Leslie, asked me to look at some land drainage problems at the castle and at the farm. The farm was managed by the late Donald McCarthy and when he died, his sons, Donald and Sandy, took over the management of the farm. Donald was a good friend of my daughter, Lewis-Ann, and they had been at agricultural college together.

I called in December to speak to Donald about the Aberdeen Angus cattle and North Country Cheviot sheep that his family had looked after for so many years. We sat in the farmhouse kitchen over a cup of coffee, where the Queen Mother had often sat, and Donald told me, "She was a great person with a wonderful sense of humour. We miss her. When she died, it seemed strange – the castle open to the public and all these people walking about. But it is what she wanted. She loved having the cattle and sheep round the castle, seeing them from her window, and she knew a good animal when she saw one. After a show or sale, she was always waiting by the phone to hear the result and was delighted if we had taken a prize."

The farm is half a mile from Castle of Mey but well into her nineties, the Queen Mother used to walk along the shore by the Pentland Firth to visit the farm. I asked Donald what his fondest memories of her were; he smiled and said, "I think it was her coming in here, when she was home in August for about six weeks. She would come down two or three times and sit in that chair and yarn away. I think that she enjoyed a good yarn, on lots of different topics, a total contrast from her life in London. She could get on old clothes here and walk wherever she wanted. Nobody bothered her."

The President of the Queen Elizabeth Castle of Mey Trust is the Queen Mother's grandson and heir to the throne, HRH Prince Charles, Duke of Rothesay. He has carried forward his grandmother's wishes for the Castle of Mey and shares her love of Caithness. During the 1980s, when inappropriate commercial forestry was claiming thousands of acres of the irreplaceable peat moorlands known as the Flow Country, I became involved in an action to protect the area. At the height of the controversy, dubbed by the press as the Battle of the Flows, those of us who were carrying on the fight were enormously encouraged to see Prince Charles on television, in the heart of the Flow Country, patiently explaining why these moorlands deserved to be preserved.

HRH Prince Charles was also a positive influence in establishing what has become one of the great Caithness success stories of recent years, the development of North Highland Products; a company formed to look after and develop the exclusive brand name Mey Selections, which sources high-quality products from local farmers and fine-food producers. I called to speak to Danny Miller, the chairman of North Highland Products, who farms at Bilbster, near Wick, and asked him how the local farming community benefited from the initiative. Danny said, "Mey Selections provides a top-quality product and also guarantees a premium to our farmers. Our customers know that, by buying Mey Selections products, a little bit more money is going back into the wider local community."

Danny, who was the local National Farmers Union chairman at the time, knew that Prince Charles was keen to help and drew together a group of thirteen Caithness farmers who put up £300 each to fund a feasibility study. The study suggested that brand promotion was the way forward. The Prince responded by offering a watercolour that he had painted of the Castle of Mey and agreed that they could use the painting as their company logo. Danny told me, "We launched in 2005 and, very quickly, the national supermarket group Sainsbury's came on board, selling our beef from their butchery counters, and, shortly thereafter, Mey Selections lamb as well."

Today, Mey Selections has seventy-five products in its range, from Barrogill Whisky to tweeds, jams, conserves, pickles, chutneys, biscuits, honey, oatcakes, cheese, beef and lamb, all produced within 100 miles of the Castle of Mey, and all subject to stringent and carefully monitored quality-control procedures. From the original thirteen farmers, the group has now expanded and includes nearly 500 members. From start-up funding of £4,000, turnover has grown to £11 million.

Danny Miller is certain that North Highland Products will continue to grow and prosper, and of the key role that HRH Prince Charles played in its foundation. He said, "Fundamental to this success is the initiative that Prince Charles brought to the project. He gave us the confidence we needed to take the first step." North Highland Products is probably the fastest growing food and drink company in Scotland and regularly wins Excellence Awards for its products. See: www.mey-selections.com/ for details. For online-ordering, email: info@mey-selections.com

Prince Charles has also carried on the tradition of attending the Mey Highland Games, held in August each year at Queen's Park, Mey. The Prince and his wife, Camilla, Duchess of Cornwall, who were married in 2005, have visited the games each year. The games grew out of the Queen Mother's suggestion that a tug-of-war competition should be held between the Castle of Mey staff and a team from the local branch of the Royal British Legion. HRH Prince Charles is the Honorary President of the games, which include Heavy Events, Track and Field events, Solo Piping and Highland Dancing.

One of the "mainstays" of the Mey Games is Charlie Simpson from Wick, who has been a member of the Royal British Legion for more than fifty years. A remarkable, multi-talented man, Charlie was, until not so long ago, a regular and successful competitor in the Heavy Events, not only at Mey, but also around the whole Highland Games circuit. Charlie is also an accomplished public speaker, always in demand for Burns Suppers and other special occasions, and plays a wide range of musical instruments. I have known Charlie for more than twenty-five years and, on occasions, had the pleasure of sharing a platform with him at Wick Burns Suppers.

The Mey Games attract more than 1,000 visitors and funds raised by the event are distributed to the Erskine Homes, which care for ex-servicemen and women, and local charities also benefit. I called to see Charlie and asked him how he became involved in the games. "I always had an interest in them but when I was in the Royal Air Force [RAF], my primary sport was boxing – won the Command Championships in 1952 and boxed for the RAF at the Royal Albert Hall. When I was home on leave in 1954, the Wick Games were on, so I went down and entered the shot-put event and won the competition. So, when I came out of the RAF, I just carried on, going to games throughout the Highlands and enjoying every minute of it."

Charlie's involvement with the Mey Games came about when the Mey Branch of the Legion asked him to join. Charlie, whose parents lived in Mey, was a policeman and he captained the Queen Mother's tug-of-war team, thus beginning an association with the Queen Mother and her family that lasts to this day. The 2008 Mey Games were held in appalling weather conditions – cold, with heavy rain. Nevertheless, Prince Charles and his wife attended, particularly to watch the tug-of-war event.

For reasons we need not go into here, the vital rope was missing and Charlie had to break the news to his Royal visitors. "I had to tell Prince Charles that the rope was missing, that it was a wee bit technical, but that there could be no tug-of-war. I suggested they would be a lot warmer in the Castle. 'Does that mean we can go?' 'Yes,' I said. 'Thank goodness for that,' replied the Prince."

Charlie has fond memories of the Queen Mother, of her kindness and courtesy to all she met. Charlie told me, "After the tug-of-war, both teams were entertained for lunch at the Castle. The Queen Mother always came along to say hello. She just seemed to know everybody and spoke to everybody. She was a very lovely person."

I left the library and made my way down the imposing staircase to the front door of the castle. The hall is furnished with many pieces the Queen Mother bought from two shops in Thurso – Miss Miller Calder's shop and Hettie Munro's shop, the Ship's Wheel; both shops were first-stop calls for the Queen Mother for tea and to catch up on all the local gossip. The Queen Mother may be gone but her memory will always be bright in the Far North. When the sun shines kindly on the Castle of Mey, Charlie Simpson always used to call it a "Queen Mother's day". That is how she is remembered in Caithness, like a sunny day.

37.
Pentland Firth Lifeboats,
"For Those in Peril on the Sea"

The wave crashed into our boat with enormous fury. As the bow climbed above it, a vast plume of spray engulfed the vessel. I stood, wedged into a tight corner on the upper deck, with my young son, Blair, clutched against my body. Astern, the lights from Scrabster Harbour in Caithness winked and faded. Ahead lay a boiling seascape of tormented blue and white water. In the distance, I glimpsed the faint outline of the red-scarred cliffs of the Island of Hoy.

The incident happened on a stormy day in 1967 when we sailed from Scrabster to Stromness in Orkney on a family holiday. This was my first meeting with one of the most famously wild seas in the world, the Pentland Firth, the narrow passage of between ten to thirteen kilometres in width that separates Mainland Scotland from the Orkney Isles. The turbulence that gives it such a fearsome reputation is caused by the clash of the Atlantic Ocean greeting the North Sea.

Many years later, I decided that I should meet some of the people who risked their lives going to the assistance of vessels in distress: the men and women of the Royal National Lifeboat Institution (RNLI), one of the most remarkable organisations in the world and whose crew members give of their time on an entirely voluntary basis.

There are forty-five RNLI stations round Scotland's shores, five of which cover the Pentland Firth area: at Wick, to the south of the firth, Thurso, operating out of Scrabster Harbour in Thurso Bay, in Orkney at Stromness in the south west, Kirkwall on Scapa Flow and at Longhope on the south east of the Island of Hoy. Last year, these five stations alone launched sixty times and saved the lives of sixty-nine people.

The Pentland Firth fills and drains the North Sea twice a day. Three million tonnes of water surge through the channel every second, from the Atlantic to the North Sea and back again. Even on a calm day, when the tide is flowing from east to west, enormous waves build up off the Caithness coast near the Castle of Mey. This display of unbridled power is known to mariners and locals as "The Merry Men of Mey" and often extends to engulf the whole of the firth.

I thought of the "Merry Men" as I crossed the firth to meet Fred Breck, coxswain of the Stromness lifeboat. Fred lectures at Orkney College, part of the University of the Highlands and Islands, and I found him at their premises near the harbour, where schoolchildren were being introduced to the basics of small boat handling.

Fred has been coxswain now for four years. There are seventeen crewmembers and every member has a pager. When the call comes, day or night, they hurry to the station. On a call, or "shout" as it is known, seven of the crew are selected to man the boat. The coxswain chooses them depending upon the type of situation involved.

Most of the Stromness crew has seafaring backgrounds and Fred himself has spent much of his working life at sea and, on one occasion in 1989, in it. He was washed over the stern during a gale when his fishing boat was retrieving its nets. All he could see when he came to the surface was the boat going full speed away from him. Fortunately, the skipper, who knew that water had come onboard, looked out of the wheelhouse and saw him, bobbing up and down in the distance.

Fred told me, "I couldn't keep up with the motion of the sea. The waves were coming over the top of me. When I went under, I was looking up, like this, ye ken, and I could see the disk of the sun. Then I would come to the surface again and gasp in some air. A kind of amusing thing was that there were wee gulls, swimming around me, wondering what's this in the water here, you know?"

The boat came back and a lifebelt was thrown. Fred grabbed it, and thought, "I'm bloody sure I'm not letting go. I have never worked so hard in my life to stay alive." Fred told me he had once been fishing about fifteen miles to the west of the Fair Isles, between Orkney and Shetland, when the hold of the boat he was working on accidentally flooded. Disaster was averted when the Lerwick lifeboat came to their aid. "I suppose," Fred said, "that by joining the lifeboat crew, I felt that I was giving something back to those who had helped me. I have never regretted doing so."

Kevin Davidson has been a crewmember of the Thurso lifeboat for eighteen years and lives in Scrabster, close to the lifeboat station at the harbour. He works in the ambulance and fire service at Dounreay Atomic Power Station but has always been fascinated by the sea. His uncle, William Farquhar, was coxswain for nineteen years (he was in the crew for thirty-three years) and, in 1999, received the RNLI Bronze Medal for service to a burning chemical tanker, *Multitank Ascania*, when dangerously close inshore at Dunnet Head.

I asked Kevin if the possibility of a call out ever preyed on his mind: "Not really," he replied, "perhaps on a bad winter night, but once out the only thing that really matters is concentrating on the job in hand." Kevin gave me a conducted tour of the Thurso boat *The Taylors* and during the tour, Thurso coxswain, William "Wing" Munro joined us. I asked him why he became involved with the lifeboat. Glancing at Kevin, he replied, "Well, it's better than being a fireman and ambulance man at Dounreay!" This humour and shared sense of comradeship was evident in everyone I met.

Although I didn't have the opportunity of visiting the Kirkwall and Longhope lifeboat stations, I was enormously impressed by their achievements. In January 1984, Coxswain William Swanson Sinclair was awarded a RNLI Bronze Medal when his lifeboat, during a storm with driving snow and very rough seas, saved the lives of three members of a fishing boat that had become stranded amongst rocks. In 2000, the Kirkwall lifeboat, in a severe gale and six-metre-high waves, used their knowledge of tides to search for and rescue a diver found sixteen kilometres away from his last known position.

The Longhope lifeboat also has an illustrious record of service. Last year, Dr Christine Bradshaw was awarded the RNLI Bronze Medal for Gallantry after going out on the Longhope lifeboat, despite not being a regular crewmember, to assist three injured men on the tanker *FR8 Venture*. In hurricane-force winds and huge seas, completely white with foam and spray, she was winched from the lifeboat onto the tanker. One man was already dead and another had received fatal injuries, but Dr Bradshaw was able to save the third man's life.

The Longhope lifeboat crew, headed by coxswain Kevin Kirkpatrick and the Coastguard helicopter crew, also received a collective Framed Letter of Thanks from the RNLI Chairman for their role in this rescue.

But in March 1969, the Longhope station had suffered one of the worst tragedies in British lifeboat history. Their boat and all of its crew were lost answering a mayday call during one of the most severe storms in the islands. They were Coxswain Daniel Kirkpatrick, Second Coxswain James Johnston, Assistant Mechanic James Swanson, and crewmembers Robert Johnston, John T. Kirkpatrick and Eric McFadyen. A memorial to them stands in Kirkhope Cemetery at South Walls.

My final visit was to Wick Lifeboat Station, where I met Coxswain Ian "Corrie" Cormack. I asked him if there was one "shout" that he particularly remembered and he talked about the night they went to assist a ferry in distress off Duncansby Head near John O'Groats.

The *St Rognvald* was sailing from Shetland to Aberdeen on 5 March 1991 when it was hit by a huge wave off the Stacks of Duncansby. The force of the wave smashed the glass on the bridge and twenty tons of water poured into the vessel. The captain received a massive electric shock and was knocked unconscious (he later made a full recovery) and the electrical systems failed. The ship lost all steering power and although the engines were still running, it was in danger of foundering in the storm.

It was dark when the call came to Wick Lifeboat Station. The crew assembled and Coxswain Walter McPhee set out into a storm-tossed sea with gale-force winds of over sixty miles per hour. Corrie was in the crew that night and told me that the lifeboat had stood by the stricken vessel for ten to eleven hours.

A Royal Air Force helicopter was called in to take off non-essential people from the *St Rognvald*. It flew past, missing both boats in the storm. Wick lifeboat put up a flare to direct the helicopter to their position. The coastguards coordinating the mission from the rescue centre on shore asked the lifeboat what conditions were like, but, in addition to the storm, it was pitch-black and difficult to be accurate. It was a south-east gale and they estimated waves were about 9m in height.

The RAF helicopter broke its entire store of high lines during the difficult manoeuvres involved in lifting passengers from the pitching ship and was replaced by a coastguard helicopter from Sumburgh in Shetland, which completed the task. There were not many people onboard the ferry, its purpose being to take cattle and trucks back and forwards between Aberdeen and Shetland, but twenty passengers were air-lifted to safety.

The RAF helicopter crew said afterwards that they had measured the waves at nearer 15m than 9m. By this time, the *St Rognvald* was barely quarter of a mile from the cliffs between Duncansby and Freswick, but the crew eventually managed to rig up an emergency steering system.

The Wick lifeboat navigated them out to sea, away from the cliffs, and then escorted the *St Rognvald* the few miles south to Sinclair Bay, where the vessel found shelter and safety from the storm. An RNLI "Thanks of the Institution Inscribed on Vellum" plaque was awarded to Coxswain McPhee for his work that night and the crew received RNLI vellum service certificates.

Corrie invited me to join his crew on a training exercise. Lifeboat crews train on a regular basis. The task that evening was to take a salvage pump out to a "sinking" fishing boat so that the crew could pump out sufficient seawater to allow the boat to be towed safely back to harbour. I stood by Corrie on the bridge as he directed the operation and was immensely impressed by the sheer professionalism of the crew. Not much was said and the crewmembers seamlessly carried out their duties.

Ashore again, Corrie told me, "There is a bond between everybody. I don't think that I have ever heard an angry word spoken in all the time I have been here. You are doing something you want to do, not something that you have been press-ganged into doing. I think that is something that people have in them. We are very lucky to have such volunteers because without their commitment, we are nothing."

As I drove homewards, I thought of the many times that I had been intimidated by the strength and fury of the uproarious Pentland Firth, and of the men and women who were ready, every hour of every day and night, to come to my assistance. I felt humbled by their courage and commitment.

The RNLI in Scotland is currently running a "train one, save many" fundraising campaign with the aim of raising £500,000 over the next two years to fund crew training at lifeboat stations around Scotland. For more information please visit, http://www.rnli.org.uk/how_to_support_us/appeals/tosm/ or email: Scotland@rnli.org.uk or call 01738 642999 quoting "Scottish Appeal".

Of the 824 members of lifeboat crews in Scotland, 774 are volunteers, allowing the charity to spend more of its funds on equipment, lifeboats and training. Every RNLI crewmember gives up their own time to undertake 150 hours of competence-based training every year. It costs an average of £1,000 a year to train each volunteer crewmember.

The Royal National Lifeboat Institution charity saves lives at sea. Its volunteers provide a twenty-four-hour search-and-rescue service around the United Kingdom and Republic of Ireland coasts. The RNLI is independent of Coastguard and government, and depends on voluntary donations and legacies to maintain its rescue service.

Since the RNLI was founded in 1824, its lifeboat crews and lifeguards have saved over 137,000 lives.

38.
The Rough Bounds of Knoydart

The small boat was busy and its decks crowded. As we set sail, children and adults chattered and jostled good-humouredly, finding a comfortable space in which to spend the journey. Once clear of the harbour, the Sound of Sleat greeted us with sparkling, blue-bright waves and I thrilled to the feeling of adventure that comes only with the salty scent of sea spray.

Kittiwake, herring gulls and black-backed gulls clustered astern, screaming their approval at our departure. Etched like snow-white flakes on the vast canvas of the silver and gold sky, gannets hovered and dived for fish. Ahead lay our destination, the tiny hamlet of Inverie on the Knoydart Peninsula, forty minutes by boat from Mallaig at the end of the Road to the Isles.

Knoydart is one of Scotland's last great wilderness areas. It enfolds 55,000 acres and lies to the west of Fort William between "heaven and hell"; the names given to the two fjord-like sea lochs, Nevis to the south and Hourn in the north, that guard it. Knoydart has been designated a National Scenic Area for its diversity of flora and fauna and for its outstanding beauty.

It is also known as the "Rough Bounds" because of the majesty of the landscape. Six Munros crown the horizon: Ladhar Bheinn (The Claw Hill), Sgurr na Ciche (The Peak of the Breast), Garbh Chioch Mhor (The Big Rough Place), Meall Buidhe (The Yellow Hill), Luinne Bheinn (The Hill of Anger) and, across Loch Hourn, Beinn Sgritheall (The Gravel Hill).

Apart from by boat, the only way in is on foot from Strathan at the end of the public road at the head of Loch Arkaig, a taxing sixteen-mile trek. The path climbs through Glen Dessary, amidst the ragged mountains where Bonnie Prince Charlie hid after his defeat at Culloden, to the ruins of Finiskig on the shores of Loch Nevis. The route then winds past Camasrory and Carnoch before climbing steeply through Gleann Meadail and down to the River Inverie.

This was my first visit to Knoydart, the only place in the land I love and call home that I had yet to explore. As our vessel, the *Western Isles*, crossed Loch Nevis, the outline of the few houses lining the shore below the massive bulk of Sgurr Coire Choinnichean took shape and form. On the port side, we passed the dramatic white statue of "Our Lady" on the rocky headland of Rubha Raonuill. A few minutes later, we were alongside the pier at Inverie.

A crowd of people awaited our arrival, to meet friends and visitors, collect supplies shipped over from Mallaig and mainland Scotland – building materials, household goods, food and drink – and all the other necessities that the people who live here depend upon to sustain their lifestyle. Cheerful greetings filled the air as the crew helped their passengers disembark.

The resident population of Knoydart amounts to some sixty people. There is a well-stocked shop, the famous Old Forge Inn – the most remote pub on the UK mainland, a primary school with nine pupils and a nursery school with two. In and around Inverie, there are a number of comfortable self-catering properties and bed-and-breakfast houses amongst the heather and ferns that cover the skirts of the hills.

The early seventeenth centrury saw the MacDonnells in control of Knoydart, but their power and influence faded after their ill-judged support of the Jacobite cause and by the nineteenth century they, like so many of their peers, began to clear the people to make way for sheep. The most fearful of those forced evictions took place in August 1853, when Josephine MacDonnell had 330 people frog-marched onto the vessel *Sillery* to be shipped to Canada.

Eleven families refused to go and some of them fled into the Rough Bounds to hide from the laird's officers and the policemen who assisted them in this brutal act. These people, sixty in number, were hunted down and bundled onboard. A few years later, the MacDonnells sold out to James Baird of Cambusdoon, a successful Ayrshire businessman.

From then onwards, a succession of wealthy individuals used Knoydart as their personal playground, the most infamous being the entirely unlamented Arthur Nall-Cain, 2nd Baron Brocket. Brocket was anti-Semitic and an ardent fan of Nazi Germany. In April 1939, five months before the outbreak of the Second World War, along with Major-General John Fuller and the Duke of Buccleuch, he travelled to Germany to celebrate Hitler's fiftieth birthday.

After the war, in 1948, Brocket again faced reprobation when a group of seven men, including war veterans, raided Knoydart and marked out sixty-five acres of arable land and 10,000 acres of hill land upon which to settle. The "Seven Men", as reported in *The Scotsman* newspaper at the time, were "invoking the Land Settlement Act, which permitted returning servicemen to take over land which was under-used and farm it as their own".

Lord Brocket was not amused and applied for a court order to remove them from his land. Hamish Henderson, one of Scotland's most articulate men of letters, wrote about the incident:

"You bloody Reds," Lord Brocket yelled,
"What's this you're doing here?
It doesn't pay, as you'll find today,
To insult an English peer,
You're only Scottish half-wits,
But I'll make you understand.
You Highland swine,
These hills are mine,
This is all Lord Brocket land."

Eventually, backed by government, Brocket won, but the Seven Men of Knoydart achieved a moral victory, which is commemorated to this day by a monument to them erected in Inverie.

The oppressive reign of insensitive landlords came to an end in the 1980s when Surrey property dealer Phillip Rhodes acquired the estate. He began selling off bits of the estate and, in doing so, was, perhaps unwittingly, the catalyst for change. The last 17,000 acres were bought by a jute manufacturing company called Titaghur and when the company went into receivership, the land was acquired by the Knoydart Foundation in a community-led buy-out. This secured the future of the area for the benefit of the people who lived and worked there.

My accommodation in Inverie was a cottage close to the "Seven Men of Knoydart" monument and in the early evening, I wandered out to see what I could see. The bay was mirror calm and several yachts lay peacefully at anchor. The smell of peat smoke filled the air, and I watched as the crews of the yachts bundled themselves into tiny dinghies and rowed ashore. Most of the occupants seemed to be heading for the Old Forge, so I followed them.

Stepping through the door, it was as though I had been transported into an entirely new world. The long bar was thronged with people who were clearly enjoying themselves enormously; two musicians, guitar and violin, were playing and singing lustily, with the rest of the assembled company joining in. At the end of each piece, loud cheers echoed round the room.

The players providing the entertainment were part of a group who had travelled by train from Glasgow, thence on to Inverie. They were mostly climbers and hillwalkers, and they were also celebrating the forthcoming marriage of one of their friends – lustily.

The Old Forge Inn is owned and run by the remarkable Ian and Jacqui Robertson and it is the "hub" of social life in Inverie. Ian told me that most of the 4,000-plus visitors who come to Knoydart each year pass through his doors, and the pub has attracted an astonishing number of accolades and awards, including the "Highlands and Islands Best Visitor Experience" in 2007.

The following morning, I met Drew Harris, the manager of the Kilchoan Estate, the western part of the old Knoydart Estate, which is now run as a sporting and recreational enterprise. I wanted to have a closer look at what the estate had to offer people afflicted with angling and, perhaps, remove a few brown trout from their natural habitat.

Drew is one of those people who does not understand the meaning of the word "impossible", and showed it through his boundless enthusiasm and obvious love for the land he looked after. As an angler, I readily accepted Drew's invitation to explore its waters. I fished remote Loch an Dubh-Lochain for wild brown trout and the delightful little Inverie River for salmon and sea-trout. Loch an Dubh-Lochain lies at the very heart of the Rough Bounds of Knoydart and is, quite simply, magnificent.

The loch is deep, dropping to a depth of almost 30m, and is one mile long by up to 400 yards wide. Look out for pretty wild brown trout that average 8–10oz in weight. But there are much larger specimens as well, including ferox trout, the aquatic "wolf" that is descended from species that have inhabited the loch since the end of the last Ice Age – along with their attendant population of Arctic charr.

Loch an Dubh-Lochain is the headwater loch of the River Inverie, a notable salmon and sea-trout fishery that is recovering from the less than welcome impact of the fish farms in Loch Nevis. Drew Harris of Kilchoan Estate is conducting a re-stocking programme that is beginning to produce encouraging results. In spite of low water levels during my visit, several sea-trout of up to and over 4lb in weight had been caught and released, and salmon parr were abundant.

There are two other trout lochs on the hill to the south of Kilchoan, Loch Bhraomisaig at Gd ref: 785973 and its unnamed satellite lochan to the west on the slopes of Lagan Loisgte. Bhraomisaig lies at about 350m and it might test your lungs a bit getting there, but it holds some excellent trout that can exceed 4lbs in weight. Neither Bhraomisaig nor its satellite surrender their residents easily but, be assured, they are there, waiting for your carefully presented fly.

But the estate is not only about stalking and fishing. It encourages hill walkers and provides first-class bunk-house facilities to accommodate them. There are whale-watching sea trips and visits to remote, uninhabited islands. You may stalk red deer with a camera, and watch otters at play in the river and along the shores of Loch Nevis. Or simply relax in the outstanding comfort of the estate's self-catering cottages. For further information, contact Drew Harris on tel: 01687 462724 or email: drewhkilchoan@onetel.com.

It was hard to leave Inverie but at 11am on a Monday morning, I found myself back on the pier awaiting the arrival of the ferry. As we headed out across Loch Nevis towards Mallaig, I watched the village fade and merge into the backdrop of blue-grey mountains. But I was quite certain that I would be back.

39.
Loch Ness Myths and Monsters

The River Ness runs through the center of "Inversneckie", the affectionate local name given to Inverness, the Scottish Highlands' capital city. Some years ago, I was walking by the banks of the river on a warm September afternoon when a considerable commotion broke out amongst those around me; people crowded the river bank, pointing excitedly to the middle of the stream, cameras clicking furiously.

After several days of heavy rain, the river was in full spate, a brown and white tumbling torrent pouring wildly out of the vastness of Loch Ness. I heard a voice exclaiming, "It's the monster! Look, look, it's the monster!" A huge back arched above the water and then plunged again into the depths. A moment later, the shape reappeared and I identified it as being the back of an enormous salmon.

But what a fish it was, and little wonder that many of the onlookers, who were mostly visitors to the north, instantly thought that they were in fact viewing the fabled Loch Ness Monster. It was impossible to tell accurately, but I estimated that the fish must have been well over 60lbs in weight and, if caught, would certainly have been the largest salmon ever landed in Scottish waters. Even after the fish had disappeared upstream, the excited chatter amongst the bystanders continued.

Scotland is famous for the quality of its salmon fishing and the Ness system is amongst the most famous of them all, on the river, the loch and on its many tributaries. These most sporting of fish return each year from their North Atlantic feeding grounds to spawn in the rivers where they were born, but once they reach Loch Ness, because of its size and depth, they are relatively safe from the ungentle administrations of anglers.

Loch Ness is renowned throughout the world because of the alleged presence of Nessie, the Loch Ness Monster. Nessie shares his/her habitat with eels, pike, stickleback, lamprey, minnows, salmon, sea-trout, brown trout and Arctic charr. The loch is some thirty-seven kilometres long by up to two and a half kilometres wide at its widest point, between Urquhart Castle on the north shore and Whitefield on the south shore. The loch lies in the grasp of the Great Glen Fault, a geological feature that is still attempting to separate the Highlands from Central Scotland. This seismic movement has been active for more than 400 million years and is evidenced by regular earthquakes; well, regular in geological terms, that is, being at the rate of about three quakes every century at level 4 on the Richter scale. The most severe earthquake occurred in 1816 when the impact was felt throughout all of Scotland.

Until the end of the last Ice Age, about 8,000 years ago, Loch Ness was glacier-filled. When the ice melted, the loch was formed and drops to a depth of almost 240m. It contains more water than all of the lakes in England and Wales put together. Loch Ness is the largest of the three lochs in the Great Glen, the other two being Loch Lochy and Loch Oich. All of these waters are linked together by the Caledonian Canal, designed by Thomas Telford to provide a safe and quicker route between Loch Linnhe in the west and the Moray Firth in the east. Work on the near 100-kilometre long project started in 1803 and the original cost was estimated to be £350,000 during a seven-year construction period. However, the construction of the canal took seventeen years and it wasn't completed until 1822 at a final cost of £840,000. There are twenty locks along the length of the canal, the most spectacular being Neptune's Staircase to the north of Fort William near Corpach. This consists of a series of eight locks that raise vessels to a height of twenty metres above sea level over a distance of 500 yards.

I first visited Loch Ness more years ago than I care to remember but I will never forget the impression it made on me then; bounded on either side by blue-grey mountains and seemingly endless; mirror calm one moment, dark and foreboding the next, ever-changing and much of the south shoreline is virtually inaccessible to all but the most determined. I walked on the beach by Dores at the north end of the loch and explored the old woodlands down to Lochend where the Caledonian Canal feeds into the system and the waters from Loch Ness hurry northwards through Loch Dochfour and the River Ness to the sea.

Another, earlier, and equally impressed visitor was Thomas Pennant (1726–1798). This dour Welshman and caustic observer of all things Highland passed this way on his tour of Scotland in 1769. He commented: "In many parts we were immersed in woods; in others, they opened and gave views of the sides and tops of vast mountains soaring above. The wild animals that possessed this picturesque scene were stags and roes, black game and grouse; and on the summits, white hares and ptarmigan. Foxes are so numerous and voracious that the farmers are sometimes forced to house their sheep, as is done in France, for fear of wolves."

The road that Pennant followed then was the only reasonable route south from Inverness down the Great Glen to Fort William. Built by General Wade (1673–1748) in the aftermath of the Jacobite rebellions of 1715 and 1719, Wade's roads were part of a network to facilitate the speedier deployment of troops to control the clans of these unruly northern lands. This tortuous road is now classified as the B852 and it parallels the south shore of the loch through Inverfarigaig to the village of Foyers. From Foyers, a well-ordered path leads steeply down to a viewpoint overlooking dramatic falls on the River Foyers; an over forty-metre-high waterfall that thunders into a spectacular gorge and leads to Loch Ness.

Scotland's bard, Robert Burns, visited the falls in 1787 and immortalised them in verse:

Among the healthy hills and ragged woods
The roaring Fyers pours his mossy floods,
Till full he dashes on the rocky mounds,
Where, thro' a shapeless breach, his stream resounds.

As high in air the bursting torrents flow,
As deep recoiling surges foam below,
Prone down the rock the whitening sheet descends,
And viewless Echo's ear, astonished, rends.

Dim-seen, through rising mists and ceaseless show'rs,
The hoary cavern wide surrounding lours:
Still thro' the gap the struggling river toils,
And still, below, the horrid cauldron boils.

Burns never mentioned the monster or Loch Ness but since early times the story has persisted. St Columba arrived from Iona in the sixth century, determined to persuade the heathen Picts to mend their ways. During his visit, he is said to have saved one of his companions, who was swimming in the River Ness, from being eaten by a fierce water monster. St Columba made the sign of the cross in the air and, in a loud voice, demanded that the monster depart, which it immediately did, thus saving the life of the terrified, floundering monk.

My own view is that the monster does exist. I don't know what kind of creature it might be but I am sure that there is something there. Indeed, I knew a young man, born and bred in Inverness, who claimed to have seen it early one morning when he was camping by the shores of the loch. His description followed similar accounts of sightings of the monster, in as much as the creature was several hundred yards offshore and glimpsed only briefly. But he recounted that it had a long neck, high above the level of the water, and that it appeared to have a long tail. I never drive along the new Inverness/ Fort William road on the north shore of the loch without keeping a weather eye open for Nessie, and I am pretty sure that most other people passing that way do the same.

One morning in May, a friend and I stopped by Urquhart Castle on the north shore to take a few pictures and generally see what we could see. "I'll let you know when I spot the monster," I announced confidently, because

Urquhart Bay has probably been the source of more sightings of the monster than anywhere else on the loch. However, the surface of the water remained stubbornly undisturbed by anything other than sudden gusts of wind and pleasure boats trailing long, white, ever-widening wakes behind them. But it was a wonderful morning and the ancient red sandstone castle on Strone Point looked magnificent. It was inhabited for centuries, by the Picts in the first millennium and thereafter by successive Clan Fraser lairds until 1689. Then, to deny its security to similarly-minded rebel forces in the future, before leaving, they blew up much of the castle and left it largely in the condition that visitors see today.

My purpose that morning lay at the end of the loch, at Fort Augustus, and we sped along the A82, through Invermoriston and Port Clair to reach our destination in goodly time for a previously arranged appointment. The name, Fort Augustus, owes its existence to the disaster that befell the area in the aftermath of the defeat of Prince Charlie's Jacobite army at Culloden on Wednesday, 16 April 1716. The battle was over in about half an hour and by midday, more than 2,000 of the Prince's followers lay dead or dying on Drumossie Moor near Inverness. The rest, including their "Bonnie" commander, were flying in disarray or lying helpless on the field of battle waiting for Cumberland's eager bayonets to end their misery. Fort Augustus became the command center for the "cleaning up" operation when Cumberland's troops raped and ravaged the surrounding countryside.

Today, Fort Augustus is an attractive, busy, welcoming town that plays host to the thousands of visitors that arrive each year to explore Loch Ness. I hoped to do the same and was excitedly looking forward to being afloat on Scotland's most famous water. I was to do so through the courtesy of a business that has been taking care of its guests for nearly fifty years, Cruise Loch Ness run by Ronald Mackenzie, whose father founded the company. Their boats are berthed at a jetty in the centre of town, below the Caledonian Canal swing bridge and next to the Clansman Centre.

I reported to Marcus Atkinson, the manager of Cruise Loch Ness, and he outlined what he planned for the visit. Marcus is a Cornishman and sailing instructor who had spent most of his life working in the Mediterranean. He arrived in the Great Glen in 1994 on a six-month summer contract, met his future wife, a local girl, and has been in Fort Augustus ever since. Nor does he have any intention of leaving. "It is a wonderful place to live and in which to bring up a family. Even although it is always busy during the summer months, there is still a great sense of community. We know most people and most people know us. I can't think of a better place to be and I have the best job in the world," he said.

Cruise Loch Ness offers their clients two distinct trips on Loch Ness: on a traditional vessel, *The Royal Scot*, a beautifully maintained and equipped boat with excellent facilities – lounge, bar, comfortable view areas – crewed by attentive, courteous and knowledgeable staff, most of whom live locally. *The Royal Scot* can also be booked for private functions, wedding receptions, anniversary celebrations and corporate entertaining purposes. The other option is to enjoy the experience of an hour or so afloat in a RIB; a unique, fast and exhilarating ride in a rigid inflatable boat (Zodiac-style) that can explore and access loch-side areas that are otherwise inaccessible to larger vessels. These boats were an instant success when Cruise Loch Ness introduced them a few years ago and are the only vessels of their type on the loch.

I quickly found out the truth of the "fast and exhilarating" bit of the description of a ride in a RIB. Within minutes of our arrival, I was kitted out in all-over wet-weather gear, complete with life jackets and goggles to protect my eyes from flying spray, and speeding down the loch at around thirty-five miles per hour. It was a magical experience; the great loch lay before us, sunlit and sparkling, and a majestic osprey circled overhead. We flew past the only island in Loch Ness, Cherry Island, in a sheltered bay close to the shore north of Fort Augustus. The island is in fact artificial, being a man-made crannog; easily defended structures that were built and inhabited some 5,000 years ago and were still in use until late medieval times. We turned homewards as dark clouds gathered over the peaks in the Glengarry and Aberchalder Forests, and arrived at the jetty thoroughly delighted with all that we had seen on the loch.

As night settled on the great loch, I drove home past a now darkened and sleeping Urquhart Castle and Invermoriston, where the busy river of that name bustles under an old bridge into the bay. Just to the north of Drumnadrochat, I glanced over the loch towards Whitefield. I thought that I saw in the gloaming a commotion on the surface of the loch, far out and barely distinguishable. What could it be? I turned to ask my friend but he was asleep. Whatever, I know that it had been something unusual but what it was I would never know.

Contact Cruise Loch Ness at Cruise Loch Ness, Knockburnie, Inchnacardoch, Fort Augustus, Inverness-shire, PH32 4BN; Tel: 01320 366277; Email: info@ cruiselochness.com; Website: http://www.cruiselochness.com/

40.
Strathnaver and the River of a Thousand Tears

One of the most inauspicious places in all of Scotland for a vehicle to break down is along the narrow, single-track, lonely road between Strath Helmsdale and Strathnaver. When I was a boy, late on an April-sharp afternoon with snow still dusting the top of Ben Klibreck, my father's car did just that during a journey from Edinburgh in the south to Bettyhill at the mouth of the River Naver in North Sutherland.

We huddled in the car whilst Father poked about, less than hopefully, under the bonnet. After an hour's grunting, things were getting desperate. Suddenly, as steely evening approached, an old man appeared riding a rusty old bicycle followed by a rusty old sheep dog. He stopped and asked Father if he could be of any assistance.

The Good Samaritan peered at the innards of the engine for a moment and fiddled under the bonnet. "Now," he said, "just you give it a turn when I give you the signal." Father returned to the driving seat but we could tell from the expression on his face that he considered the matter to be a lost cause. "Now!" came the command.

Father turned the key in the ignition and the engine sprang to life, whirring vigorously and sounding as healthy and as happy as a new-born lamb. Relieved, Father tried to reward our benefactor, who politely refused. "You must be a mechanic?" Father inquired. "Oh, no," came the reply. "I am a Mackay from Strathnaver."

The people of Clan Mackay have lived in Strathnaver for almost 1,000 years and the evidence of their tenure fills the glen; the tumbled stones of their townships and hard-won fields; the place where the 93rd Highlanders regiment was raised; Donald Macleod's monument near to the ruins of the township of Rossal, cleared of its tenants by Patrick Sellar in 1814 during the cruel Strathnaver evictions. Macleod wrote later:

> I was present at the pulling down and burning of the house of William Chisholm in which was lying his wife's mother, an old, bed-ridden woman of nearly one hundred years of age. I told Sellar that the old lady was too ill to be moved. "Damn her!" Sellar replied. "The old witch, she has lived too long, let her burn!" The old woman's daughter arrived whilst the house was on fire and assisted the neighbours in moving her mother out of the flames and smoke, presenting a picture of such horror which I shall never forget . . . she died within five days.

Betsy Mackay was born at Skail, in the middle of Strathnaver, near the old Neolithic burial chamber in the little birch wood. She remembered that Sellar had burned the hill to prepare the land for sheep, destroying spring grazing for the cattle, and that the beasts had wandered far in search of food. Her sister, who had just given birth, was one of the first to be evicted. They lived in the township of Grumore on the shores of Loch Naver. When she asked Patrick Sellar where they should go, he replied that they could go where they liked, so long as it was not Strathnaver.

Bell Cooper lived at Achness, "the cornfield by the cascade", where the tumbling River Mallart meets the River Naver. She remembered children crying all night on the bare hill, watching the smoldering ruins of their homes. Grace Macdonald of Langdale was nineteen years old when her family was burned out. "There was no mercy or pity shown to young or old. All had to clear away and those who could not get their effects removed to a safe distance had them burnt before their eyes."

The architect of the Clearances was an Edinburgh lawyer named James Loch, Commissioner for the Sutherland Estates. He claimed that,

"The adoption of the new system, by which mountainous districts are converted into sheep pastures, even if it should unfortunately occasion the emigration of some individuals, is, upon the whole, advantageous to the nation at large."

The "some individuals" amounted to more than 15,000 men, women and children, evicted from their ancient homes to make way for sheep so that Loch's masters, the Sutherland family, already amongst the most wealthy families in Europe, could become even more wealthy. Patrick Sellar, their Factor, was the compassionless instrument by which the new system was put into effect.

The best place to begin your journey of discovery down Strathnaver is at the museum at Farr Church near Bettyhill. It was in this church that the Rev. Hugh Mackenzie urged his flock to quit without fuss. He told them, "The truly pious acknowledge the mighty hand of God in the matter. In the sight of God, they humble themselves and receive the chastisement of his hand." Mackenzie received rather more for his support of the Duke: a fine manse and the best ground.

Farr Museum displays an account of the Strathnaver Clearances, largely prepared by the children of Farr School. By spending time in the museum, you will be better able to understand the magnitude of the human suffering that the Clearances caused. The museum is dominated by the imposing pulpit from which Mackenzie preached his sycophantic sermon and, propped against the wall, almost unnoticed and dust-covered, is one of the few surviving portraits of Patrick Sellar himself.

Strathnaver was populated before the arrival of Clan Mackay and these earlier people, Mesolithic hunter-gatherers, Neolithic and Iron Age tribes, Picts and others, have left behind them a wide range of monuments and artifacts. The Farr Stone, lying against the west wall of Farr Museum, for example, is a glorious, finely carved, Pictish symbol stone that probably dates back to before the ninth century.

Across the mouth of the River Naver at Bettyhill, partly hidden in the sands of a raised beach, there are the outlines of no less than twenty-six Neolithic hut circles, occupied some 4,500 years ago, and on a hill overlooking settlements stands the ruins of the first of the famous Strathnaver brochs. The sites of these brochs zig-zag south up the river from Invernaver past Loch Naver to Mudale, a distance of twenty-three miles.

The brochs were built over a relatively brief period of time, from approximately 200 BC until AD 100, and their true purpose remains a mystery. They were massive, dry-stone structures, nine to twelve metres in height, enclosing an area of some twelve metres in diameter. The double walls were four and a half metres thick, containing a circular staircase. There was only one small, easily defended entrance. The Romans never invaded Sutherland; the brochs were in place before the Vikings attacked the Scottish coast. Why these massive defensive forts were needed is a matter of pure speculation.

At the east side of the iron bridge over the River Naver, drive south for half a mile to the ruins of the township of Achanlochy, which lie on the hill above Lochan Duinte. There were eight families living at Achanlochy when it was cleared in the spring of 1819, forty-nine souls in all – forty-two of whom shared the same surname, Mackay.

The most extensive post-clearance ruins are at Rossal, further down the strath near Syre, where Patrick Sellar set himself up in a grand house from which he administered the 75,000 acres he eventually rented from the Sutherland Estate; a reward for the results of his efforts on their behalf. A well-marked route leads round the remains of Rossal and there are informative display panels describing how the people lived.

Stop also at the 93rd Highlanders monument. In 1800, when the call came for volunteers, within twenty-four hours 2,000 men had responded. Two hundred and fifty of them were from Strathnaver and 104 were named William Mackay. The Countess of Sutherland promised them "her protection in all time coming and provision for their sons upon their return home". The reality was eviction and destitution.

During the Crimean War, when the cry went up for more "cannon-fodder" for the British Army, the Duke of Sutherland himself hurried north to drum up recruits. There was not a single volunteer. An old man told the Duke why: "How could you expect to find men where they are not? But one comfort you have. Though you cannot find men to fight, you can supply those who will fight with plenty of mutton, beef and venison."

Today, a new breed of laird rules the strath: absentee landlords, devoted to their private preserve of salmon fishing in the river and deer stalking on the hill. The ancient lands of Clan Mackay have been stolen from the people. But in spite of everything, the Mackays have survived and they will still greet you with gentle Highland courtesy, proud to proclaim, "I am a Mackay from Strathnaver."

41.
The 93rd Sutherland Highlanders and "the Thin Red Line"

I sat at a green baize-covered table in the library of Stirling Castle. Beside me lay a tumble of books and folders containing artifacts and documents from one of Scotland's most illustrious regiments, the 93rd Sutherland Highlanders. The coffee in my cup was untouched and cold. As the December day eased towards evening, embracing the grey walls of the ancient fortress in gathering darkness, I turned the final page and wondered: what land makes such men, what nation deserves such trust?

In May 1800, with snow still clinging to the high tops of Ben Klibreck, Major-General David Douglas Wemyss and Major Gordon Clunes of Cracaig cantered up the banks of the Helmsdale River through the spring-awakened Strath of Kildonan. Their purpose was to raise a regiment of Highlanders to reinforce Britain's canon-fodder-hungry army, depleted by the recent ferocious battles against the French in Europe.

The men they sought were sons of the tenants of the Countess of Sutherland; prior to Wemyss' arrival, a survey had been carried out by the Countess' Ground Officer, Donald Bruce, of the "disposable population" living on her land. These men were summoned to parade before the recruiting officers and reminded of the duty they owed to their Clan Chief and to their Sovereign, King George III.

But hidden behind this patriotic appeal was a threat. Tenants who refused to give up their sons would be evicted. To encourage recruitment, the Countess promised "her protection in all time coming and provision for their sons on their return home". Few came home. Those who did soon discovered the truth of their Chief's fine words: empty straths, cleared of people to make way for more profitable sheep.

As spring lengthened into summer, the recruiting parades continued throughout the Countess' vast domain. In the Parish of Farr at the mouth of the River Naver, men were selected by drawing white and black balls from a box. Murdo Macdonald's two brothers each drew black balls and had to enlist. By mid-August, General Wemyss had his canon-fodder. Shortly thereafter, the call came and 600 young men tramped south to assemble at Fort George near Inverness.

For almost 300 years since then, the Regiment has fought Britain's battles, one of the most notable being the Battle of Balaclava on 25 October 1854, where the 93rd formed the famous "thin red line" to receive a furious Russian cavalry charge. As they waited for their guests to arrive, Sir Colin Campbell, the commander of the Highland Brigade, shouted: "There is no retreat from here, men, you must die where you stand."

"Aye, Sir Colin, and needs be we'll do that," they replied.

One of the greatest disasters to befall the 93rd occurred in 1815 at the Battle of New Orleans. The peace that had existed between Great Britain and America since the end of the War of Independence was shattered by a dispute over which country had been responsible for a sea-fight between a British man-of-war and an American battleship. Britain decided to teach the colonists a lesson. The 93rd were embarked, under the command of Major-General Sir John Keane, to take part in an attack on the south coast of America. The assault force assembled on 23 November at Nigril Bay in Barbados and the whole fleet, amounting to some fifty vessels, set sail on 8 December and anchored off Ship Island in the Gulf of Mexico.

The intention was to capture the rich prize of New Orleans by outflanking garrison forts along the Lower Mississippi. By the end of December, the army was established on the Isle aux Pois, a swampy inlet at the east end of the Pearl River, and final orders were given for the attack. A coordinated assault was planned, both frontal and on the left bank of the river, by moving troops up a shallow lagoon and landing them at Bayou Bienvenue. On the night of 7 January, a force of 1,600 men under Col Thornton set off to occupy that position. It was a hazardous affair, the bayou was a boat-width wide and troops had to land by using the boats as a bridge, passing from one to another until they reached the shore.

As this force advanced inland from the tall reeds fringing the bayou, the ground became firmer and soldiers moved more easily through a forest of cypress trees, sugar cane and orange groves. But the element of surprise was lost when pickets, fleeing from Thornton's approach, raised the alarm.

As dawn broke on the morning of 8 January, Major-General Andrew Jackson's 3,600-strong militia was ready, and the defeat of General Pakenham's 12,000 seasoned British troops was at hand. The main attack was to be launched when Col Thornton's column fired a signal rocket to indicate the success of their left-flanking movement, but the main force, for some inexplicable reason, began its advance too early. Lieutenant C. H. Gordon of the 93rd wrote:

The 93rd moved from its bivouac and advanced in close column. As we neared the enemy lines, day began to dawn. By this time, the enemy could perceive us plainly advancing and no sooner got us within 150 yards of their works than a most destructive and murderous fire was opened on our column of round, grape, musketry, rifle and buckshot. Not daunted, however, we continued our advance, which in one minute would have carried us into their ditch, when we received a peremptory order to halt.

This indeed was the moment of trial, the officers and men being mown down by rank, impatient to get at the enemy at all hazard, yet compelled for want of orders to stand still, and neither to advance or retreat, galled as they were by this murderous fire of an invisible enemy. Not a single American soldier did we see that day, they kept charging their muskets and rifles without lifting their faces above the parapet, the fire from their muzzles being only visible over the parapet.

Meanwhile, Col Thornton and his men pushed on and stormed Morgan's Redoubt and fired the signal rocket; whereupon the American commander, Paterson, spiked his guns and retired, being pursued for about two miles by Thornton's party until the theory of the main attack caused the latter to halt. Thornton himself was wounded and had eighty-three other ranks killed and wounded. He secured the only trophy brought back by this expedition, a small American flag.

Captain Simpson, a naval officer wounded and captured by the defending force, wrote: "Having remained during the whole day in the American field hospital, I had an opportunity of observing the consternation caused to my enemy by Col Thornton's attack on the opposite bank, which was totally unexpected. Conceive my indignation on looking round to find the two leading regiments had vanished as if the earth had opened and swallowed them up."

Col Lambert, who assumed command when General Pakenham was killed, held a council of war. Taking into consideration that a third of the army on the left bank had been killed or wounded and another third was unfit for further fighting, and the danger that Thornton's detachment might be cut off, he ultimately sent a flag of truce to ask for a suspension of hostilities to bury the dead and collect the wounded. Jackson granted an armistice until noon on 9 January. After dark, Lambert, having destroyed his heavy guns, withdrew his troops to the bivouac of the previous night.

An unknown eyewitness of the battle – from the American side – observed, "According to the evidence available, when General Lambert rode forward to assume command, standing in the center, 100 yards from the enemy were the 93rd, proud, eager, helpless and enduring; the only corps which had kept its formation. And we can understand how it was that to the exalting Americans the 93rd Highlanders appeared as firm and immovable as a brick wall."

In later years, the daughter of one of the American defenders recounted in a letter to Lt Col Nightingale of the 93rd: "I have often heard my father say that both officers and men gave proof of the most intrepid gallantry and that it moved him to tears as he saw man after man of the magnificent Highlanders mowed down by the murderous artillery and rifle balls. After the battle, my father took a bible from the body of one of the Highlanders. It had his name but no address and had been given him by his mother."

The 93rd lost 568 men, three-quarters of their strength. The Highlanders lie buried on the field of battle, their final resting place still marked by a grove of cypress trees. Murdo Macdonald's two brothers, who had drawn the black balls at Farr, died together, side by side. The greatest tragedy was that the battle could have been avoided. A preliminary peace treaty was signed on 14 December 1814 and, had news of this been sent promptly to the opposing forces, the battle need never have happened.

The 93rd's Colours, carried during the battle, have a place of honour in Stirling Castle, the present Headquarters of the Regiment, and I paid silent tribute to them before thanking the staff for their courtesy. They told me that a letter had arrived at the Castle that morning from a descendant of one of those who had taken part in the battle – apologising for the unnecessary deaths of so many brave Highlanders.

As I drove north to my home in "Duthaich Mhic Aoidh" – the land of Clan Mackay – I said a prayer for the souls of these Sutherland men and for those who have followed so honorably in their footsteps.

42.
The Black Isle

The Black Isle encapsulates everything that is precious to me about the Scotland I love. It may not have the rugged grandeur of other Highland areas, but for me it irrevocably marries the land to the people who live and work there. It is a peninsula, not an island, separating the Moray Firth in the south from the Cromarty Firth to the north. During winter months, the Black Isle is often snow-free when the rest of Easter Ross and Inverness-shire is blanketed white, hence the name "Black Isle". Until recent times, residents and visitors relied mostly upon passage by sea to get to and from the Black Isle. Ferries were a vital mode of transport amidst the fjord-like coastline of Easter Ross.

However, not everyone was impressed by the safety or efficiency of these vessels. One notable ferry user, Lord Henry Cockburn, an Edinburgh High Court Circuit Judge who traveled the far north administering justice during the nineteenth century, had this to say about Highland ferries: "They are disgraceful! Passengers, cattle and carriages are just lifted and thrown into clumsy, crazy boats, and jerked by bad rowers with unsafe oars, amidst a disorderly tumult of loud, discordant, half-naked and very hairy Celts, who, however, expecting whisky, are at least civil."

Even today, one small, two-car ferry remains, plying between Cromarty and Nigg on the north shore of the Cromarty Firth, although travelers are more comfortably catered for now than they were in 1825. Back then, according to contemporary reports, "Passengers on the Cromarty Ferry had to be carried ashore on a woman's back at the Nigg side."

The most important ferry was at Kessock, sailing between Inverness and the Black Isle. Boats serviced this route from the early years of the fifteenth century. The ferry survived until the building of the Kessock Bridge in 1982, when, "On the final trip to North Kessock, the two ferries were accompanied by small sailing craft, a wind surfer, water skier and a canoeist. Pipe Major Andrew Venters played his own specially composed tune, 'Farewell to Kessock Ferry.'"

One of my favourite places in the Black Isle is the raised beach near Eathie on the north shore of the Moray Firth. These beaches were formed 10,000 years ago, when sea levels fluctuated as the last Ice Age retreated, leaving sand and gravel deposits high above the present level of the sea. Here, I retrace the footsteps of the Black Isle's most famous son, Hugh Miller, a stonemason and geologist born in Cromarty in 1802.

Miller's cottage, built in 1711, is the only remaining thatch-roofed dwelling in Cromarty. It is now a museum that recounts the life and work of this humble man. Miller is a hero of mine. He discovered and explored the fossil fish of the Black Isle Syncline, rocks of the Old Red Sandstone period. Make your own pilgrimage to Hugh Miller's fossil beds to discover for yourself the heart and soul of the Black Isle.

A wooden stile near Eathie Mains Farm leads to a track bordered by a field of barley and an old forest. Along the way, you pass the tumbled stones of a ruined croft on the margins of a reed-fringed pond, alive with the buzz of insects. After a few hundred yards, from the top of the cliff, you will see the blue waters of the Moray Firth and the raised beach below.

The track plunges down the cliff face through banks of heather and yellow ragwort to reach the shore at the Eathie salmon-fishing bothy. The view toward Inverness frames the lighthouse-tipped finger of Chanonry Point, where the seventeenth-century prophet, Brahan Seer, was allegedly boiled in a barrel of tar after bearing bad tidings to the Countess of Seaforth about her husband's infidelity.

Across the firth, the gaunt symmetry of Fort George bulks the horizon. The fort was built by the government in the aftermath of Bonnie Prince Charlie's failed uprising in 1745 to help "control and contain" rebellious Highlanders. It has been used as military barracks ever since. The nearby oilrig platform construction yards at Ardersier throw up steel steeples against the sky.

The fossil-beds are a short walk east from Eathie. Hugh Miller worked here more than 100 years ago, but I feel his presence and hear the sharp tap of his busy hammer every time I pass by. The jagged rocks, as old as time itself, are red, black, blue, white and grey, finely weathered into fantastic shapes and patterns. Strange marks scar the surface of the rocks, painting in the imagination a picture of embryonic life struggling from the ocean.

They are, as Hugh Miller described, "calcareous shales, containing hard limey nodules with occasional fragments of primitive armour-plated fish". I have personal experience of Black Isle rocks and soil. When I managed a land drainage company, we installed field drainage systems in more than 1,000 acres around Munlochy. On my days off, I hiked miles over Munlochy cliffs, searching for the elusive herd of wild goats that live there, but never found them. Their forbears could have been introduced to the Black Isle by Neolithic settlers 5,000 years ago. They feed on gorse, heather and leaves – and everything else that takes their fancy. Which is what goats are for.

In winter months, draining the land was cold, hard work, stamping about misty stubble fields, serenaded by visiting flocks of Arctic greylag geese and Icelandic whooper swans. The Black Isle is renowned for its populations of migrants. But during my work, and in spite of the cold, I got to know the Black Isle intimately, from the toes of my muddy boots to my freezing hands, which were invariably encrusted with rich Black Isle soil.

I felt kinship not only with Hugh Miller, but also with my Scottish ancestors who had felt the same soil trickling through their fingers. After the Iron Age, a Pictish tribe, known to the Romans as the Decantae, cultivated these fields. But the Roman advance of AD 79 stopped short of the Black Isle, and the Decantae were left to their own devices until Viking invaders arrived to "absorb" them into a Norse culture.

One of Scotland's least-sung patriots, Andrew de Moray (d. 1297), was born near the fishing village of Avoch on the Black Isle. Don't ask local people the way to Avoch. Nobody will understand you. It is pronounced "auk". While

William Wallace was raising the south of Scotland in opposition to the usurping Edward I of England, de Moray did the same in the north. Wallace and de Moray eventually defeated Edward's forces at the famous Battle of Stirling Bridge, during which de Moray received his "deathbed" wound.

By the end of the thirteenth century, Cromarty, the principal town of the Black Isle at the northeast tip of the peninsula, had been made a Royal Burgh. David I (1080–1153) began the practice of granting towns Burgh status. This gave them important, exclusive trading privileges and, in the case of a Royal Burgh, the right to be represented in the king's councils. The town was the main trading port in the region up until the nineteenth century, exporting highly prized Black Isle grain, oats, bere (an early type of barley), wheat, linen, pigs, whisky and salted herring to London markets and across the North Sea to Baltic ports.

Rocky headlands, the Soutors of Cromarty, guard the approach to the harbour. "Soutor" is the old Scots word for shoemaker. Two giants, shoemakers, worked on the headlands and shared tools by tossing them to each other across the bay . . . so the story goes.

Cromarty captures the essential spirit of the Black Isle. Walking its narrow streets evokes a sense of timelessness; the old courthouse and gaol, with its distinctive clock tower; the Georgian symmetry of Cromarty House; the brewery building and fishermen's cottages; a Gaelic church, built to meet the religious needs of the Highland men and women who worked in Cromarty during the great years of the herring fishings. It is as though, in spite of "progress", nothing really has changed substantially. They are the same people, with the same hopes and aspirations as those who trod this way before.

Another place that evokes an enormous sense of peace is Fortrose Cathedral. My in-laws lived close by and when visiting them, I would recharge my spiritual batteries amidst the graceful sandstone ruins. A stone figure lies on top of the most important tomb on the grounds of the cathedral: Euphemia, Countess of Ross. Euphemia, after she was widowed in 1382, was married to Alexander Stewart, the illegitimate son of King Robert II, infamously known as "The Wolf of Badenoch".

Alex was much more interested in Euphemia's property than in acquiring a bride, and the minute he got what he wanted, he deserted Euphemia in favour of an accommodating mistress. The countess complained about her treatment to the Bishop of Moray, who threatened Alexander with excommunication. The Wolf decided to teach the Bishop a lesson and burned the Moray towns of Forres and Elgin, including Elgin Cathedral, adjudged to be the most beautiful cathedral in the civilised world. Euphemia is still waiting to reclaim her inheritance, while her "estranged" husband lies uneasily asleep in Dunkeld Cathedral, Perthshire.

The Jacobite Mackenzie Earls of Seaforth lie nearby. In 1880, a hoard of 1,100 silver coins was found, buried in the cathedral green. Could they have been part of the money sent from France in 1746 to Bonnie Prince Charlie and, allegedly, buried at the west end of Loch Arkaig to the north of Fort William?

The Black Isle holds golden memories for me and I always find it hard to leave. I have tramped its rocky shores and marveled at its flora and fauna for many years. There is in the Black Isle a sense of continuity, of order and permanence. It is as though no matter what the future might hold for my native land, this special corner of Scotland, with its wondrous woodlands and fertile fields, will forever remain true to itself, and to the people who call the Black Isle home.

43.
Of Guns, Rods and Gillies

The bedrock of a Scottish boy's life consists of rugby, gold and fishing. It is impossible to grow up in Scotland without becoming embroiled in these activities. I still hear, to this day, our school sportsmaster yelling at me, "Lie on the ball, Sandison, kill it!" Thus I learned the proper function of a fullback in an extreme emergency: to "kill" the ball when it is dangerously adjacent to the goal line whilst twenty-nine of my blood-crazed compatriots gathered round to kick the living daylights out of me.

Consequently, quickly developing a compelling interest in golf was easy. My father gave me four wooden-shafted clubs and a couple of grizzled balls, then let me loose on Swanston Golf Course in the Pentland Hills near Edinburgh. The smell of bacon and eggs cooking in the clubhouse kitchen on a cold morning is an enduring memory. As is the memory of the hours and hours I spent searching for these two, irreplaceable balls. Dad was notoriously short-tempered: "For God's sake, keep your eye on the ball, Bruce! It is the last one you will get from me."

So I decided to concentrate my mind on fishing and the great outdoors. It seemed to me to be the most sensible thing to do. No one else in my family fished, or hunted, or stalked the moors. Here, at least, I would be absolutely free to do my own thing and make my own mistakes well out of range of maniac rugby masters, prickly gorse bushes and outraged green-keepers. I acquired an old greenheart rod, an antiquated silk line, a small brass reel and a dozen tattered flies. Within a few weeks, I had taught myself how to cast and was off to the river.

That, I suppose, is the story of my life. I had discovered a joy that has comforted me for, well, decades. In the process, I also discovered my native land and its vibrant, often violent history. And I found Scotland's lonely places, amidst its blue-grey mountains and heather-covered moors. I learned to speak to statuesque red deer, rocketing grouse and cautious wildcat. My friends were playful otters, golden eagle and peregrine. I splashed and swam in remote summer-corrie lochans and saw sunsets and dawns that I will never forget.

Along the way, I also have had the pleasure of getting to know many of my fellow countrymen who care for and nurture Scotland's priceless natural heritage: the gillies, keepers and stalkers without whose hard work and dedication my native land would be a much poorer place. The Gaelic word "gille" means: a lad; a young man; servant man. The word has been corrupted in English usage as "gillie" but it means the same: a Highland chief's attendant, or the guide of hunting and fishing sportsmen. But it is "gillie" and never, ever "ghillie".

Myths and legends abound about the character, morals and humour of Scotland's gillies and, believe me, every single story is true; indeed, some are even truer. Their alleged love of whisky, *uisge beatha,* is well known, but in my time, I have met many more *uisge-beathaed* sportsmen than I have met under-the-weather gillies. The fact of the matter is that, like driving, whisky and looking after often-inexperienced guns or rods simply do not mix. The gillie needs a clear head in order to steer his guest out of trouble and to give him the best opportunity of sport.

Nevertheless, a decent dram is useful and sporting gentlemen in Scotland are well advised to carry a suitable supply. I was having such a dram one evening with a senior gillie when I asked him what was the worst thing that had ever happened to him during his time as a gillie. He paused, in the middle of a reflective sip, and considered my question: "Well, do you know, once I had a Gentleman out with me and after a while I realised that he had brought no whisky with him." As though still stunned by the memory, he was quiet for a few moments.

"What did you do?" I asked, shocked.

"Oh that was easy. I just took him to where there were no fish."

One of the most remarkable sporting sights in Scotland used to be the ballroom at Mar Lodge, near Balmoral on Deeside, which contained the heads of more than 2,000 stags. Tragically, the lodge was burned down some years ago and the ballroom destroyed. However, Donald MacDonald of Ballater, who was head keeper on the Invercauld Estate and whose father was a keeper at Mar, remembers being told about special deer drives when King George V used to come over from Balmoral for the occasion: "I have heard my father say that often twenty or thirty stags would be shot in a day, and I myself have seen as many as seventeen ponies going up the hill to collect them."

An Invercauld colleague of Donald's, Tom MacPhearson, told me about a day grouse shooting when he found the laird, Captain Farquharson, crouched on the floor of his butt, his jacket shredded as though it had been put through a mincer: "It's not safe, Tom," said the laird. "Some idiot is shooting at me, not at the damn birds." Tom worked with the laird the next day and soon found the culprit. It was a guest from China, in the neighboring butt, who was less than familiar with safety procedures and shooting etiquette.

As the grouse rocketed past the butts, Tom watched the Chinese guest. His loaded gun swung round to the left, following the flight of the incoming birds far beyond the safety point and in line with the laird's butt. Tom yelled a warning as the Chinaman's gun blasted shot in their direction and he and the laird flopped to the floor. Tom accosted the culprit: "Now, Sir," Tom said, "that was very nearly your best shot of the day – the laird and his head keeper with one barrel!"

The late Jock McAskill of Invergarry, in the Great Glen, was another expert stalker. Three generations of McAskills worked at Invergarry, starting before the First World War with Jock's grandfather. Jock began his stalking career on the Brae Roy Estate in Glen Roy, where the head keeper was getting on in years and his eyesight beginning to fail. On the first morning on the hill, he said to Jock: "Now then, lad, just give me a good nudge if you see anything." Jock was also an expert angler, his last great expedition being when he took four salmon in a morning from Loch Oich, the heaviest of which weighed 17lbs.

One of the most famous angling developments in the middle years of the century was that of greased line fishing for salmon, invented on the River Dee at Cairnton by legendary angler Arthur Wood. Wood claimed great success fishing for salmon in low water conditions by using a line that floated on the surface of the water, rather than using a sinking line that "swims" below the surface. His most successful pattern of salmon fly, he alleged, was a small pattern called the Blue Charm and every angling magazine in Britain was full of the story.

However, Jimmy Ross of Rothes told me a different story. As a young man, Jimmy used to gillie at Aboyne on the Dee and knew Arthur Wood's gillie. In the pub one night, Jimmy plied his colleague with drams and quizzed him about all these fish supposedly being killed on a wee Blue Charm fished by Arthur Wood on a floating line. "Don't you believe it!" replied Wood's gillie. "It's a great big Jock Scott on a sinking line that he is doing all the damage, and everybody for miles around lashing away with wee Blue Charms catching nothing!"

David Hanton was one of Scotland's most respected keepers. The Hanton family served the Cortachy Castle Estate in Angus for many years. David's grandfather was head keeper for nearly sixty years and two of his sons worked for the estate. David's own father had been head keeper and David himself worked on the estate all his life, on the moor and as a gillie on the River South Esk.

When I first met David, he had been retired for several years but he was still as bright and spry as a spring morning. A coal fire burned in the grate and the living room was scattered with the memorabilia of a lifetime spent out of doors. With a twinkle in his eye, he complained to me: "Do you know, when I was a boy of seventeen, I joined the Gordon Highlanders and I can remember it as clearly as though it were yesterday. Now, last week I put away two spools of fishing nylon and I'm damned if I can remember where I put them."

David began fishing in Glen Clova, one of the five glorious glens of Angus, in the Burn of Heughs by the side of his grandfather's house: "What a grand place for a young lad! There was a stream in front of the lodge, which came down from Ben Tirram, and it had fine pools with a trout under every stone." David was injured on Vimy Ridge during the First World War and he told me: "I was hit by a whiz-bang . . . it was like being hit by the side of a house. As I fell to the ground, I remember thinking, 'well, that's the end of your keepering days, my lad,' but I recovered and I have been a keeper ever since."

Another well-loved South Esk gillie was Ned Coates, who started his keepering days with Big Bill Robertson, a farmer and potato merchant and owner of the House of Dunn: "Noo, Ned, whit wages do you get?" asked Robertson of the young man seeking employment. "Ten pounds a week," Ned replied. "Well, I'll gie ye the same, with free milk, free tatties and a free house. Dinna call me Bill or Sir. Just call me Boss." Ned has never owned a pair of trousers in his life and always wears the kilt. "It's a bit sharp in the spring, wading out to land a fish, but the kilt just floats up around me and soon dries out again afterwards."

Today, on moor, loch, river and hill, I am constantly surprised by just how young Scotland's gillies are. And as the seasons pass, they seem to get even younger, year by year. This is a great mystery to me because I have stayed the same age, from the time I lay in the mud on that rugby field until the present day. I have not changed one iota. I believe I owe this attitude to the happy days I spend amidst the cathedral-like wilderness of the land I love, and to the excellent company of the kindest and most courteous breed of men that I have ever met, Scotland's gillies.